한국 인권문제

민주화 관련
기타 자료 3

한국 인권문제

민주화 관련 기타 자료 3

한국학술정보

| 머리말

일제 강점기 독립운동과 병행되었던 한국의 인권운동은 해방이 되었음에도 큰 결실을 보지 못했다. 1950년대 반공을 앞세운 이승만 정부와 한국전쟁, 역시 경제발전과 반공을 내세우다 유신 체제에 이르렀던 박정희 정권, 쿠데타로 집권한 1980년대 전두환 정권까지, 한국의 인권은 이를 보장해야 할 국가와 정부에 의해 도리어 억압받고 침해되었다. 이런 배경상 근대 한국의 인권운동은 반독재, 민주화운동과 결을 같이했고, 대체로 국외에 본부를 둔 인권 단체나 정치로부터 상대적으로 자유로운 종교 단체에 의해 주도되곤 했다. 이는 1980년 5·18광주민주화운동을 계기로 보다 근적인 변혁을 요구하는 형태로 조직화되었고, 그 활동 영역도 정치를 넘어 노동자, 농민, 빈민 등으로 확대되었다. 이들이 없었다면 한국은 1987년 군부 독재 종식하고 절차적 민주주의를 도입할 수 없었을 것이다. 민주화 이후에도 수많은 어려움이 있었지만, 한국의 인권운동은 점차 전문적이고 독립된 운동으로 분화되며 더 많은 이들의 참여를 이끌어냈고, 지금까지 많은 결실을 맺을 수 있었다.

본 총서는 1980년대 중반부터 1990년대 초반까지, 외교부에서 작성하여 30여 년간 유지했던 한국 인권문제와 관련한 국내외 자료를 담고 있다. 6월 항쟁이 일어나고 민주화 선언이 이뤄지는 등 한국 인권운동에 많은 변화가 있었던 시기다. 당시 인권문제와 관련한 국내외 사안들, 각종 사건에 대한 미국과 우방국, 유엔의 반응, 최초의 한국 인권보고서 제출과 아동의 권리에 관한 협약 과정, 유엔인권위원회 활동, 기타 민주화 관련 자료 등 총 18권으로 구성되었다. 전체 분량은 약 9천여 쪽에 이른다.

2024년 3월

한국학술정보(주)

| 일러두기

· 본 총서에 실린 자료는 2022년 4월과 2023년 4월에 각각 공개한 외교문서 4,827권, 76만 여 쪽 가운데 일부를 발췌한 것이다.

· 각 권의 제목과 순서는 공개된 원본을 최대한 반영하였으나, 주제에 따라 일부는 적절히 변경하였다.

· 원본 자료는 A4 판형에 맞게 축소하거나 원본 비율을 유지한 채 A4 페이지 안에 삽입 하였다. 또한 현재 시점에선 공개되지 않아 '공란'이란 표기만 있는 페이지 역시 그대로 실었다.

· 외교부가 공개한 문서 각 권의 첫 페이지에는 '정리 보존 문서 목록'이란 이름으로 기록물 종류, 일자, 명칭, 간단한 내용 등의 정보가 수록되어 있으며, 이를 기준으로 0001번부터 번호가 매겨져 있다. 이는 삭제하지 않고 총서에 그대로 수록하였다.

· 보고서 내용에 관한 더 자세한 정보가 필요하다면, 외교부가 온라인상에 제공하는 『대한 민국 외교사료요약집』 1991년과 1992년 자료를 참조할 수 있다.

| 차례

정리보존문서목록					
기록물종류	일반공문서철	등록번호	2020020060	등록일자	2020-02-10
분류번호	734.29	국가코드		보존기간	준영구
명　칭	세계인권편람 자료 검토, 1991				
생 산 과	국제연합과	생산년도	1991~1991	담당그룹	
내용목차	* 영국 Economist사에서 발간 * 우리 인권 상황에 관한 설문서 회신 포함				

0001

주 영 대 사 관

영국(정) 723-36   1991. 7. 19.

수신 : 장관

참조 : 국제기구조약국장

제목 : 세계인권편람

1. 당지 Economist 사에서 발간되는 세계인권편람(World Human Rights Guide)
   의 집필인 Mr. Charles Humana 는 91.7.5(금)자 서한으로 아국의 인권상황에 대한
   설문서를 작성해 줄것을 요청하여 왔는바, 동 서한 및 설문서 양식을 별첨 송부
   하오니 작성후 당관에 회송하여 주시기 바랍니다.

2. 동 집필인은 유엔개발계획(UNDP)의 1991년도 인권보고서가 동인의 인권지표에
   기초하였다 함을 참고바랍니다.

첨부 : 1. 서한 사본 1부.
       2. 설문서 사본 1부. 끝.

예고 : 91.12.31.일반

일반문서로 재분류(1991. 12. 31

주 영 대

자			결		
접수일시 1991. 7. 25	번호 4395		재 공람		
서 리 과					

0002

기 안 용 지

분류기호 문서번호	국연 2031 - 1886	(전화:)	시 행 상 특별취급	
보존기간	영구·준영구· 10. 5. 3. 1	장 관		
수 신 처 보존기간				
시행일자	1991. 7. 30.			

보조 기관	국 장	전 결	협 조 기 관	
	과 장			
기안책임자		송영완		

경 유	
수 신	법무부장관
참 조	법무실장
제 목	세계인권 편람

1. 영국의 유력주간지 Economist 사에서 발간되는 세계

인권편람 (World Human Rights Guide)의 집필자인 Mr. Charles

Humana는 주영대사에게 아국의 인권상황에 대한 설문서를 작성해

줄 것을 요청하여 왔는 바, 동 설문서 및 1985-1986년도의 아국

인권상황 작성 예를 별첨 송부하오니 설문서를 영문으로 작성,

8.7(수)한 당부로 회송하여 주시기 바랍니다.

/ 계속 /

0003

2. 동 세계인권 편람 집필자는 유엔개발계획(UNDP)의

1991년도 인권보고서가 동인의 인권지표에 기초하였다 함을

참고하시기 바랍니다.

첨 부 : 1. 설문서 1부.

2. 서한사본 1부.

3. 설문서 작성 예 (85-86년 세계인권편람에 수록된

아국인권상황) 1부. 끝.

일반문서로재분류(1991 12.31.

0004

기 안 용 지

분류기호 문서번호	국연 2031 2010	(전화:)	시 행 상 특별취급	
보존기간	영구·준영구· 10. 5. 3. 1		장 관	
수 신 처 보존기간				
시행일자	1991. 8. 26.			

보조기관	국 장	전 결	협조기관		문서통제
	심의관				1991. 8.
	과 장				발송인
기안책임자		황준국			1991. 8. 27 외무부

경 유		
수 신	법무부장관	발신명의
참 조		

제 목   세계인권편람

1. 국연 2031-1886 (91.7.30)과 관련입니다.

2. 귀부 검토자료를 참고하여 별첨과 같이 설문서를

작성하였는 바, 특별한 의견있으면 가급적 9.3(화)까지 회신

하여 주시기 바랍니다.

일반문서로 재분류(1991. 12. 31.)

첨 부 : 동 설문서 1부. 끝.

0005

기 안 용 지

분류기호 문서번호	국연 2031 - 2089	(전화:)	시 행 상 특별취급	
보존기간	영구·준영구/ 10. 5. 3. 1/		장 관	
수 신 처 보존기간				
시행일자	1991. 8. 26.			

보조 기관	국 장	전 결	협 조 기 관	
	심의관			
	과 장			
기안책임자		황준국		

경 유		발 신 명 의	
수 신	대통령비서실장		
참 조	외교안보보좌관, 정책조사보좌관		
제 목	세계인권편람		

1. 영국 Economist사에서 발간되는 세계인권편람

(World Human Rights Guide)의 집필자인 Mr. Charles Humana는

주영대사에게 우리의 인권상황에 관한 설문서에 답해 줄 것을

요청해 왔는 바 이에 대한 법무부 의견을 참조하여 별첨과 같이

설문서를 작성,회신코자 하오니 특별한 의견있으면 가급적

9.3(화)까지 알려주시기 바랍니다.

/ 계속 /

0006

2. Mr. Humana에 의하면 유엔개발계획(UNDP)의

인권지표(Human Freedom Index)가 동 세계인권편람에 기초

하였다 함을 참고하시기 바랍니다.

첨 부 : 1. 동 설문서

~~2. 법무부의견~~

2. 세계인권편람측 요청서한.   끝.

일반문서로재분류(1991 12. 31)

```
┌─────────────────────────────────────┐
│   영국 이코노미스트지 인권설문서 검토자료   │
└─────────────────────────────────────┘
```

1991. 8.

법 무 부 인 권 과

I. 검토개관

○ 인권상황 설문서 내용중 당부와 관련된 부분의 자료는 첨부
  내용과 같음

○ 1986년도 아국에 대한 평가내용을 살펴보면, 아국에서는
  동성애의 권리가 보장되지 아니하며 불법이라고 하는 등
  그 평가에 있어서 명백한 오류를 범한 부분이 다수 있음

○ 따라서, 위 설문에 대한 종합답변서 작성시에는, 1986년
  이후 현재까지의 아국내의 정치. 경제. 사회. 문화 전반의
  변화상황, 특히 인권관련 발전사항 등에 관해 그 변화된
  내용을 답변서 모두에 기재하는 등의 방법으로 명백히
  인식시킬 필요가 있음

○ 그 개괄적인 변화상황으로는, 1987.10.29, 헌법 및 대통령
  선거법 개정으로 인한 대통령의 국민직선제 실시로 제6공화국이
  탄생하였고, 인권보장의 제도적 장치 마련을 위해 헌법재판소를
  설치하고('88.8), 국제인권규약에 가입하였으며('90.4.10,
  '90.7.10 부터 발효), 나아가 형사절차상의 인권보호를 위해
  서는 국가보안법 및 사회보호법과 사회안전법 등의 개정으로
  보안처분 등의 남용소지를 제거하는 등 종래 소위 민주악법
  이라고 칭하여지던 다수의 법률이 개정 또는 폐지되는 커다란
  변화가 있었음

1

0009

o 참고로, 최근 대한변협회장이 제3회 법의 지배를 위한 변호사
  대회에서 행한 인권관련 연설내용중 한국의 인권개념이 독재
  집권자의 자의적인 처벌로부터의 인권개념에서 정보화, 고도
  산업사회 구조하에서의 인권개념으로 시각의 전환을 필요로
  한다는 부분은, 이제까지 주로 아국의 인권상황을 평가함에
  있어 기존의 일방적으로 왜곡되고, 부정적인 측면만을 확대,
  강조하는 측면에서의 인권상황 평가에서 탈피하여야 할 필요
  성에 대해 언급한 것으로서, 이건 평가와 관련해서도 외국
  인권단체의 왜곡.편향된 시각을 시정하는데 시사하는 바가
  크다고 생각됨

2

II. 관련 질문내용 및 답변자료

(* 이 건 문항은 1986년 평가보고서에 No로-Yes중 일부포함-
   평가된 부분임)

질 문 내 용

1. 국외로의 여행의 자유가 보장되고 있는가

2. 평화적인 집회.결사의 자유가 보장되고 있는가

3. 학문의 자유(대학) 및 출판, 정보자유가 보장되고 있는가

4. 국가기관에 의한 각종 고문, 탄압행위 여부

5. 사형제도

6. 불법 및 장기감금 여부

7. 언론에 대한 검열이 있는가 (주무관서:공보처)

8. 우편, 전화에 대한 도청 및 검열이 있는가 (주무관서:공보처)

9. 평화롭게 정부입장에 반대할 수 있는 권리가 보장되는가

10. 비밀, 평등, 보통선거를 통한 다수정당의 각종 선거참여가
    이루어지고 있는가 (주무관서:내무부)

3

0011

11. 여성에 대한 정치적, 법적 평등보장 여부 (주무관서:정무제2)

12. 여성에 대한 경제적, 사회적 평등보장 여부 (주무관서:정무제2)

13. 언론의 자유가 보장되는가 (주무관서:공보처)

14. 출판의 자유가 보장되는가 (주무관서:공보처)

15. 라디오. TV 방송국의 자치운영, 편성 등 자치권이 인정되는가
    (주무관서:공보처)

16. 독자적인 노동조합의 존재 및 활동 가능여부

17. 유죄판결을 받을 때까지 무죄로 추정되는가

18. 민간인들이 공개재판을 받고 있는가

19. 신속한 재판을 받고 있는가

20. 혼인, 이혼 등 가족관계에서의 여성의 평등이 이루어지고
    있는가 (주무관서:정무제2)

21. 개인 사생활 등에 국가가 관여하는가 (주무관서:내무부)

4

답 변 내 용

1. 국외로의 여행의 자유

   ○ 보장되고 있음

   ○ 헌법 (the constitution, 1987.10.29 전문개정) 제14조는
     "모든 국민은 거주(residence). 이전(move)의 자유를 가진
     다"라고 규정하여 국외이주의 자유와 해외여행의 자유를
     보장하고 있음

   ○ 따라서, 정치적 반대인물이라 하여 위 헌법규정과 달리
     국외로의 여행의 자유를 제한할 어떠한 제도적 장치도
     없으며, 실제 달리 취급하고 있지 아니함

   ○ 단지, 전염병 환자나 형사재판 진행중인 자 등만 일부
     제한되고 있음

5

0013

2. 평화적인 집회.결사의 자유

  ○ 보장되고 있음.

  ○ 헌법 제21조 제2항은 '언론.출판에 대한 허가나 검열과
     집회.결사에 대한 허가는 인정되지 아니한다"고 규정하고
     있고, 집회및시위에관한법률 (the Act Concerning
     Assembly and Demonstration, 1989.3.29 개정) 제6조
     제1항은 '옥외집회 또는 시위를 주최하고자 하는 자는
     그 목적, 일시, 장소, 주최자 ... 를 기재한 신고서를
     옥외집회 또는 시위의 48시간전에 관할 경찰서장에게
     제출하여야 한다'고 규정하고 있음

  ○ 따라서 신고를 마친 평화적인 시위인 경우 그 내용이
     정부를 비난하는 것일지라도 허용되고 있음

  ○ 다만, 집회.시위와 관련하여 처벌받는 경우는 신고를 하지
     않거나 화염병, 돌을 던지는 폭력행위 등의 경우 뿐임

3. 학문과 정보의 자유

　o 보장되고 있음.

　o 헌법 제22조 제1항은 '모든 국민은 학문과 예술의 자유를
　　가진다'고 규정하고 있음

　o 대학은 감시하에 있지 않으며, 대학의 자유를 최대한 보장
　　하기 위해 정부는 학교당국이 불법폭력사태를 수습할 수
　　없어 총학장이 경찰력 투입을 요청하거나 동의하는 경우
　　에만 경찰력을 투입하고 있음

　o 진보적인 사상을 가지고 있거나 북한 출판물을 소지하고
　　있다고 하여 처벌되는 것이 아니라, 급진좌익이론에 따라
　　폭력적 방법에 의한 계급혁명을 선동하는 행위나, 아국
　　내에서 민중봉기에 의한 폭력혁명을 선동하는 북한 출판물
　　만이 규제되고 있음

7

4. 국가기관에 의한 고문과 탄압으로부터의 자유

o 보장되고 있음.

o 헌법 제12조 제2항은 '모든 국민은 고문을 받지 아니하며,
  형사상 자기에게 불리한 진술을 강요당하지 아니한다'고
  규정하고 있고, 형법 제125조에서는 '재판. 검찰. 경찰
  기타 인신구속에 관한 직무를 행하는 자 또는 이를 보조
  하는 자가 그 직무를 행함에 당하여 형사피의자 또는 기타
  사람에 대하여 폭행 또는 가혹한 행위를 가한 때에는 5년
  이하의 징역과 10년 이상의 자격정지에 처한다'고 규정
  하고 있으며, 형사소송법 제309조는 '피고인의 자백이
  고문, 폭행, 협박, 신체구속의 부당한 장기화 또는 기망
  기타의 방법으로 임의로 진술한 것이 아니라고 의심할
  만한 이유가 있는 때에는 이를 유죄의 증거로 하지
  못한다(any confession extracted by torture, violence,
  threat, unjustifiably prolonged detention or which
  is suspected to have been made involuntarily, shall
  not be admitted as evidence of guilt)'고 규정하고 있음

o 정부는 각종 고문, 가혹행위 등 인권침해사례가 발생하지
  않도록 수사기관 종사자들에게 수시 주의를 촉구하고 있
  으며 ('88.8.4. 법무부장관의 '인권침해사례 근절을 위한
  지시' 등) 인권침해행위를 저지른 공무원에 대하여는 가중
  처벌하고 있음

8

0016

5. 사형으로부터의 자유

   ○ 일부 중죄에 대하여 사형제도가 유지되고 있음

   ○ 사형제도의 존치여부에 대해 활발한 논의가 전개되고 있고
     살인, 강도 등 사람의 생명 및 신체에 대한 법익을 침해
     하는 범죄 이외의 범죄에 대해서는 "사형"을 폐지하는
     방향으로 법률을 개정해 나가고 있음

   ○ 그 일환으로 1990.12.31 법률개정에 의하여 '특정범죄가중
     처벌등에관한법률 (the Act Concerning Additional
     Punishment for Specified Crimes)'의 4개조문 (뇌물죄,
     관세포탈죄, 무면허수출입죄, 산림절도죄 등),
     '특정경제범죄가중처벌등에관한법률 (the Act Concerning
     Additional Punishment for Specified Financial Crimes)'
     의 3개조문 (특정재산범죄의 가중처벌, 재산국외도피의죄,
     금융기관 임직원의 수재등의 죄 등)에 법정형으로 규정되어
     있는 "사형"을 삭제하였음

9

0017

6. 불법적인 장기구금으로부터의 자유

o 보장되고 있음

o 헌법 제12조 제1항은 '모든 국민은 신체의 자유를 가진다.
누구든지 법률에 의하지 아니하고는 체포(arrested),
구속(detained), 압수(seized), 수색(searched) 또는
심문(interrogated)을 받지 아니하며, 법률과 적법한
절차에 의하지 아니하고는 처벌.보안처분(preventive
restrictions) 또는 강제노역을 받지 아니한다'고 규정
하고 있고, 형법 제124조에서는 '재판. 검찰. 경찰 기타
인신구속에 관한 직무를 행하는 자 또는 이를 보조하는
자가 그 직권을 남용하여 사람을 체포 또는 감금한 때에는
7년 이하의 징역과 10년 이하의 자격정지에 처한다'고
규정하고 있음

o 정부는 수사기관 종사자들의 불법적인 체포.감금사례가
발생하지 않도록 수시 교육시키고 있음

o 또한, 수사단계에서 피의자 구속기간도 엄격히 제한되어
일반범죄의 경우 최대 30일 (경찰수사단계 10일, 검찰수사
단계 20일)을 초과할 수 없고 (형사소송법 제202조,제203조,
제205조), 국가보안법 위반범죄의 경우 최대 50일로 제한됨
(국가보안법 제19조)

o 위 구속기간 제한에 대한 예외는 전혀 인정되지 아니하며,
기간초과의 경우는 그 즉시 석방하고 있음

10

0018

9. 평화적인 정치적 반대의 권리

 ㅇ 보장되고 있음

 ㅇ 북한과의 협상이나 비군사적인 해결방안을 주장하는 사람
   들이 전복행위자들로 간주된다는 것은 명백한 오해임

 ㅇ 북한의 대남혁명전략에 동조하여 그 전술을 실행하는
   경우에 처벌하고 있을 뿐이며, 정부의 방침과는 다른
   북한과의 협상 또는 교류, 통일방안을 주장한다고 하여
   전복행위자로 간주하는 사례는 없음

 ㅇ 일례로, 자유롭게 정부의 방침을 비판하고 새로운 방안이
   제안되는 경우를 언론에서 자주 볼 수 있음

11

0019

16. 독립적인 노조활동의 자유

  o 보장되고 있음

  o 헌법 제33조 제1항은 '근로자는 근로조건의 향상을 위하여
    자주적인 단결권. 단체교섭권 및 단체행동권 (the right
    to association, collective bargaining and collective
    action)을 가진다'고 규정하고 있고, 노동조합의 설립은
    노동조합법 (the Labor Union Act) 제13조에 따라 설립
    신고서를 행정관청에 제출함으로써 가능하게 되어 있음

  o 다만, 조합원의 임금 등 근로조건 향상을 목적으로 해야
    하는 노조의 성격이 변질되는 것을 막기 위해 개별적인
    정치활동은 자유롭게 보장되지만 노조명의의 정치활동이나
    정치자금 징수 등은 금지되고 있음 (노동조합법 제12조)

  o 파업을 해산시키기 위한 폭력의 사용에 정부가 개입하고
    있지 않으며, 그러한 폭력행위는 구속하여 엄벌하고 있음

12

0020

17. 유죄판결을 받은 때까지 무죄로 추정될 법적 권리

   ○ 보장되고 있음

   ○ 헌법 제27조 제4항은 '형사피고인은 유죄의 판결이 확정될 때까지는 무죄로 추정된다'고 규정하고 있음

   ○ 국가전복행위나 북한관련 범죄라고 하여 위 헌법규정과 달리 취급할 어떠한 제도적 장치도 없으며, 실제 달리 취급하고 있지 아니함

18. 공개재판을 받을 권리

 ○ 일반적으로 보장되고 있음

 ○ 헌법 제109조는 '재판의 심리와 판결은 공개한다. 다만
   심리는 국가의 안전보장 또는 안녕질서를 방해하거나
   선량한 풍속을 해할 염려가 있을 때에는 법원의 결정으로
   공개하지 아니할 수 있다'고 규정하고 있음

 ○ 실제에 있어 안보관련범죄나 전복행위관련 범죄는 전부
   공개되고 있으며, 강간사건과 같이 피해자의 명예가
   보호되어야 하는 소수의 사건에서만 법원의 결정으로
   비공개되는 경우가 있음

14

19. 신속한 재판을 받을 권리

○ 일반적으로 보장되고 있음

○ 헌법 제27조 제3항은 '모든 국민은 신속한 재판을 받을
  권리를 가진다. 형사피고인은 상당한 이유가 없는 한
  지체없이 공개재판을 받을 권리를 가진다'고 규정하고
  있음

○ 또한, 소송촉진등에관한특례법 (Special Act for Speedy
  Proceedings) 제21조도 '판결의 선고는 제1심에서는 공소
  가 제기된 날로부터 6월 이내에, 항소심 및 상고심에서는
  기록을 송부받은 날로부터 각 4월 이내에 하여야 한다'고
  규정하여 구속기간을 엄격히 제한하고 있음

○ 따라서, 아무리 중한 범죄라 하더라도 구속재판기간은
  최장 6개월을 초과하지 못하며, 그 예외는 전혀 인정되지
  아니함

15

0023

분류번호	보존기간

발 신 전 보

번   호 : WUK-1557   910826 1912 FN   종별 : _____

수   신 : 주   영국   대사. 총영사 *****
                        (국연)

발   신 : 장 관

제   목 : 세계인권편람

대 : 영국(정) 723-36 (91.7.19)

대호, 현재 관계부처와 협의 설문서 작성중에 있으며
9월초순에는 귀관에 송부될 수 있을 것으로 예상되~~는 바~~, 하겸. 참고바람.
~~세계인권편람측에 우선 등보바람~~.   끝.

(국제기구조약국장 문동석)

~~인권~~

앙고재	91년 8월 26일 국연과	기안자 성명	과 장 심의관	국 장	차 관	장 관

보 안 통 제	
외신과통제	

0024

42381

기 안 용 지

분류기호 문서번호	국연 2031 -	(전화:)	시 행 상 특별취급	지급
보존기간	영구·준영구· 10. 5. 3. 1		장 관	

수 신 처 보존기간	
시행일자	1991. 8. 29.

보 조 기 관	국 장	전결
	심의관	
	과 장	
기안책임자		황준국

협
조
기
관

문서통제
결열
1991. 8. 29
발송인

경 유	
수 신	통계청장
참 조	

발신명의

의무부

제 목   통계자료 협조요청

외국인권기관이 당부에 요청해 온 우리나라 관련

통계자료에 대하여 관련부처들에 문의한 결과 아래와 같은

통계수치가 나왔는 바, 동수치가 옳게 되었는지 귀청에서

확인해 주실 것을 요망하오니 가급적 9.4(수)한 회시하여

주시기 바랍니다.

- 아   래 -

1. 인 구 : 43,520,199명

0025 /계속/

(2)
2. 평균수명 : 72세
3. 영아사망율(0-1세 1,000명당) : 11명
4. 1인당 국민소득 : US$5,569
5. 국가가 지출하는 보건비가 GNP에서 차지하는 비율 : 0.5%
6. 국가가 지출하는 교육비가 GNP에서 차지하는 비율 : 3.6%
7. GNP 대비 군사비 비율 : 4.7%. 끝.
0026

통 화 요 록

통화일시 : 91.8.29(목) 16:00

송 화 자 : 법무부 인권과 정기용 검사

수 화 자 : 외무부 유엔과 황준국 사무관

내 용 : 세계인권편람관련 외무부측 공문(국연 2031-2090)에 대한
        법무부측 의견

    o 12번 항목 코멘트 추가 : Court not authorized to sentence
                                     corporal punishment

    o 17번 항목 : the government or the president를 the government
                         including the president로

    o 28번 항목 : YES를 yes로 (복수노조 및 직접적 정치활동 불인정)

    o 31번 항목 : state run legal aid for the indigent 추가. 끝.

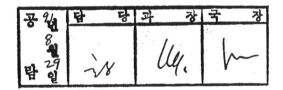

0027

통 계 청

자관 10852-2462 　　　　720-2788 　　　　1991. 9. 3.
수신 외무부장관
제목 통계자료 협조요청에 대한 회신

　　　1. 국연 2031-42381('91. 8. 29)호와 관련입니다.

　　　2. 귀 기관에서 확인 요청한 통계수치에 대한 검토 결과를 별첨과 같이
회신 합니다.

첨부 : 통계수치 검토결과및 비율산출 근거자료 1부. 끝.

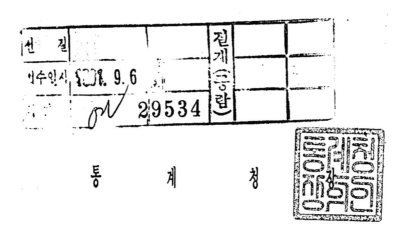

통 계 청

0028

통 계 수 치 검 토 결 과

구 분	당초 자료	확인 자료	비 고
1. 인구	43,520,199 명	43,268,301 명	'91년 연앙추계
2. 평균수명	72세	70.8세	'89년 남자 : 66.9세 여자 : 75.0세
3. 영아 사망율	11명	12.5명	'90년 추정치
4. 1인당 국민소득(GNP)	US $ 5,569	US $ 5,569	'90년 잠정치
5. 국가가 지출하는 보건비가 GNP에서 차지하는 비율	0.5%	0.66%	'90년 가결산 자료
6. 국가가 지출하는 교육비가 GNP에서 차지하는 비율	3.6%	3.32%	'90년 가결산 자료
7. GNP대비 군사비 비율	4.7%	4.07%	'90년 가결산 자료

※ 1,2,3항은 통계청 자료, 4항은 한국은행 자료, 5,6,7항은 재무부 가결산
자료를 한국은행의 GNP에 대한 비율을 계산한 것임.

비 율 산 출 근 거 자 료

구 분	금 액 (10억원)	비 율 (%)	비 고
G N P	168,437.8	-	한국은행
- 보건	1,111.8	0.66	재무부
. 보건	248.1	0.15	재무부
. 사회복지	863.7	0.51	재무부
- 교육	5,586.0	3.32	재무부
- 국방	6,856.2	4.07	재무부

0029

기 안 용 지

분류기호 문서번호	국연 2031	(전화 :)	시 행 상 특별취급	
보존기간	영구·준영구· 10. 5. 3. 1	장 관		
수 신 처 보존기간				
시행일자	1991. 9. 7.			

보조기관	국 장	전 결	협조기관		문서통제
	심의관				1991. 9. 09
	과 장				통제
기안책임자	황준국				발송 1991. 9. 9 외무부

경 유		발신명의	
수 신	주영대사		
참 조			
제 목	세계인권편람		

대호 세계인권편람 설문서를 작성 별첨 송부합니다.

첨부 : 동 설문서 1부. 끝.

일반문서로 재분류(1991. 12. 31.

0030

기안용지

분류기호 문서번호	국연 2031 -	(전화 :)	시 행 상 특별취급	
보존기간	영구·준영구· 10. 5. 3. 1	차 관		장 관
수 신 처 보존기간		(초장)		
시행일자	1991. 9. 7.			

보 조 기 관	국 장	∿	협 조 기 관	제1차관보(초장)	문서통제
	심의관				
	과 장	∿			
기안책임자		황준국			발 송 인

경 유		발신명의	
수 신	내부결재		
참 조			
제 목	세계인권편람		

　

영국 Economist사에서 발간되는 세계인권편람(World

Human Rights Guide)의 집필자인 Mr. Charles Humana는 주영

대사에게 우리의 인권상황에 관한 설문서에 답해 줄 것을

요청하여 왔는 바, 법무부, 청와대, 통계청등 관계부처와

협조하여 별첨과 같이 설문서를 작성, 회신코자 하오니 재가

하여 주시기 바랍니다.

0031

/ 계속 /

첨 부 : 1. 동 설문서

        2. 세계인권편람측 요청서한.   끝.

일반문서로 재분류(1991 .12. 31.

0032

Country : <u>The Repulbic of Korea</u>

Population : 43,520,199

Life expectancy : 70.8

Infant mortality
(0-1 year) per 1,000 births : 12.5

Form of government : executive presidency

United Nations covenants : a list attached

Income per head : US $5,569

% of GNP spent by state
on health : 0.66

% of GNP spent on military : 4.07

% of GNP spent by state on
education : 3.32

Factors affecting human rights :

- Advancement of democratization in all quarters of the society since 1988
  when the 6th Republic was inaugurated by direct presidential election

- Significant amendments to relevant laws including the National Security
  Law to strengthen legal and institutional protection of basic human rights

- Accession to International Covenant on Economic, Social and Cultural
  Rights and International Covenant on Civil and Political Rights and its
  Optional Protocol in July 1990

- Unique security situation unchanged with North Korean threat remaining
  formidable

FREEDOM TO :		COMMENTS
1. Travel in own country	YES	1. No restrictions
2. Travel outside own country	YES	2. No special regulations against political opponents
3. Peacefully associate and assemble	YES	3. All kinds of peaceful demonstrations are allowed if those have been properly reported to the police beforehand in accordance with the law
4. Teach ideas and receive information	YES	4. Police involvement in universities only when they request so. North Korean publications banned only when their content is explicitly seditious in favor of Communist revolution

0033

5. Monitor human rights violations	YES	5. Free activities of monitoring groups are allowed
6. Publish and educate in ethnic language	YES	6. Insignificant minorities

FREEDOM FROM :

7. Serfdom, slavery, forced or child labour	YES	
8. Extrajudicial killings or 'disappearances'	YES	
9. Torture or coercion by the state	YES	9. Any confession obtained by torture or coercion not admitted as evidence of guilt. Law enforcement officers strictly instructed not to inflict coercion in the performance of their official duties
10. Compulsory work permits or conscripted labour	YES	
11. Capital punishment by the state	NO	11. Premature to eliminate death penalty in that heinous crimes are being committed. Crimes subject to death penalty now more limited
12. Court sentences of corporal punishment	YES	
13. Indefinite detention without charge	YES	13. Indefinite detention without charge not allowed in any case
14. Compulsory membership of state organisations or political parties	YES	
15. Compulsory religion or state ideology in schools	YES	
16. Deliberate state policies to control artistic works	YES	
17. Political censorship of press	YES	17. No Guidelines. Direct criticism of the government or the president rather normal
18. Censorship of mail or telephone-tapping	YES	

0034

FREEDOM FOR OR RIGHTS TO :			COMMENTS
19. Peaceful political opposition	YES		19. Expression of political opinions in a peaceful manner is perfectly all right
20. Multi-party elections by secret and universal ballot	YES		20. Executive president for a 5-year term directly elected by the people. Multi-party politics by universal, equal, direct and secret voting guaranteed by the Constitution
21. Political and legal equality for women	YES		21. Discriminatory elements of the Family Law revised in 1989 reflecting most of the women's requests
22. Social and economic equality for women	yes		22. Traditional Confucian ideas in favor of male domination still remaining
23. Social and economic equality for ethnic minorities	YES		
24. Independent newspapers	YES		24. No guidelines
25. Independent book publishing	YES		25. Restrictions by the law may be imposed when endangering national security or survival, or the free and democratic order
26. Independent radio and television networks	YES		26. No one can interfere with the making of a program or the operation of a broadcasting company without complying with the conditions prescribed by law
27. All courts to total independence	YES		27. Free from political manipulation
28. Independent trade unions	yes		28. Direct political activities in the name of trade unions banned

LEGAL RIGHTS

29. From deprivation of nationality	YES		
30. To be considered innocent until proved guilty	YES		30. Clearly stated in the Constitution
31. To free legal aid when necessary and counsel of own choice	YES		31. Lawyers, free of charge, assigned by the state

0035

32. From civilian trials in secret	YES	32. In practice trials for subversion are open but trials that may harm personal privacy are sometimes in secret by the decision of the court
33. To be brought promptly before a judge or court	YES	33. Detention by a police officer and a prosecutor prior to indictment limited to 10 days each (exceptional cases : a total of 50 days) Detention and trial by a court shall not exceed 2 months (exceptional cases : maximum 6 months)
34. From police searches of home without a warrant	YES	
35. From arbitrary seizure of personal property	YES	
PERSONAL RIGHTS :		
36. To inter-racial, inter-religious or civil marriage	YES	
37. Equality of sexes during marriage and for divorce proceedings	YES	37. Significantly enhanced by the amendments to the Family Law in 1989
38. To practise any religion	YES	
39. To use contraceptive pills and devices	YES	39. Government support
40. To non-interference by state in strictly private affairs	YES	

COMPULSORY DOCUMENTS FOR CITIZENS

Legally required at all times   :   ID Card

For employment in own country   :   ID Card

When applying for passport   :   ID Card

Period of validity of passport   :   5 years

Countries forbidden to holder   :   Countries that have no diplomatic relations with the Republic of Korea

0036

Republic of Korea

International Covenant on Economic, Social and Cultural Rights (1966), United Nations, *Treaty Series*, Vol. 993, p. 3. Entered into force on 3 January 1976.

International Covenant on Civil and Political Rights (1966), United Nations, *Treaty Series*, Vol. 999, p. 171. Entered into force on 23 March 1976.

Declaration regarding Article 41 of the International Covenant on Civil and Political Rights (concerning the competence of the Human Rights Committee to receive and consider communications by one State Party against another). Entered into force on 28 March 1979.

Optional Protocol to the International Covenant on Civil and Political Rights (1966), United Nations, *Treaty Series*, Vol. 999, p. 171. Entered into force on 23 March 1976.

International Convention on the Elimination of All Forms of Racial Discrimination (1965), United Nations, *Treaty Series*, Vol. 660, p. 195. Entered into force on 4 January 1969.

Convention on the Prevention and Punishment of the Crime of Genocide (1948), United Nations, *Treaty Series*, Vol. 78, p. 277. Entered into force on 12 January 1951.

Convention for the Suppression of the Traffic in Persons and of the Exploitation of the Prostitution of Others (1950), United Nations, *Treaty Series*, Vol. 96, p. 271. Entered into force on 25 July 1951.

Convention relating to the Status of Stateless Persons (1954), United Nations, *Treaty Series*, Vol. 360, p. 117. Entered into force on 6 June 1960.

Convention on the Political Rights of Women (1952), United Nations, *Treaty Series*, Vol. 193, p. 135. Entered into force on 7 July 1954.

Convention on the Elimination of All Forms of Discrimination against Women (1979), GA Res. 34/180. Entered into force on 3 September 1981.

0037

Geneva Convention for the Amelioration of the Condition of the Wounded and Sick in Armed Forces in the Field (1949), United Nations, *Treaty Series*, Vol. 75, p. 31. Entered into force on 21 October 1950.

Geneva Convention for the Amelioration of the Condition of Wounded, Sick and Shipwrecked Members of Armed Forces at Sea (1949), United Nations, *Treaty Series*, Vol. 75, p. 85. Entered into force on 21 October 1950.

Geneva Convention relative to the Treatment of Prisoners of War (1949), United Nations, *Treaty Series*, Vol. 75, p. 135. Entered into force on 21 October 1950.

Geneva Convention relative to the Protection of Civilian Persons in Time of War (1949), United Nations, *Treaty Series*, Vol. 75, p. 287. Entered into force on 21 October 1950.

Additional Protocol to the Geneva Conventions of 12 August 1949 relating to the Protection of Victims of International Armed Conflicts (Protocol I) (1977). Entered into force on 7 December 1978.

Additional Protocol to the Geneva Conventions of 12 August 1949 relating to the Protection of Victims of Non-International Armed Conflicts (Protocol II) (1977). Entered into force on 7 December 1978.

0038

WORLD HUMAN RIGHTS GUIDE

Compiler: Charles Humana
World Human Rights Guide
38 Greyhound Road
London W6 8NX
Tel: (071) 229 8978, (☒☒☒☒☒☒☒☒☒
☒☒☒☒☒☒☒☒☒☒☒☒☒☒
Fax UK: 0753 646746

His Excellency Mr Jay Hee Oh
Ambassador
Embassy of the Republic of Korea
4 Palace Gate
LONDON
W8 5NF

5th July, 1991

Excellency,

You may be familiar with my human rights guide, which is now internationally known. You may also be aware that the Human Development Report 1991 of the UNITED NATIONS Development Programme has based its recently introduced Human Freedom Index on my work.

I was invited last month by the Development Report to New York to discuss a new edition of the guide, which I am now compiling. In view of this, I am sure you will appreciate that it is more important than ever that my facts are accurate and unbiased.

To achieve this high standard, I need the help and goodwill of the representatives of the United Nations member states. With this in mind, I am enclosing my usual questionnaire, with a copy of the 1985/86 entry in the guide, which I hope you or the appropriate member of your staff will be able to complete.

The 4-point scale I use is a straightforward method of assessing human rights performance. It is as follows:

        YES = No violations
        yes = Occasional violations

        no = Frequent violations
        NO = Constant violations

If there are questions that cannot be answered, or the answers will mean a long wait for information, please return the partly completed questionnaire. It would be appreciated, however, if you could update the section on Compulsory Documents.

I look forward to receiving the questionnaire for your country. I accept that you may feel constrained in answering some of the questions but I am also sure that you share my wish for the highest possible degree of accuracy.

                Yours sincerely,

                Charles Humana

                Charles Humana

Published by: ECONOMIST PUBLICATIONS, 40 Duke Street, London WI
    PAN BOOKS, Cavaye Place, London SW10
    FACTS ON FILE, 460 Park Avenue South, New York, NY 10016, USA
    BUCHET-CHASTEL, 18 Rue de Condé, Paris 75006, France

PEN

0039

Korea, South

Human rights rating: 59%

Population: 41,999,000
Life expectancy: 67
Infant mortality (0–1 year)
              per 1,000 births: 32
Form of government: executive presidency
United Nations covenants:
signed – Convention on equality for
women.

Income per head: US$2,010
% of GNP spent on military: n/a
% of GNP spent by state on health: n/a
% of GNP spent by state on education: n/a

		40
YES	14	
yes	9	
NO	7	
no	10	

FACTORS AFFECTING HUMAN RIGHTS

Since 1948, when the country was divided between North and South, the priority of adequate military defences against the communist north has dominated the policy of the government of the Republic of Korea. In this it is supported by the presence of a large US military force following the war of 1950–2. The improving economic standards and the possibility of a liberalisation after the next presidential election of 1988, when the present incumbent has promised to stand down, have meant a less oppressive human rights situation. Recent National Assembly elections improved the prospects of the limited opposition.

FREEDOM TO:

			COMMENTS:
1	Travel in own country	yes	Except in North Korea frontier zone
2	Travel outside own country	yes	But denied to political opponents of the president
3	Peacefully associate and assemble	NO	No demonstrations against the government. students have received long prison sentences and have paid heavy fines for participating in peaceful rallies
4	Teach ideas and receive information	no	Universities under strict surveillance. Free-thinking students a constant challenge to the authorities; however, some banned professors recently reinstated. Imprisonment for possessing North Korean publications
5	Monitor human rights violations	yes	The US government has used its influence to help the work of monitoring groups. Some human rights activists released from prison under an amnesty
6	Publish and educate in ethnic language	YES	Insignificant minorities

FREEDOM FROM:

			COMMENTS:
7	Serfdom, slavery, forced or child labour	YES	Rights respected

158

0040

FREEDOM FROM: COMMENTS:

8 Extrajudicial killings or **YES** Rights respected
'disappearances'

9 Torture or coercion by the **no** Slight reduction in worst excesses because of
state international publicity but beatings still continue

10 Compulsory work permits or **YES** Rights respected
conscription of labour

11 Capital punishment by the **NO** By hanging or shooting. For treason, murder, etc
state

12 Court sentences of corporal **YES** Rights respected
punishment

13 Indefinite detention without **NO** Some prisoners of conscience detained since 1971
charge but recent pattern is of repeated short detentions
for local activists

14 Compulsory membership of **YES** Rights respected
state organisations or parties

15 Compulsory religion or state **YES** Rights respected
ideology in schools

16 Deliberate state policies to **YES** Rights respected
control artistic works

17 Political censorship of press **no** Severe guidelines. Editors and journalists
dismissed. No criticism of the president

18 Censorship of mail or **NO** Extensive surveillance. Constant alertness
telephone-tapping because of North Korean infiltration

FREEDOM FOR OR RIGHTS TO: COMMENTS:

19 Peaceful political opposition **no** Fear of North Korean influences has meant that
those advocating compromise or non-military
solutions are seen as subversives

20 Multi-party elections by secret **no** Executive president for a 7-year term indirectly
and universal ballot elected by electoral college of 5,271 members.
New political parties for the National Assembly,
which has little influence on the president, were
formed for the 1985 elections

21 Political and legal equality for **no** No women in the most senior government posts.
women Nationality is decided by patriarchal lineage

22 Social and economic equality **no** Professions and commerce are male dominated.
for women Traditional Confucian ideas emphasising
women's subservience still evident. 2 lawyers in
every 1,000 are women

23 Social and economic equality **YES** Rights respected
for ethnic minorities

24 Independent newspapers **yes** But subject to severe guidelines. No direct
criticism of the president

25 Independent book publishing **yes** Frequent bannings. Government approval of
many books a prepublication precaution

0041   159

FREEDOM FOR OR RIGHTS TO: COMMENTS:

26 Independent radio and television networks — **no** — Close government supervision for subversive broadcasts and communist influences

27 All courts to total independence — **yes** — But political cases likely to be manipulated to suit the government

28 Independent trade unions — **no** — No involvement in politics. Violent strike-breaking gangs encouraged by government

LEGAL RIGHTS: COMMENTS:

29 From deprivation of nationality — **YES** — Rights respected

30 To be considered innocent until proved guilty — **no** — Not when offence is considered 'subversive' or bearing on North Korean issues

31 To free legal aid when necessary and counsel of own choice — **yes** — Means test. Lawyers appointed by court

32 From civilian trials in secret — **NO** — If civilian involved in security or subversion, trial may be in secret

33 To be brought promptly before a judge or court — **NO** — The National Security Law may hold back case for long interrogations

34 From police searches of home without a warrant — **yes** — Constitution not always honoured. Special 'stability laws' may cover police violations

35 From arbitrary seizure of personal property — **YES** — Rights respected

PERSONAL RIGHTS: COMMENTS:

36 To inter-racial, inter-religious or civil marriage — **YES** — Rights respected

37 Equality of sexes during marriage and for divorce proceedings — **yes** — But in practice women are victims of both Confucian traditions and modern social prejudice

38 To practise any religion — **YES** — Rights respected

39 To use contraceptive pills and devices — **YES** — Government support

40 To practise homosexuality between consenting adults — **NO** — Illegal

COMPULSORY DOCUMENTS FOR CITIZENS
Legally required at all times: ID card
For employment in own country: ID card
When applying for passport: Proof of purpose abroad (work, business, etc). ID card and birth certificate
Period of validity of passport: 1 year. Tourism usually only for citizens over 50
Countries forbidden to holder: All communist countries and South Africa

0042

Country .... —........

Population:

Life expectancy:

Infant mortality
(0-1 year) per 1,000 births:

Form of government:

United Nations covenants:
(ratified)

(signed)

Income per head:

% of GNP spent by state
on health:

% of GNP spent on
military:

% of GNP spent by
state on education:

Factors affecting human rights:

FREEDOM TO:

1. Travel in own country

2. Travel outside own
   country

3. Peacefully associate
   and assemble

4. Teach ideas and
   receive information

5. Monitor human rights
   violations

6. Publish and educate
   in ethnic language

FREEDOM FROM:

7. Serfdom, slavery,
   forced or child labour

COMMENTS

0043

COMMENTS

8. Extrajudicial killings
   or 'disappearances'

9. Torture or coercion
   by the state

10. Compulsory work permits
    or conscripted labour

11. Capital punishment
    by the state

12. Court sentences of
    corporal punishment

13. Indefinite detention
    without charge

14. Compulsory membership
    of state organisations
    or political parties

15. Compulsory religion or
    state ideology in
    schools

16. Deliberate state
    policies to control
    artistic works

17. Political censorship
    of press

18. Censorship of mail or
    telephone-tapping

FREEDOM FOR OR RIGHTS TO:

19. Peaceful political
    opposition

20. Multi-party elections
    by secret and universal
    ballot

21. Political and legal
    equality for women

22. Social and economic
    equality for women

0044

23. Social and economic
    equality for ethnic
    minorities

24. Independent newspapers

25. Independent book
    publishing

26. Independent radio and
    television networks

27. All courts to total
    independence

28. Independent trade
    unions

LEGAL RIGHTS

29. From deprivation of
    nationality

30. To be considered
    innocent until proved
    guilty

31. To free legal aid when
    necessary and counsel
    of own choice

32. From civilian trials
    in secret

33. To be brought promptly
    before a judge or court

34. From police searches of
    home without a warrant

35. From arbitrary seizure
    of personal property

0045

PERSONAL RIGHTS: COMMENTS

36. To inter-racial,
    inter-religious or
    civil marriage

37. Equality of sexes
    during marriage and
    for divorce proceedings

38. To practise any
    religion

39. To use contraceptive
    pills and devices

40. To non-interference by
    state in strictly
    private affairs

COMPULSORY DOCUMENTS FOR CITIZENS

Legally required
at all times:

For employment in
own country:

When applying for
passport:

Period of validity
of passport:

Countries forbidden
to holder:

0046

정 리 보 존 문 서 목 록

기록물종류	일반공문서철	등록번호	2021090130	등록일자	2021-09-27
분류번호	734.26	국가코드		보존기간	30년
명 칭	인종차별철폐협약(CERD) 당사국 회의, 제14차. New York, 1992.1.15				
생 산 과	국제연합2과	생산년도	1991~1992	담당그룹	
내용목차	* 수석대표 : 신기복 주유엔대표부 차석대사 - 인종차별철폐위원 선거(총 18명중 9명 선출)				

0001

주 제 네 바 대 표 부

제네(정) 2031-**863**

1991. 9. 4

수신 : 장관

참조 : 국제기구국장

제목 : 인권관계 위원회 위원 입후보 지지 요청

91. 9. 6

    당지 불가리아 대표부는 별첨 공한을 통하여 Garvalov 불가리아 제 1외무
차관이 인종차별 철폐 위원회 위원으로 재선되도록 지지하여 줄 것을 요청하여 온바,
검토, 그 결과를 당관에 알려 주시기 바랍니다.

    첨부 : 상기 공한 사본 1부.   끝.

주 제 네 바 대 사

선결		간		
접수일시	1991. 9. 13	전		
처리과	**50931**	(공람)		

0002

MISSION PERMANENTE DE LA RÉPUBLIQUE
DE BULGARIE AUPRÈS DE L'OFFICE DES NATIONS UNIES
ET DES ORGANISATIONS INTERNATIONALES

CHEMIN DES CRÊTS-DE-PREGNY 16
1218 GRAND-SACONNEX/GENÈVE
TÉL. 798 03 00

0|◌̣̇

Geneva, August 27th, 1991

No. 1437

The Permanent Mission of the Republic of Bulgaria to the United Nations Office and the International Organizations at Geneva presents its compliments to the Permanent Missions of UN Member States accredited at Geneva and Parties to the International Convention on the Elimination of All Forms of Racial Discrimination and has the honour to notify them that the Government of the Republic of Bulgaria has decided to present the candidature of Ambassador Ivan GARVALOV, First Deputy Foreign Minister, for re-election as Member of the Committee on the Elimination of Racial Discrimination at the elections to be held in New York in January 1992.

Since 1970 Ambassador Ivan Garvalov's involvement in UN activities is a rich one. Particularly distinguished is his effort for the promotion of international co-operation in the human rights field. His Curriculum Vitae is enclosed.

In presenting this candidature, the Bulgarian Government attaches prime importance to the work of the Committee on the Elimination of Racial Discrimination, regarding it as a most authoritative international body for the protection of human rights and fundamental freedoms. Bulgaria is convinced that, in his expert capacity in the field of international protection of human rights, Mr. Ivan Garvalov will continue to make a substantial contribution towards the enhancement of its efficiency.

The Ministry of Foreign Affairs of the Republic of Bulgaria would highly appreciate it, if the Governments of the States Parties to the International Convention on the Elimination of All Forms of Racial Discrimination will lend their support to this candidature.

The Permanent Mission of the Republic of Bulgaria avails itself of this opportunity to renew to the Permanent Missions of UN Member States and Parties to the International Convention on the Elimination of All Forms of Racial Discrimination, the assurances of its highest consideration.

PERMANENT MISSION OF THE
REPUBLIC OF KOREA
20, Route de Pre-Bois
Case postale 566
1215 Geneve 15

0003

IVAN GARVALOV

Curriculum Vitae

<u>Place and Date of Birth</u>: Sofia, Bulgaria, 1930;
<u>Education</u>: Graduate of "St. Kliment Ohridsky" Sofia University;

<u>DIPLOMATIC CAREER</u>:
Served tenures at Bulgaria's Embassies in New Delhi, Jakarta, Cairo, and twice at the Permanent Mission of the Republic of Bulgaria in New York, including as Ambassador, Deputy Permanent Representative of Bulgaria to the United Nations from 1982 till 1989);

1989 - 1990: Director of the Human Rights Department, Ministry of Foreign Affairs;
1990: Director of the United Nations and Disarmament Department, Ministry of Foreign Affairs;

<u>Currrent post, since January 1991</u>: First Deputy Minister of Foreign Affairs

<u>ACTIVITY AT THE UNITED NATIONS:</u>
1970 - 1990: Member of the Bulgarian delegations at the regular sessions of UN General Assembly; Member of Bulgarian delegations at UN special sessions and conferences on disarmament, international economic relations, racial discrimination, youth, women, etc.;

1978 - 1982: Representative of Bulgaria to the UN Commission on Human Rights;

1986 -1987: Deputy Representative of Bulgaria to the Security Council;

<u>Elections in UN bodies</u>:
1973: <u>Elected Rapporteur</u> of the Fourth Main Committee of the United Nations General Assembly (decolonization);
1980: <u>Elected Chairman</u> of the Third Main Committee of the UN General Assembly (social and humanitarian issues);
1982: <u>Elected Chairman</u> of the UN Commission on Human Rights;
1983: <u>Elected Chairman</u> of the United Nations Committee on the Enhancing of the Principle of the Non-Use of Force;
1985: <u>Elected Vice-President</u> of ECOSOC, Chairman of the Social Committee;
1988 - 1992: <u>Member</u> of the Committee on the Elimination of Racial Discrimination;

<u>Sofia, 15 August 1991</u>

0004

주 제 네 바 대 표 부

재네(정) 2031-783

수신 : 외무부장관

참조 : 국제기구국장

제목 : 인종차별 철폐위원회 위원 선출

1991. 9. 9

91. 9. 13

     UN 사무총장은 별첨 사본의 외무장관앞 공한을 통해 92. 1. 19로 임기만료 되는 인종차별 철폐위원회의 위원 9명에 대한 후임위원 선거와 관련, 후보추천을 요청해 왔음을 보고하오니, 검토하시기 바랍니다.

    첨부 : 상기 공한 및 동 첨부물 1부. 끝.

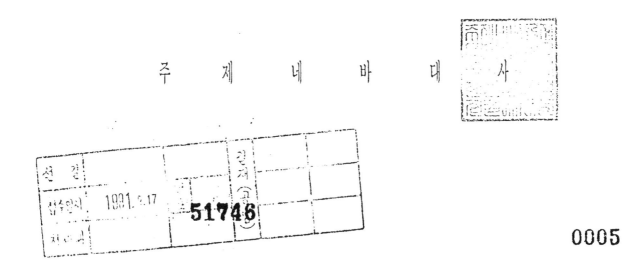

주 제 네 바 대 사

51746

0005

OFFICE DES NATIONS UNIES A GENÈVE

UNITED NATIONS OFFICE AT GENEVA

CENTRE POUR LES DROITS DE L'HOMME

CENTRE FOR HUMAN RIGHTS

Téléfax: (022) 733 98 79
Télégrammes: UNATIONS, GENÈVE
Télex: 28 96 96
Téléphone: 734 60 11   731 02 11
RÉF. Nº: G/SO 237/2 (3)
(à rappeler dans la réponse)

Palais des Nations
CH-1211 GENÈVE 10

COPIE - COPY

The Secretary-General of the United Nations presents his compliments to the Minister for Foreign Affairs of the Republic of Korea and has the honour to refer to article 8 of the International Convention on the Elimination of All Forms of Racial Discrimination relating to the election of the members of the Committee on the Elimination of Racial Discrimination, the full text of which appears in annex I to the present note.

As determined at the First Meeting of States Parties to the Convention held in 1969, the terms of office of nine members of the Committee, listed in annex II, will expire on 19 January 1992. The Secretary-General, therefore, in accordance with paragraph 3 of article 8, has the honour to invite His Excellency's Government to submit its nomination c/o the Centre for Human Rights, United Nations Office at Geneva, not later than 30 October 1991, having regard to the provisions of paragraphs 1 and 2 of article 8.

Paragraph 1 of article 8 provides that the members of the Committee shall be "experts of high moral standing and acknowledged impartiality elected by States Parties from among their nationals who shall serve in their personal capacity, consideration being given to equitable geographical distribution and to the representation of the different forms of civilization as well as of the principal legal systems".

Paragraph 2 stipulates that "each State Party may nominate one person from among its own nationals". In this connection, attention is drawn to annex III which lists the names of members of the Committee who will continue to serve on it until 19 January 1994.

After 30 October 1991, the Secretary-General will, in accordance with paragraph 3 of article 8, prepare a list in alphabetical order of all persons nominated, indicating the States Parties which have nominated them, and forward it to His Excellency's Government together with information concerning the exact date, place and time of the Meeting of the States Parties to elect the members of the Committee.

30 August 1991

0006

International Convention on the Elimination of All Forms of Racial Discrimination

Article 8

1. There shall be established a Committee on the Elimination of Racial Discrimination (hereinafter referred to as the Committee) consisting of eighteen experts of high moral standing and acknowledged impartiality elected by States Parties from among their nationals, who shall serve in their personal capacity, consideration being given to equitable geographical distribution and to the representation of the different forms of civilization as well as of the principal legal systems.

2. The members of the Committee shall be elected by secret ballot from a list of persons nominated by the States Parties. Each State Party may nominate one person from among its own nationals.

3. The initial election shall be held six months after the date of the entry into force of this Convention. At least three months before the date of each election the Secretary-General of the United Nations shall address a letter to the States Parties inviting them to submit their nominations within two months. The Secretary-General shall prepare a list in alphabetical order of all persons thus nominated, indicating the States Parties which have nominated them, and shall submit it to the States Parties.

4. Elections of the members of the Committee shall be held at a meeting of States Parties convened by the Secretary-General at United Nations Headquarters. At that meeting, for which two thirds of the States Parties shall constitute a quorum, the persons elected to the Committee shall be nominees who obtain the largest number of votes and an absolute majority of the votes of the representatives of States Parties present and voting.

5. (a) The members of the Committee shall be elected for a term of four years. However, the terms of nine of the members elected at the first election shall expire at the end of two years; immediately after the first election the names of these nine members shall be chosen by lot by the Chairman of the Committee.

(b) For the filling of casual vacancies, the State Party whose expert has ceased to function as a member of the Committee shall appoint another expert from among its nationals, subject to the approval of the Committee.

6. States Parties shall be responsible for the expenses of the members of the Committee while they are in performance of Committee duties.

CERD/C/Misc.1
GE. 89-16985

0007

ANNEX II

The nine members of the Committee whose terms
expire on 19 January 1992

Mr. Eduardo FERRERO COSTA   (Peru)

Mr. Isi FOIGHEL   (Denmark)

Mr. Ivan GARVALOV   (Bulgaria)

Mr. Yuri A. RECHETOV   (Union of Soviet Socialist Republics)

Mr. Jorge RHENAN SEGURA   (Costa Rica)

Mrs. Shanti SADIQ ALI   (India)

Mr. SONG Shuhua   (China)

Mr. Kasimir VIDAS   (Yugoslavia)

Mr. Mario Jorge YUTZIS   (Argentina)

0008

ANNEX III

List of the other nine members who will continue to
serve on the Committee until 19 January 1994

Mr. Mahmoud ABOUL-NASR   (Egypt)

Mr. Hamzat AHMADU   (Nigeria)

Mr. Michael Parker BANTON   (United Kingdom of Great Britain
                                          and Northern Ireland)

Mr. Régis de GOUTTES   (France)

Mr. George O. LAMPTEY   (Ghana)

Mr. Carlos LECHUGA HEVIA   (Cuba)

Mr. Agha SHAHI   (Pakistan)

Mr. Michael E. SHERIFIS   (Cyprus)

Mr. Rüdiger WOLFRUM   (Germany)

0009

EMBASSY OF BULGARIA
SEOUL

№ 290

NOTE   VERBALE

The Embassy of the Republic of Bulgaria in Seoul presents its compliments to the honorable Ministry of Foreign Affairs of the Republic of Korea and has the honour to communicate to it that the Government of the Republic of Bulgaria has decided to present the candidature of Ambassador Ivan Garvalov, First Deputy Minister of Foreign Affairs of the Republic of Bulgaria for reelection as member of the Committee on the Elimination of Racial Discrimination at the elections scheduled to be held in January 1992 in New York.

Ambassador Garvalov has a long and fruitful experience in the field of international cooperation on human rights matters. Ambassador Garvalov has been the Representative of Bulgaria to the UN Commission on Human Rights, its Chairman, Vice President of the ECOSOS and at the moment he is a member of the Committee on the Elimination of Racial Discrimination.

Please find enclosed herewith the c.v. of Mr. Ivan Garvalov.

The Government of the Republic of Bulgaria attributes a primary attention to the work of the Committee on the Elimination of Racial Discrimination as one of the most important mechanisms for the protection of human rights and fundamental freedoms.

0010

EMBASSY OF BULGARIA
SEOUL

The Government of the Republic of Bulgaria is convinced that Mr. Garvalov, as a well-known expert in the field of the international protection of human rights is in-a-position-to contribute significantly to the effective functioning of the committee.

The Ministry of Foreign Affairs of the Republic of Bulgaria would be grateful if the Government of the Republic of Korea decides to render its support to the candidature of Ambassador Ivan Garvalov during the forthcoming elections at the meeting of the states parties to the International Convention on the elimination of all forms of racial discrimination that is to be held in January 1992 in New York.

The Embassy of the Republic of Bulgaria avails itself of this opportunity to renew to the honorable Ministry of Foreign Affairs of the Republic of Korea the assurances of its highest considerations.

3. September 1991

To the Ministry of Foreign Affairs
of the Republic of Korea

0011

CURRICULUM   VITAE   OF

IVAN   GARVALOV

Place and Date of Birth : Sofia, Bulgaria, 1930

Education   : Graduated from "St. Kliment Ohridfsky" Sofia University.

Diplomatic Career : Served tenures at Bulgaria, Embassies in
New Dalhi (1956-1958), Jakarta (1958-1961), Cairo (1964-
1969), and twice at the Permanent Mission of the Republic
of Bulgaria in New York, including as Ambassador, Deputy
Permanent Representative of Bulgaria to the United Nations
(1971-1977, 1982-1989).

Dealt with bilateral relations of Bulgaria with Asia and
Arab countries, UNESCO, Cultural Issues, Human Rights,
United Nations Problems and Disarmament.

1989-1990   Director of the Human Rights Department
   1990   Director of the United Nations and Disarmament
Department
Current Post, since January 1991
First Deputy Minister of Foreign Affairs

Activity at the United Nations :

1970-1990   Member of the Bulgarian Delegation at the
Regular Sessions of UN General Assembly,
Member of the Bulgarian Delegation at UN Special
Sessions and Conferences on Disarmament,
International Economic Relations, Racial Dis-
crimination, Youth, Women, etc.

1978-1982   Representative of Bulgaria to the UN Commission
on Human Rights

1986-1987   Deputy Representative of Bulgaria to the
Security Council

0012

<u>Elections in UN Bodies</u>   :

1973	Elected Rapporteur of the Fourth Main Committee of the United Nations General Assembly (Decoloniyation).
1980	Elected Chairman of the Third Main Committee of the UN General Assembly (Social and Humanitarian Issues).
1982	Elected Chairman of the UN Commission on Human Rights.
1983	Elected Chairman of the United Nations Committee on the Enhancing of the Principle of the Non-Use of Force.
1985	Elected Vice-President of ECOSOC, Chairman of the Social Committee.
1988-1992	Member of the Committee on the Elimination of Racial Discrimination.

0013

주 제 네 바 대 표 부

제네(정) 2031-83   1991. 9. 20

수신 : 장관

참조 : 국제기구국장

제목 : 인종차별 철폐 위원 입후보지원 요청

　　　　연 : 제네(냉) 2031-783

　　　당지 주재 아르헨티나 대표부는 별첨 당관앞 공한으로 92. 2월 있을

예정인 인종차별 철폐위원 개선 관련 자국 입후보에 대한 지지를 요청해 온바,

동 공한 사본을 별첨 송부하니 검토 바랍니다.

　　　첨부 : 상기 입후보 지지 요청 공한 사본 1부.　끝.

주 제 네 바 대 　　사

0014

Misión Permanente
de la República Argentina
ante los
Organismos Internacionales en Ginebra
EMP/jg
V/100-8/700
No.155/91

The Permanent Mission of the Republic of Argentina to the International Organizations in Geneva presents its compliments to the Permanent Mission of the Republic of Korea and has the honour to inform the latter that the Government of Argentina has decided to present the candidacy of Mr. Mario Jorge Yutzis for re-election as a member of the Committee on the Elimination of Racial Discrimination.

The Government of Argentina attaches great importance to the Committee and would be most grateful if the Government of the Republic of Korea could lend its valuable support to the candidacy of Mr. Mario Jorge Yutzis, at the elections scheduled to be held next January 1992, in New York.

The curriculum vitae of Mr. Mario Jorge Yutzis is enclosed herewith.

The Permanent Mission of the Republic of Argentina to the International Organizations in Geneva avails itself of this opportunity to renew to the Permanent Mission of the Republic of Korea the assurances of its highest consideration.

Geneva, 12 September 1991.

To the Permanent Mission
of the Republic of Korea
G e n e v a

0015

CURRICULUM VITAE OF Mr. MARIO JORGE YUTZIS

Argentine, born in Buenos Aires, 26 July 1936.

Married to Teresita Grach Felkar. Two sons.

<u>Vicar</u> of the United Lutheran Church in Argentina

<u>Master of Theology</u>, José C. Paz Lutheran Faculty of Tehology, Buenos Aires, Argentina.

<u>Doctor of Sciences of Religion</u>, Faculty of Protestant Theology, University of Strasbourg, France.

<u>Studies of Psychology and Anthropology</u>, Buenos Aires and Montevideo, Uruguay.

<u>Studen Chaplain</u>, Studen Christian Movement of Argentina (1960).

<u>Studies Secretary</u> of the Latin American Executive Committee of the World Studen Christian Federation (1973-1976).

<u>Member of the Executive Committee</u> of the World Studen Christian Federation.

<u>Human Rights Adviser</u> to the Lutheran World Federation (1978-1979).

<u>Co-editor</u> of the Newsletter "Human Rights Concern" of the Lutheran World Federation (1978-1983).

<u>Professor of Philosophical Anthropology</u> at the Buenos Aires Higher Evangelical Institute for Theological Education (ISEDET).

<u>Professor of Contemporary Ideologies</u> at ISEDET.

<u>Professor of Psychoanalysis and Religion</u> at ISEDET.

<u>Professor of Christian Ethics</u> at the José C. Paz Lutheran Faculty of Theology, Buenos Aires (1963-1964).

<u>Professor of Fundamental Psychology</u>, Young Men's Christian Association of Argentina (1973-983).

<u>Visiting Professor</u>, Hamma School of Theology, Springfield, Ohio (1969).

<u>Visiting Professor</u>, St. Paul Seminary, St. Paul, Minnesota (1985).

0016

Visiting Professor, Dayton University, Columbus, Ohio (1969).

Visiting Professor, Washington Ecumenical Consortium (1981).

Visiting Professor, Vancouver (Canada) School of Theology (1984).

Visiting Professor, Ecumenical Institute of Bossey (Celigny, Vaud, Switzerland) (1978-1979).

Assistant Professor in the field of Adult Education, University of Geneva, Switzerland (1978-1979).

Member of CERD (1984-1988).

Vice-Chairman of CERD (1986-1988).

Member of CERD (1988-1992).

Publications

La noción de la persona en la antropología de Unamuno ("The notion of person in Unamuno's anthropology"). Salamanca.

La construcción social de la enfermedad ("The social construction of illness"). Buenos Aires.

Identidad nacional y democracia ("National identity and democracy"). Buenos Aires.

Derecho Internacional, multilateralismo y la paz en el mundo ("International law, multilateralism and world peace"). Buenos Aires.

Derechos humanos y la hermenéutica de la fe cristiana ("Human rights and the hermeneutics of Christian faith"). Buenos Aires.

Ideología y cambio social ("Ideology and social change"). Geneva.

Algunas reflexiones en torno al lenguaje de la fe cristiana ("Some reflections on the language of Christian faith"). Buenos Aires.

*   *   *

0017

인종차별철폐위원회 위원 입후보현황

1991. 9. 27.

양 년 고 월 재 일	담 당	과 장	국 장
	(서명)	*(서명)*	

1. 인종차별철폐위원회 구성
   o 설치근거
     - 인종차별철폐협정(CERD) 제8조의 규정에 의하여 설치

   o 구 성
     - 당사국 회의에서 선출하는 임기 4년의 18명의 전문가로 구성

   o 위원선출 절차
     - 당사국은 자국국민중에 후보자 1명을 지명할 수 있음.
     - 당사국 회의(정족수 2/3)의 비밀투표에서 출석, 투표한 국가의
       최대 다수표 및 절대다수표를 얻은 후보자가 위원으로 당선
     - 동입후보 마감 : 91.10.30.
     - 협약당사국회의 : 92.1월, 뉴욕

   o 위원회의 임무
     - 각 당사국이 2년마다 제출하는 정기보고서를 심의
     - 당사국이 제출한 각종 보고와 정보를 검토, 이를 근거로 제의와
       일반적인 권고를 하며, 위원회 활동사항을 매년 유엔총회에 보고
     - 위원은 개인자격으로 활동

2. 입후보지지 요청현황
   o 92.1월 임기만료국 : 페루, 덴마크, 불가리아, 소련, 코스타리카,
                          인도, 중국, 유고, 알젠틴

   o 94.1월 임기만료국 : 에집트, 나이제리아, 영국, 프랑스, 가나, 쿠바,
                          파키스탄, 사이프러스, 독일

   o 입후보지지요청국
     - 불가리아(재선) : 주제네바대표부 경유
     - 알젠틴(재선) : 주제네바대표부 경유

3. 대책방안
   o 91.11월까지 지지요청 접수후 방침결정. 끝.

0018

주 제 네 바 대 표 부

제네(정) 2031-860   1991. 10. 4

수신 : 장관

참조 : 국제기구국장

제목 : 인종차별 철폐위 위원 입후보

     당지 소련대표부는 인종차별 철폐협약 당사국 대표부앞으로 보내는 회람 공한을 통하여 자국의 Yuri A. Rechetov 인종차별 칠페위 위원이 제출마함을 통보하여 온바, 이를 별첨 송부합니다.

     첨부 : 상기 공한   끝.

주 제 네 바 대  사

0019

Постоянное Представительство СССР
при Отделении ООН и других
международных организациях в Женеве

Mission permanente de l'URSS
auprès de l'Office des Nations Unies
et des autres organisations internationales
ayant leur siège à Genève

———

15, avenue de la Paix
Téléphone : 733 18 70
Téléfax : 734 40 44
GENEVE

No. 499

        The Permanent Mission of the Union of Soviet
Socialist Republics presents its compliments to the
Permanent Missions of the States-Parties to the
Convention on Elimination of All Forms of Racial
Discrimination and has the honour to inform that the
Soviet Government has decided to present the
candidature of Mr. Yuri A. RECHETOV to be re-elected
to the Committee on Elimination of Racial
Discrimination at the Meeting of the States Parties
to the Convention in January 1992, in New York.

        The curriculum vitae of Mr. Y. RECHETOV is
attached.

        The Permanent Mission of the Union of Soviet
Socialist Republics avails itself of this opportunity
to renew to the Permanent Missions of the States-
Parties to the Convention on Elimination of All Forms
of Racial Discrimination the assurances of its
highest consideration.

                              Geneva, September 23 , 1991

Permanent Missions of
the States-Parties to
the Convention on Elimination
of All Forms of Racial
Discrimination to the United
Nations Office in Geneva

G e n e v a

0020

Yuri Alexandrovich RECHETOV (USSR)

Born on 10 January 1935, in the city of Gorky (Nizhny Novgorod).

Graduated from the Moscow State Institute of International Relations in 1959 and from the Diplomatic Academy in 1971. Ph.D. in philosophy, Doctor of Law, speaks English, French, German, Swedish, Danish and Icelandic.

From 1959 to 1975 worked in the Scandinavian Countries Department and in the International Economic Organizations Department of the Ministry of Foreign Affairs of the USSR, and also in the Soviet Embassies in Iceland and Denmark. Participated in the proceedings of the European Conference on Security and Co-operation during the Geneva round in 1974-1975.

From 1975 to 1980 headed the Prevention of Discrimination and Protection of Minorities Unit of the Human Rights Department of the UNOG Secretariat, worked as a Secretary of the Sub-Commission on Prevention of Discrimination and Protection of Minorities.

From 1980 to 1986 worked in the Institute of State and Law of the USSR Academy of Sciences. Y. Reshetov is a prominent expert in the field of international law. He is the author of more than 100 publications on human rights issues, on relations between nationalities, on international crimes, on the United Nations role in the field of human rights, etc.

Since 1986 Y. Reshetov has been Deputy Chief of the Division for Humanitarian Issues of the Ministry of Foreign Affairs of the USSR. His duties concern mainly the solution of humanitarian problems, and especially the perfection of the Soviet legislation.

Since 1988 Y. Rechetov heads the Directorate on International Humanitarian Cooperation and Human Rights of the Ministry of Foreign Affairs of the USSR. He headed the USSR Delegations at the CSCE meeting in Copenhagen and at the 47th session of the UN Commission on Human Rights.

0021

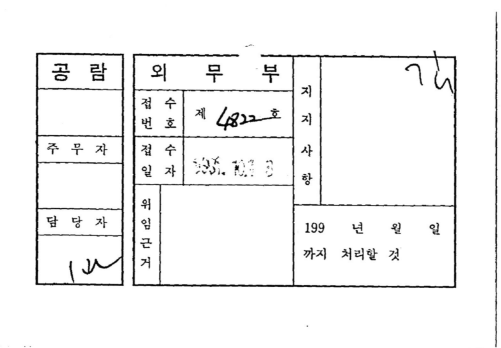

공 람	외 무 부		
	접 수 번 호	제 4822 호	지 지 사 항
주 무 자	접 수 일 자		
담 당 자	위 임 근 거		199 년 월 일 까지 처리할 것

EMBAJADA DEL PERU
SEÚL, COREA

M/29

The Embassy of Peru presents its compliments to the Ministry of Foreign Affairs and has the honor to inform the latter that the Government of Peru has decided to present the candidacy of Dr. Eduardo Ferrero, to the Committee on the Elimination of Racial Discrimination of the United Nations.

The elections for the above-mentioned will be held next January in New York.

Dr. Ferrero, a jurist and scholar specialist of International Law has been working as legal adviser for several institutions and international organizations, having a wide experience on International Law and Racial Discrimination issues. His Curriculum Vitae is attached to this note.

The Government of Peru will be very grateful if the Korean Government grants its support to the candidacy of Dr. Ferrero, who is at present member of the Committee on the Elimination of Racial Discrimination.

The Embassy of Peru avails itself of this opportunity to renew to the Ministry of Foreign Affairs the assurances of its highest consideration.

Seoul, 15 october 1991

TO
THE MINISTRY OF FOREIGN AFFAIRS
S E O U L

0023

EMBAJADA DEL PERU
SEÚL, COREA

PERUVIAN CANDIDATE TO REELECTION AT THE COMMITTEE FOR
THE ELIMINATION OF RACIAL DISCRIMINATION

DR. EDUARDO FERRERO

I. PERSONAL DATA
Nationality   : Peruvian
Place and Date of Birth : Lima, Peru, October 26, 1946
Civil Status   : Married with four children

II.   TITLES AND ACADEMIC DEGREES

Bachelor of Arts in Law (1970)
Lawyer (1970)
Doctoral Degree in Law (1974)

III. PRESENT OCCUPATIONS

- Executive President of Peruvian Center for International Studies
  - CEPEI (1983 to date)
- Member of the United Nations' Committee for the Elimination of
  Racial Discrimination.
- Member of the Consultive Committee of External Relations at the
  Ministry of External Relations of Peru
- Member of the Consultive Committees of Public International Law
  and Law of the Sea at the Bar Association of Lima
- Member of the Board at the Joint Studies on International
  Relations of Latin America - RIAL
- Member of the Editors' Board at the 'Ocean Development and
  International Law Journal', U.S.A. (from 1974); 'Marine Policy',
  Great Britain (from 1987); 'Omagua Series' Europa Instituut
  Universiteit van Amsterdam (from 1988); International Legal
  Materials, American Society of International Law.

IV.   ACADEMIC AND RESEARCH EXPERIENCE

Universidad Católica del Perú:
- Professor at the Law Department and the Masters Course in
  Economic International Law.
- Lecturer on Public International Law, International Treaties and
  Controversy Solving.

Diplomatic Academy of Peru
- Professor of Public International Law (1973-1983)

0024

2

Wisconsin University (U.S.A.)
- Associated Professor at the Law Department.
  Scholarship by the Ford Foundation for Research on International
  Law (1971-1972). Granted a scholarship by the Ford Foundation.

University of California, San Diego (U.S.A.)
- Researcher at the Sripps Institute of Oceanography: Research on
  Law of the Sea (1972)

Inter American Juridical Committee (OAS)
- Visiting Professor at the Law Department and the Center of Latin
  American Studies (1987)

Center for High Military Studies (CAEM) and Naval Warfare Superior
School (Peru)
- Lecturer (from 1975 to date)

V. OTHER PROFESSIONAL ACTIVITIES

Universidad Católica del Perú
- President of the Students Union at the Law Department,
  Co-president of the Students Federation and Students'
  Representative at the University Council (1969-1970)
Estudio Luis Echecopar G. (Echecopar Lawyers Office)
- Associated Lawyer (1972-1973)
Ministry of Industry, Commerce, Tourism and Integration
- Legal Adviser to the Minister (1974-1975)
- General Director of the Legal Affairs (1976)
SENATI (National Service for Industrial Training)
- Member of the Board of Directors (1975-1976)
Petroleos del Peru (Peruvian National Oil Enterprise)
- Member of the Board of Directors (1976)
Estudio Ferrero & Ferrari Asociados (Ferrero & Ferrari Lawyers)
- Partner (from 1977 to 1980)

Ministry of External Relations of Peru
- Legal Adviser (1981-1982)
- Representative of Peru to the Legal Commission of the Permanent
  Commission of South Pacific (1978-1982)
- Adviser of the Peruvian Delegation to the III Conference of
  United Nations on Law of the Sea (1979-1982)
- Member of various national committees of the public sector and
  Honorary adviser of official Peruvian delegations to
  International Conferences (from 1975 to date)

0025

3

National Institute of Planning (Peru)
- Member of the National Consultive Council (1986-1989)
Organization of American States (OAS)
- International Observer and adviser of the Secretary-General of OAS in the elections of Costa Rica, Nicaragua and Dominican Republic (1990)
International Conferences
- International Expositor at Academic Seminars and International events hold in Peru and other countries, on subjects concerning International Law and International Relations (1972 to date)

V. PUBLICATIONS
   BOOKS
   - Public International Law: Cases and Teaching Materials (2 volumes), Universidad Católica del Perú, 1972
   - Industrial Legislation of Peru (4 volumes), Banco Industrial del Perú (1979)
   - The New Law of the Sea: Peru and the 200 miles, Fondo Editorial Universidad Católica del Perú, 456 pag., 1980
   - Peru in front of the New Trends of International Trade (editor), Centro Peruano de Estudios Internacionales (CEPEI),1984.
   - Peru and the Foreign Capital: Debt and Investment, (editor), Centro Peruano de Estudios Internacionales (CEPEI), 1986
   - Peru and the Law of the Sea Convention, Working Document No. 5, Centro Peruano de Estudios Internacionales (CEPEI), Lima, 1986
   - International Relations of Peru with the United States, (co-author and editor), Centro Peruano de Estudios Internacionales (CEPEI), Lima, 1987
   - Relations of Peru with the neighboring countries, (co-author and editor), Centro Peruano de Estudios Internacionales (CEPEI), 1988
   - Latin America, Peru and the New Structure of the International Economic Relations, (co-author and editor) Centro Peruano de Estudios Internacionales (CEPEI), 1988
   - Latin America, Peru and the Changes on the International System (editor) CEPEI, 1989
   - The Fishing Agreements signed by Peru with the Soviet Union (co-author and editor) CEPEI, 1989
   - Relations of Peru with Chile and Bolivia (co-author and editor) CEPEI, 1989
   - Peruvian relationships in the International Financial System (co-author and editor) CEPEI, 1990
   - Security of Peru in front of the New International Context (co-author and editor) CEPEI, (in press)

0026

4

SIGNIFICANT ACADEMIC DOCUMENTS
- The Latin American position on legal aspects of maritime jurisdiction and oceanic research, in: " Freedom of Oceanic Research", book edited by Warren S. Wooster, Crane Russak and Co., New York (1973)
- Human Rights, Journal of the Bar Association of La Libertad, Trujillo, Peru (1974)
- Principles of Maritime Sovereignty of Peru to the 200 miles, Law review , Pontificia Universidad Católica del Perú N. 32. Lima, Peru (1974)
- Introduction to the Study of Human Rights in a Global Perspective, Review of the Diplomatic Academy of Peru N. 9, Lima (1974)
- The New Law of the Sea : Legal Nature of the Exclusive Economic Zone, Review of the Permanent Committee of South Pacific, N. 8, (1978)
- Latin American Contribution to the New Law of the Sea: 200 miles and the Economic Zone, (German version), in the book " " Seerechtskonferenz and Dritte Welt", Institut fur Allegmeine Uberseeforschung, Hamburg, Germany
- Evolution of the Law of the Sea.- in : Permanent Committee of South Pacific, Review N. 9 (1980)
- Legal nature of the Exclusive Economic Zone, Symposium on Maritime Legislation, Caracas-Venezuela, 1980.
- Latin American Integration Law on a New Decade, (Sub Regional Andean Integration) in: Contemporary International Law Perspective 3, Instituto de Estudios Internacionales de la Universidad de Chile, Santiago, Chile (1981)
- Peru and the Convention of the Law of the Sea.- in : Commercial and Maritime Law Review of the Asociación Peruana de Derecho Marítimo N. 6, Lima 1981
- Covenant in Latin America: The case of the Law of the Sea.- Establishing new ways of International Links ; Instituto de Estudios Internacionales de la Universidad de Chile, 1985
- Peru and the Convention of the Law of the Sea, in Marine Policy, Vol. II, N. I, January 1987
- Foreign Policy of Peru, 1985-1986, in Latin American Foreign Policy Yearbook 1986, edit. Heraldo Munoz, Argentina (1987)
- International Mediation: Theory and Practice, "Law" Magazine, Law Department of Universidad Católica, Lima, 1987
- Peruvian Foreign Policy: Current Trends, Constraints and Opportunities, Vol. 29, N. 2, Summer 1987
- USA-Japan and the Pacific Ocean Resources and Ocean Law: A Latin American Perspective, in Ecology Law Quarterly, University of California, Berkeley, Vol. 16, N. 1 (1989)

0027

5

- Peruvian Relations in the Pacific Basin. Magazine of the Instituto de Estudios Internacionales in Universidad de Chile, Year XXII, 1989, N. 88, Santiago, Chile
- Foreign Fishing in the Maritime Domain of Peru.- in: Latin America and The Law of the Sea. Permanent Committee of South Pacific, Bogota, 1988.
- Peru in 1988: International Crisis and Foreign Policy. Latin American Foreign Policy Yearbook. Caracas, 1989, Venezuela
- Political and Economic Changes on the Main Players of the International System: A First Approach. National Defense Review of the Center for High Military Studies (CAEM), Lima, Peru (1989)
- Legislation and Recent Experience regarding Fishing by Foreign Vessels within Peruvian Jurisdictional Waters. Pacific Economic Cooperation Conference (PECC), Fisheries Task Force Coordinator. Pacific America.

Seoul, October 15   1991

0028

주 국 련 대 표 부

주국련2031214-
825

수신 장관

참조 국제기구국장

제목 CERD 위원 후보지지 요청

91. 10. 24.

1991. 10. 2 5

　　당지 불가리아대표부 및 중국대표부는 1992.1. 뉴욕개최 인종차별 철폐협약
당사국회의에서 선출예정인 인종차별 철폐위원회(The Committee on the Elimination
of Racial Discrimination)위원 선출과 관련, 자국인 후보의 지지를 요청하여
왔는바, 동 공한 사본을 별첨 송부합니다.

　첨　부 : 1. 중국대표부 공한 1부.

　　　　　2. 불가리아대표부 공한 1부. 끝.

주 국 련 대

60763

0029

PERMANENT MISSION OF
THE PEOPLE'S REPUBLIC OF CHINA
TO THE UNITED NATIONS

No. CMS (91)32

The Permanent Mission of the People's Republic of China to the United Nations presents its compliments to the Permanent Missions of the States Parties to the Convention on the Elimination of All Forms of Racial Discrimination and has the honour to inform the latter that the Chinese Government has decided to nominate Mr. SONG Shuhua for reelection to the Committee on the Elimination of Racial Discrimination (CERD), at the elections to be held at the meeting of States Parties to the Convention on the Elimination of All Forms of Racial Discrimination, in New York in January 1992.

The Chinese Govervment would be grateful if the valuable support could be accorded to this important candidature by the States Parties to the Convention on the Elimination of All Forms of Racial Discrimination.

Enclosed is a copy of Mr. SONG's curriculum vitae.

The Permanent Mission of the People's Republic of China to the United Nations avails itself of this opportunity to renew to the Permanent Missions of the States Parties to the Convention on the Elimination of All Forms of Racial Discrimination of the assurances of its highest consideration.

11 October 1991, New York

The Permanents Mission of
the States Parties to the Convention
on the Elimination of All Forms of Racial
Discrimination

New York

0030

PERMANENT MISSION

OF THE .   REPUBLIC OF BULGARIA

TO THE UNITED NATIONS

11 EAST 84TH STREET

NEW YORK. N.Y. 10028

(212) 737-4790

September 1, 1991

1040

     The Permanent Mission of the Republic of Bulgaria to
the United Nations presents its compliments to the Permanent
Observer Mission of the Republic of Korea to the United Nations
and has the honor to inform the latter that the Government of the
Republic of Bulgaria has decided to nominate Ambassador Ivan
Garvalov, First Deputy Foreign Minister of the Republic of
Bulgaria, for re-election to the Committee on the Elimination of
Racial Discrimination at the forthcoming elections in January of
1992.

     Ambassador Ivan Garvalov has a long-standing experience
in international cooperation on human rights issues. He has
served as representative of Bulgaria to the UN Commission on
Human Rights, as Chairman of the latter, as Vice-President of
ECOSOC, and is at present a member of the Committee on the
Elimination of Racial Discrimination.

     The Republic of Bulgaria attaches great significance to
the activities of the Committee on the Elimination of Racial
Discrimination as one of the most authoritative international
mechanisms for protecting the human rights and basic liberties.
The Republic of Bulgaria is confident that Mr. Garvalov, being an
internationally acknowledged expert in the protection of human
rights, is capable of making a substantial contribution to the
efficient work of this Committee.

     The Ministry of Foreign Affairs of the Republic of
Bulgaria would be most grateful if the Government of the Republic
of Korea would support Mr. Ivan Garvalov's candidature at the
forthcoming elections.

     Enclosed herewith please find the Curriculum Vitae of
Mr. Ivan Garvalov.

     The Permanent Mission of the Republic of Bulgaria to
the United Nations avails itself of this opportunity to renew to
the Permanent Observer Mission of the Republic of Korea to the
United Nations the assurances of its highest consideration.

Permanent Observer Mission of
the Republic of Korea
to the United Nations
866 United Nations Plaza, Suite 300
New York, N.Y. 10017

0031

주 제 네 바 대 표 부

제네(정) 2031-948   1991. 11. 8.

수신 : 장   관

참조 : 국제기구국장

제목 : 인종차별 철폐위 위원 입후보

      당지 코스타리카 대표부가 보내온 자국인의 표제 입후보 관련 지지요청
공한을 벌첨 송부합니다.

      첨부 : 상기 공한 1부.   끝.

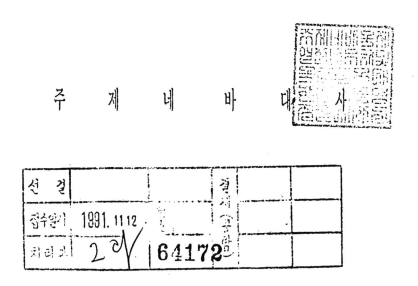

주 제 네 바 대   사

0032

*Misión Permanente
de Costa Rica
Ginebra*

Geneva, October 21, 1991

MCR/200/91

  The Permanent Mission of the Republic of Costa Rica to the United Nations Office and the International Organizations in Geneva presents its compliments to the Permanent Missions of UN Member States accredited in Geneva and Parties to the International Convention on the Elimination of All Forms of Racial Discrimination and has the honour to notify them that the Government of the Republic of Costa Rica has decided to present the candidature of Ambassador Jorge RHENAN-SEGURA for re-election as Member of the Committee on the Elimination of Racial Discrimination at the elections to be held in New York in January 1992.

  Dr RHENAN-SEGURA, whose curriculum vitae is attached, is an eminent jurist and has a wide experience in human rights, particularly distinguished is his effort for the promotion of international cooperation in the field of human rights. The Government of Costa Rica is convinced that, in his expert capacity in the field of International protection of human rights, Mr Jorge RHENAN-SEGURA will continue to make a substantial contribution to the work of this Committee.

  The Ministry of Foreign Affairs of the Republic of Costa Rica would highly appreciate the support of the Governments of the States Parties to the International Convention on the Elimination of All Forms of Racial Discrimination to this candidature.

  The Permanent Mission of the Republic of Costa Rica avails itself of this opportunity to express its high consideration to the Permanent Missions of UN Member States and Parties to the International Convention on the Elimination of All Forms of Racial Discrimination.

0033

Curriculum Vitae
de
Embajador Jorge Rhenán Segura

Apellidos: Rhenán Segura

Nombre: Jorge

Fecha y lugar de Nacimiento: 6 de octubre de 1956. San José de Costa Rica

Estudios Superiores

UNIVERSIDAD DE LA SORBONNA

- Doctor en Ciencias Políticas (Summa Cum Laude)

- DEA (Master) del Instituto de Estudios de América Latina. Paris III

UNIVERSIDAD DE GINEBRA

-DEA (Master) del Instituto de Estudios Europeos

-Estudios en Derechos Humanos y Humanitario

UNIVERSIDAD DE COSTA RICA

- Licenciatura en Derecho Público
- Licenciatura en Ciencias Políticas
- Master en Historia de las Rel. Internacionales
- Notario Público

UNIVERSIDAD AUTONOMA DE CENTRO AMERICA

- Licenciatura en Periodismo

Cargo actual

-Diplomático de carrera del Servicio Exterior de Costa Rica. Actualmente con rango de Embajador.

-Embajador. Representante Permanente Alterno de Costa Rica ante la Oficina Europea de Naciones Unidas.

-Embajador ante la Conferencia de Desarme.

-Miembro del Comité de Discriminación Racial.

-Miembro de la Comisión Académica (Com. sobre Migración) del Institut de Droit Humanitaire de Sanremo, Italia,(1990).

-Profesor con permiso Universidad de Costa Rica (actualmente dirige trabajos de graduación, en la Esc. de Ciencias Políticas, U.C.R.).

TRABAJOS REALIZADOS

0034

-Representante de Costa Rica en la segunda Conferencia Internacional contra la Discriminación Racial (1983).

-Representante de Costa Rica a las sesiones del Consejo Económico y Social (ECOSOC) (1983-1991).

-Representante de Costa Rica a la VII UNCTAD, Ginebra. (1987).

-Consejero Jurídico sobre la Adhesión de Costa Rica al Acuerdo General (GATT) (1987-1989).

-Vice-presidente de la segunda Conferencia para el examen de la Convención de Armas Biológicas (1986).

-Representante Especial de Costa Rica, Jefe de Delegación ante la Conferencia Internacional de Paris sobre la Prohibición de Armas Químicas. Protocolo de Ginebra. Enero de 1989.

-Jefe Alterno de Costa Rica, 43 Asamblea General de las Naciones Unidas, 1988.

-Jefe de Delegación, 42 y 43 Conf. Int. de Educación. Ginebra, (1989) - (1990).

-Representante de Costa Rica en la Conferencia Int. sobre Refugiados Indochinos, Ginebra, Junio de 1989.

-Jefe de la Delegación del Gob. de Costa Rica encargado de presentar el II Informe Períodico al Comité de Derechos Económicos Sociales y Culturales (Dic. 1990) y de la Delegación encargada de presentar el III Informe ante el Comité de Derechos Civiles y Políticos (Abril. 1990).

-Representante del Gob. de Costa Rica en las reuniones especiales del Grupo de Trabajo encargado de la redacción de la Convención sobre Derechos del Niño (1983-1989).

-Rep. del Gob. de Costa Rica ante el Grupo de trabajo Encargado de elaborar un programa int. eficaz en materia de delincuencia y justicia penal (Viena, Agosto de 1991)

PARTICIPACION EN ASOCIACIONES Y DIVERSOS

-Miembro del Colegio de Abogados de Costa Rica.

-Miembro del Colegio de Ciencias Políticas de Costa Rica.

-Miembro de la Asociación de Autores de Obras Científicas y Literarias de Costa Rica

-Ex-Miembro del Comité del Consejo Consultativo Int. de la Asociación Internacional contra la Tortura.

0035

-Asistente en la Facultad de Ciencias Sociales y Jurídicas, Universidad de Costa Rica (1974-1979). (T. del Estado, Pol. Internacional, D. Constitucional)

-Asistente del Centro de Estudios de América Latina de Universidad Nacional (1977).

-Investigador en el Centro de Política Internacional de Esc. Ciencias Politicas, U. de Costa Rica (1979-1982).

-Profesor en la Esc. de Ciencias Políticas.(Pol. Internacional) Universidad de Costa Rica (1979-1982)

-Profesor en Esc. Relaciones Internacionales (Derecho Internacional y Económico Int.) Universidad Nacional (1979-1982)

-Director de la Oficina de Asuntos Internacionales (Esc. Rel. Internacionales, U. Nacional de Costa Rica. (1981)

-Consejero Jurídico (Programa P.N.U.D) -Ministerio de Planificación y Política Económica (1981).

-Consejero Jurídico de la Misión Permanente de Costa Rica ante los Org. especializados de Nac. Unidas. (1982-1987).

-Encargado de Negocios de la Misión Permanente de Costa Rica ante Naciones Unidas (1987-1988).

-Ministro-Consejero de la Misión Permanente de Costa Rica ante Nac. Unidas (1988-1990).

-Miembro Adjunto de la Subcomisión de Prevención y Protección a las Minorías de O.N.U. (1988- 1990).

-Miembro Experto del Grupo de Trabajo de Naciones Unidas sobre los territorios no autónomos del Pacífico y el Oceáno Indíco (1988-)-

ACTIVIDADES DIPLOMATICAS

-Embajador. Representante Permanente Alterno de Costa Rica ante la Comisión de Derechos Humanos (1983-1991).

-Consejero Técnico a las Conferencias Internacionales de Trabajo (1983-88), y Jefe Alterno de la LXXV y LXXVI Confs. Internacional de Trabajo (1990-91).

-Jefe de Delegación al Consejo de Administración de la O.I.T (1990-91) y Coordinador del Grupo Gubernamental en la O.I.T. (1990-)

-Consejero Jurídico ante el Alto Comisionado para los Refugiados, Comité Intergubernamental de Migraciones y la Cruz Roja (1983-1990).

-Representante Alterno de la segunda Conferencia Int. sobre la situación Palestina (1983).

0036

-Miembro del Comité de Expertos para la Prevención de la Tortura en las Américas, C.E.P.T.A.

-Colaborador del Diario La Nación de Costa Rica (Política Internacional y Problemas Económicos).

-Ha participado en varias reuniones, seminarios, coloquios y mesas redondas sobre los Derechos Humanos y política Internacional organizados en las Universidades de Costa Rica, Ginebra, La Sorbonna, Sevilla, y San Marcos de Lima.

-Profesor en el Instituto de Derecho Humanitario de San Remo, Italia, en los cursos de Discriminación Racial, y el papel de la policía y los derechos Humanos (1988).

-Profesor en el Instituto Interamericano de Derechos Humanos, en el curso sobre Discriminación Racial (1989).

-Ha dirigido en la Esc. de Ciencias Políticas (UCR) trabajos finales (tesis) de investigación a estudiantes. (1988-1990)

-Asesor del Presidente Arias para la Cumbre Hemisférica de Presidentes Americanos (Octubre de 1989)

-Jefe de delegación al Seminario Regional sobre Migración y cooperación internacional de la O.I.M (La Paz, Bolivia, 1990)

El Dr. Rhenán-Segura es autor de varios libros sobre política Internacional y derecho internacional, y autor de varias decenas de artículos sobre derechos humanos y política internacional en revistas especializadas.

0037

UNITED
NATIONS

 International Convention
on the Elimination
of all Forms of
Racial Discrimination

Distr.
GENERAL

CERD/SP/41
8 November 1991

ENGLISH
Original: ENGLISH

MEETING OF THE STATES PARTIES
Fourteenth Meeting
New York, 15 January 1992

PROVISIONAL AGENDA

Submitted by the Secretary-General

1.   Opening of the Meeting by the representative of the Secretary-General

2.   Election of the Chairman

3.   Adoption of the agenda

4.   Election of other officers of the Meeting

5.   Election of nine members of the Committee on the Elimination of Racial
     Discrimination to replace those whose terms of office will expire on
     19 January 1992, in accordance with article 8, paragraphs 1 to 5, of the
     Convention (CERD/SP/42)

6.   Provision of sufficient resources to ensure the effective functioning of
     the Committee on the Elimination of Racial Discrimination (CERD/SP/43)

7.   Other matters

GE.91-18294/7840a

0038

**UNITED
NATIONS**

 **International Convention
on the Elimination
of all Forms of
Racial Discrimination**

Distr.
GENERAL

CERD/SP/42
8 November 1991

ENGLISH
Original: ENGLISH, FRENCH
SPANISH

MEETING OF THE STATES PARTIES
Fourteenth Meeting
New York, 15 January 1992

ELECTION OF NINE MEMBERS OF THE COMMITTEE ON THE ELIMINATION OF
RACIAL DISCRIMINATION TO REPLACE THOSE WHOSE TERMS WILL EXPIRE
ON 19 JANUARY 1992 IN ACCORDANCE WITH THE PROVISIONS OF
ARTICLE 8 OF THE CONVENTION

<u>Note by the Secretary-General</u>

1.   In pursuance of article 8, paragraph 4, of the International Convention
on the Elimination of All Forms of Racial Discrimination, the Fourteenth
Meeting of States Parties to the Convention will be convened by the
Secretary-General at United Nations Headquarters on 15 January 1992 to elect
nine members of the Committee on the Elimination of Racial Discrimination to
replace those whose terms are due to expire on 19 January 1992 (see annex I
below).   The names of the other nine members who will continue to serve on
the Committee until 19 January 1994 appear in annex II.

2.   In accordance with article 8, paragraph 3, of the Convention, the
Secretary-General, in a note verbale dated 30 August 1991, invited the States
parties to submit their nominations for the election of nine members of the
Committee within two months, namely, by 30 October 1991.   Listed below in
alphabetical order are the nominees and the States parties which have proposed
them:

Mr. Theodoor Cornelis van Boven	(Netherlands)
Mr. Ion Diaconu	(Romania)
Mr. Eduardo Ferrero Costa	(Peru)
Mr. Ivan Garvalov	(Bulgaria)
Mr. Yuri A. Rechetov	(Union of Soviet Socialist Republics)
Mr. Jorge Rhenan Segura	(Costa Rica)
Mrs. Shanti Sadiq Ali	(India)
Mr. Song Shuhua	(China)

GE.91-18300/3944B

0039

Mr. Luis Valencia Rodriguez   (Ecuador)
Mr. Kasimir Vidas   (Yugoslavia)
Mr. Mario Jorge Yutzis   (Argentina)

3. Biographical data of the nominees, as furnished by the States parties concerned, are contained in annex III to this document. Any further nominations and biographical data which may be received by the Secretary-General will be brought to the attention of the States parties in addenda to this document.

0040

Annex I

THE NINE MEMBERS OF THE COMMITTEE WHOSE TERMS EXPIRE
ON 19 JANUARY 1992

Mr. Eduardo Ferrero Costa	(Peru)
Mr. Isi Foighel	(Denmark)
Mr. Ivan Garvalov	(Bulgaria)
Mr. Yuri A. Rechetov	(Union of Soviet Socialist Republics)
Mr. Jorge Rhenán Segura	(Costa Rica)
Mrs. Shanti Sadiq Ali	(India)
Mr. Song Shuhua	(China)
Mr. Kasimir Vidas	(Yugoslavia)
Mr. Mario Jorge Yutzis	(Argentina)

0041~~0040~~

Annex II

LIST OF THE OTHER NINE MEMBERS WHO WILL CONTINUE TO SERVE
ON THE COMMITTEE UNTIL 19 JANUARY 1994

Mr. Mahmoud Aboul-Nasr	(Egypt)
Mr. Hamzat Ahmadu	(Nigeria)
Mr. Michael Parker Banton	(United Kingdom of Great Britain and Northern Ireland)
Mr. Régis de Gouttes	(France)
Mr. George O. Lamptey	(Ghana)
Mr. Carlos Lechuga Hevia	(Cuba)
Mr. Agha Shahi	(Pakistan)
Mr. Michael E. Sherifis	(Cyprus)
Mr. Rüdiger Wolfrum	(Germany)

Annex III

BIOGRAPHICAL DATA OF THE NOMINEES

Theodoor Cornelis van Boven (Netherlands)

Born in 1934 in Voorburg (Netherlands)

University degrees

1959   Master of Law, University of Leiden, Netherlands

1960   Master of Comparative Law, Southern Methodist University, Dallas, Texas, USA

1967   Doctor of Law, University of Leiden, Netherlands

Previous positions

Official of the Netherlands Ministry of Foreign Affairs (1960-1977)

Netherlands representative on the United Nations Commission on Human Rights (1970-1975)

Member of the United Nations Sub-Commission on Prevention of Discrimination and Protection of Minorities (1975-1976, 1986-1991)

Director of the Division of Human Rights of the United Nations (1977-1982)

Visiting Professor at Harvard School of Law (1987) and New York University School of Law (1990)

Present positions

Professor of Law at the University of Limburg, Maastricht, Netherlands

Special Rapporteur of the United Nations Sub-Commission on the right to restitution, compensation and rehabilitation for victims of gross violations of human rights and fundamental freedoms

Member of the Group of Independent Experts of the International Labour Organisation to monitor sanctions and other measures against apartheid

Vice-President of the International Institute of Human Rights, Strasbourg, France

Member of the Board of Trustees of the European Human Rights Foundation

Member of the International Council of International Alert, London, UK

0043

Publications

Books:

International Protection of Religious Liberty, Assan, 1967

People Matter, Views on International Human Rights Policy, Amsterdam, 1982

Numerous articles on human rights and humanitarian issues

Honours

Laureate of the Louise Weiss Prize, Strasbourg (1982)

Doctor honoris causa of the Catholic University of Louvain-la-Neuve, Belgium (1982), the Erasmus University of Rotterdam, Netherlands (1988) and the University of New York at Buffalo, USA (1991)

Recipient of the Right Livelihood Honorary Award, Stockholm (1985)

<u>Ion Diaconu</u> (Romania)

Born on 23 October 1938

Married, two children

<u>Education</u>

1956-1960   Faculty of Law, Bucharest

1965-1968   Doctoral studies at the Institut de Hautes Etudes Internationale of
            Geneva

1971   Doctor ès science politique of the University of Geneva, thesis on
            "Imperative norms in international law (<u>jus cogens</u>)"

<u>Professional activities</u>

1960-1980   Ministry of Foreign Affairs, Department of Legal Matters and
            Treaties

1965-1968   Doctoral studies in Geneva

1980-1981   Counsellor at the Embassy of Romania in Brussels

1981-1986   Minister counsellor at the Permanent Mission of Romania to the
            United Nations in New York; vice-chairman of the Sixth Committee
            in 1983, chairman of working group of the Committee

1986-1990   Deputy director in the Ministry of Foreign Affairs, Department of
            Economic External Relations, Treaties and International
            Organizations

From 1990   Director of the Department of Legal Affairs and Treaties

            Professor of International Law at the National School of Political
            Science, University of Bucharest

1962-1991   Member of Romanian delegations to various international meetings of
            the United Nations, UNESCO, FAO, WHO and CSCE; to conferences of
            codification of international law; to United Nations, UNESCO and
            CSCE meetings of experts on human rights and humanitarian issues

1988-1991   Member of the Sub-Commission on Prevention of Discrimination and
            Protection of Minorities

From 1990   Member of the Permanent Court of Arbitration

From 1972   Member of the Romanian Association for International Law and
            Relations

0045

Publications

> Les normes impératives en droit international (jus cogens), thèse de doctorat, Genève, 1971; revised edition (in Romanian), 1977, Bucharest
>
> New rules of international multilateral negotiations (in Romanian), 1977, Bucharest
>
> Machinery for the peaceful settlement of disputes between States (in Romanian), 1982, Bucharest
>
> Human Rights (in Romanian), to be published, 1991, Bucharest
>
> Articles on international law in various Romanian and foreign journals and publications

0046

Eduardo Ferrero Costa (Peru)

Biographical data

Nationality: Peruvian

Born: Lima, 26 October 1946

Civil status: Married, four children

Academic qualifications

Bachelor of Law (1970)

Admission to the Bar (1970)

Doctor of Law (1974)

Current positions

Executive President of the Peruvian Centre for International Studies
(CEPEI) (1983 to present)

Member of the United Nations Committee on the Elimination of Racial
Discrimination (CERD)

Member of the Advisory Committee on Foreign Affairs of the Peruvian
Ministry of Foreign Affairs

Member of various Peruvian and foreign institutions connected with
international law and international relations

A full list of memberships may be consulted in the files of the
Secretariat.

Teaching and research

Catholic University of Peru:

Professor of the Faculty of Law and of Master's studies in
International Economic Law

A full list of teaching assignments and lecturing activities may be
consulted in the files of the Secretariat.

Other previous relevant activities

Ministry of Foreign Affairs:

Legal Adviser (1981-1982)

Permanent Representative of Peru to the Legal Committee of the
Permanent South Pacific Commission (1978-1982)

0047

Adviser of the Peruvian delegation to the Third United Nations
Conference on the Law of the Sea (1979-1982)

Member of various national commissions in the public sector and
honorary adviser to official Peruvian delegations at international
conferences (1975 to present)

Peruvian National Planning Institute:

Member of the National Planning Advisory Board (1986-1989)

Organization of American States (OAS):

International observer and adviser to the Secretary-General of OAS at
the elections in Costa Rica, the Dominican Republic and Nicaragua (1990)

International conferences:

International speaker at numerous academic seminars and international
events, both in Peru and abroad, on questions of international law and
international relations (1972 to present)

A full list of positions held may be consulted in the files of the
Secretariat.

Publications

Books:

Derecho Internacional Público: Casos y Materiales de Enseñanza (Public
international law: cases and teaching materials), 2 vols., Catholic
University of Peru (1972)

Relaciones del Perú con los Estados Unidos (Peru's relations with the
United States) (co-author and editor), CEPEI, 440 pp., 1987

Relaciones del Perú con los Países Vecinos (Peru's relations with its
neighbours) (co-author and editor), CEPEI, 220 pp., 1988

América Latina, el Perú y la Nueva Estructura de las Relaciones
Económicas Internacionales (Latin America, Peru and the new structure
of international economic relations) (co-author and editor), CEPEI,
320 pp., Lima, 1988

América Latina, el Perú y los Cambios del Sistema Internacional
(Latin America, Peru and the changes in the international system)
(editor), CEPEI, 280 pp., 1989

Relaciones del Perú con Chile y Bolivia (Peru's relations with Chile
and Bolivia), (co-author and editor), CEPEI, 200 pp., 1989

La Reinserción del Perú en el Sistema Financiero Internacional, (Peru's
reintegration into the international financial system) (co-author and
editor), CEPEI, 320 pp., 1990

0048

La Seguridad del Perú frente al Nuevo Contexto Internacional (The security of Peru in the new international context) (co-author and editor), CEPEI (in press)

Significant academic articles:

"Los Derechos Humanos" (Human rights), Revista del Colegio de Abogados de la Libertad, Trujillo, 1974

"Introducción al Estudio de los Derechos Humanos en el Plano Universal" (Introduction to the study of human rights at world level), Revista de la Academia Diplomática del Perú, No. 9, Lima, 1974

"El Derecho de la Integración Latinoamericana frente a la Nueva Década (Integración Sobregional Andina)" (The right to Latin American integration in the new decade (Andean subregional integration)), Perspectivas del Derecho Internacional Contemporáneo (3), edited by Francisco Orrego Vicuña, Institute of International Studies, University of Chile, Santiago, 1981

"Política Exterior del Perú, 1985-1986" (Peru's foreign policy, 1985-1986), Anuario de Políticas Exteriores de América Latina, 1986, edited by Heraldo Muñoz, Grupo editorial Latinoamericano, Buenos Aires, 1987

"La Mediación Internacional: Teoría y Práctica" (International mediation: theory and practice), Derecho, Faculty of Law of the Catholic University of Peru, Lima, 1987

"Peruvian Foreign Policy: Current Trends, Constraints and Opportunities", Journal of Interamerican Studies and World Affairs, Vol. 29, No. 2, Summer 1987

"Relaciones del Perú en la Cuenca del Pacífico" (Peru's relations in the Pacific Basin), Estudios Internacionales, Institute of International Studies, University of Chile, XXII year, No. 88, Santiago, 1989

"El Perú en 1988: Crisis Interna y Política Exterior" (Peru in 1988: internal crisis and foreign policy), Anuario de Políticas Exteriores de América Latina 1988, edited by Heraldo Muñoz, Editorial Nueva Sociedad, Caracas, 1989

"Los Cambios Políticos y Económicos en los Principales Actores del Sistema Internacional: una Primera Aproximación" (Political and economic changes among the main protagonists in the international system: an initial approach), Defensa Nacional, Centre for High Military Studies (CAEM), Lima, 1989

A full list of publications may be consulted in the files of the Secretariat.

0049

Ivan Garvalov (Bulgaria)

Born in Sofia, Bulgaria, 1930

Education

Graduate of "St. Kliment Ohridsky", Sofia University

Diplomatic career

Served tenures at Bulgaria's embassies in New Delhi, Djakarta, Cairo and twice at the Permanent Mission of the Republic of Bulgaria to the United Nations in New York, including as Ambassador, Deputy Permanent Representative from 1982 until 1989

1989 - 1990	Director of the Human Rights Department, Ministry of Foreign Affairs
1990	Director of the United Nations and Disarmament Department, Ministry of Foreign Affairs
Current post (since 1/91)	First Deputy Minister of Foreign Affairs

Activity at the United Nations

1970 - 1990	Member of the Bulgarian delegations at the regular sessions of the General Assembly; member of Bulgarian delegations at General Assembly special sessions and conferences on disarmament, international economic relations, racial discrimination, youth, women, etc.
1978 - 1982	Representative of Bulgaria to the United Nations Commission on Human Rights
1986 - 1987	Deputy Representative of Bulgaria to the Security Council

Positions in United Nations bodies

1973	Elected Rapporteur of the Fourth Committee of the United Nations General Assembly (decolonization)
1980	Elected Chairman of the Third Committee of the United Nations General Assembly (social and humanitarian issues)
1982	Elected Chairman of the United Nations Commission on Human Rights

0050

1983   Elected Chairman of the United Nations Committee on the
                Enhancing of the Principle of the Non-Use of Force

1985   Elected Vice-President of the Economic and Social Council,
                Chairman of the Social Committee

1988 - 1992   Member of the Committee on the Elimination of Racial
                Discrimination

0051

Yuri Alexandrovich Rechetov (USSR)

Born on 10 January 1935, in the city of Gorky (Nizhny Novgorod)

Graduated from the Moscow State Institute of International Relations in 1959 and from the Diplomatic Academy in 1971. Ph.D. in philosophy, Doctor of Law, speaks English, French, German, Swedish, Danish and Icelandic.

From 1959 to 1975 worked in the Scandinavian Countries Department and in the International Economic Organizations Department of the Ministry of Foreign Affairs of the USSR, and also in the Soviet embassies in Iceland and Denmark. Participated in the proceedings of the Conference on Security and Co-operation in Europe during the Geneva round in 1974-1975.

From 1975 to 1980 headed the Prevention of Discrimination and Protection of Minorities Unit of the Human Rights Division of the United Nations Secretariat (Geneva); acted as Secretary to the Sub-Commission on Prevention of Discrimination and Protection of Minorities.

From 1980 to 1986 worked in the Institute of State and Law of the USSR Academy of Sciences. Y. Rechetov is a prominent expert in the field of international law. He is the author of more than 100 publications on human rights issues, on relations between nationalities, on international crimes, on the United Nations role in the field of human rights, etc.

Since 1986 Y. Rechetov has been Deputy Chief of the Division for Humanitarian Issues of the Ministry of Foreign Affairs of the USSR. His duties concern mainly the solution of humanitarian problems, and especially the perfection of Soviet legislation.

Since 1988 Y. Rechetov has headed the Directorate on International Humanitarian Cooperation and Human Rights of the Ministry of Foreign Affairs of the USSR. He headed the USSR delegations at the CSCE meeting in Copenhagen and at the forty-seventh session of the United Nations Commission on Human Rights.

0052

Jorge Rhenán Segura (Costa Rica)

Date and place of birth: 6 October 1956, San José, Costa Rica

Higher education

La Sorbonne, University of Paris:

Doctorate in Political Sciences (summa cum laude)

Master's Degree of the Institute of Latin American Studies, Paris III

University of Geneva:

Master's Degree of the Institute of European Studies

Studies in human rights and humanitarianism

University of Costa Rica:

Degree in Public Law

Degree in Political Sciences

Master's Degree in History of International Relations

Notary public

Autonomous University of Central America:

Degree in Journalism

Present post

Career diplomat in Costa Rica's Foreign Service, currently with rank
of Ambassador

Ambassador. Deputy Resident Representative of Costa Rica to the
United Nations Office at Geneva

Ambassador to the Conference on Disarmament

Member of the Committee on the Elimination of Racial Discrimination

Member of the Academic Committee (Committee on Migration) of the
International Institute of Humanitarian Law, San Remo, Italy (1990)

Professor on sabbatical of the University of Costa Rica (currently
supervising graduate studies at the University's School of Political
Sciences).

0053

Previous functions

Representative of Costa Rica to the Second International Conference on Racial Discrimination (1983)

Representative of Costa Rica at sessions of the Economic and Social Council (1983-1991)

Legal Adviser on the accession of Costa Rica to the General Agreement on Tariffs and Trade (GATT) (1987-1989)

Representative of the Government of Costa Rica at the special meetings of the Working Group on a draft convention on the rights of the child (1983-1989)

Representative of the Government of Costa Rica to the Intergovernmental Working Group on the Creation of an Effective International Crime and Justice Programme (Vienna, August 1991)

A full list of professional assignments may be consulted in the files of the Secretariat.

Membership of associations, etc.

Member of the Costa Rican Bar Association

Member of the Costa Rican Political Sciences Association

Former member of the International Advisory Board of the International Association against Torture

Legal Adviser, Permanent Mission of Costa Rica to the Specialized Agencies of the United Nations (1982-1987)

Chargé d'Affaires, Permanent Mission of Costa Rica to the United Nations (1987-1988)

Minister-Counsellor, Permanent Mission of Costa Rica to the United Nations (1988-1990)

Alternate member of the Sub-Commission on Prevention of Discrimination and Protection of Minorities, Commission on Human Rights (1988-1990)

Expert member of the United Nations Working Group on non-self-governing territories of the Pacific and Indian Oceans (1988-   )

A list of teaching assignments and lecturing activities may be consulted in the files of the Secretariat.

0054

Diplomatic functions

Ambassador, Deputy Permanent Representative of Costa Rica to the United Nations Commission on Human Rights (1983-1991)

Technical Adviser to the International Labour Conference (1983-1988) and deputy head of delegation to the LXXV and LXXVI International Labour Conferences (1990-1991)

Head of delegation to the Governing Body of the International Labour Organisation (ILO) (1990-1991) and Coordinator of the Governmental Group at ILO (1990-   )

Member of the Committee of Experts for the Prevention of Torture in the Americas (CEPTA)

Participant in numerous meetings, seminars, colloquiums and round-tables on human rights and international politics at the Universities of Costa Rica, Geneva, Paris (La Sorbonne), Seville and San Marcos de Lima

Professor at the International Institute of Humanitarian Law, San Remo, Italy, lecturing in courses concerned with racial discrimination, and the role of the police and human rights (1988)

Professor at the Inter-American Institute of Human Rights, lecturing in the course on racial discrimination (1989)

A full list of diplomatic assignments may be consulted in the files of the Secretariat.

Dr. Rhenán Segura is the author of several books on international politics and international law and of several dozen articles on human rights and international politics which have appeared in specialized reviews.

0055

Shanti Sadiq Ali (India)

Born 18 November 1924

Education

1940 - 1942   Vasant College
Theosophical Society,
Banaras, Uttar Pradesh, India.

1942 - 1944   Women's College, Banaras
Hindu University, Varanasai, India.

Joined Masters Degree course. Discontinued studies to join students' movement
in freedom struggle under Indian National Congress. Drafted to All India
Congress Committee Office (AICC), Allahabad, New Delhi.

Awards

1953 - 1954   Awarded United Nations Fellowship on recommendation of
Government of India in recognition of work for refugees from
Pakistan and particularly resettlement of abducted women in
camps under the Indian National Congress. Visited Geneva,
United Kingdom, France and Greece

Experience in African affairs

1963 - 1972   Drafted as Executive Secretary to Indian Council for Africa
(established in 1960 and now Indian Centre for Africa under
the Indian Council for Cultural Relations).

                    Supervised publication of Africa Quarterly. Organized and
participated in seminars. Commentator on African Affairs on
All India Radio, Doordarshan (TV).

1977 - 1982   Member, Governing Body, Indian Council for Cultural
Relations as an authority on African affairs.

1978   India's representative at the 1978 United Nations Symposium
on the Exploitation of Blacks in South Africa and Namibia
and on prison conditions in the South African jails,
Lesotho; elected Rapporteur.

1978 - 1979   Member, Indian National Committee to observe the
United Nations International Anti-Apartheid Year and
Convener of the Maharashtra State Committee.

1979   Member of the Indian delegation to the thirty-fourth session
of the United Nations General Assembly.

1979 - 1981   Executive Editor, Africa Quarterly, organ of the Indian
Centre for Africa, Indian Council for Cultural Relations.

1980   Elected to United Nations Committee on the Elimination of Racial Discrimination for four-year term; re-elected in 1984. Represented CERD and presented papers at the following seminars/conferences:

United Nations Regional Seminar, Bangkok, 2–13 August 1982. Presented paper on "The Universal Relevance of the International Convention on the Elimination of Racial Discrimination".

United Nations International Seminar, 20 June – 1 July 1983 at the Palais des Nations, Geneva. Presented paper on "Experience in Developing Public Awareness of the Provisions of International Standards on Human Rights" (working paper).

Colloquium on the "International Protection of Human Rights Institutions and Reality", Thessalonika, Greece, 28–30 September 1984. Presented paper on "Human Rights in the Socio-Economic Environment of a Developing Country: India, A Case Study".

1980   Chairman of the Committee for International Seminar on "India and East African Littoral, Hinterland and Indian Ocean Island States: Areas of Co-operation" held in Goa. Co-author of edited papers of Seminar.

1984   Elected first President African Studies Society of India (ASSI) (Registered in May 1984).

Positions held currently

President, African Studies Society of India

Rapporteur, United Nations Committee on the Elimination of Racial Discrimination

Member, Indian Council of World Affairs

Member, Institute of Defence Studies and Analyses

Honorary Member, University Women's Association, Pune.

Honorary Member, Seminar Committee, Area Studies Centre in the Indian Ocean Region, Osmani University, Hyderabad.

Member, Board of School of International Studies, Jawaharlal Nehru University, New Delhi

Elected Editor in Chief, Africa Newsletter, Journal of the African Studies Society of India, at Annual Conference, Jaipur, 15 February 1987

Member, Advisory Panel on Africa, Centre for Africa, ICCR

0057

Published books

India and the Western Indian Ocean States: Towards Regional Cooperation
Development. Co-authored with Professor R.R. Ramchandani (Allied
Publishers).

India and Africa through the Ages (National Book Trust).

Africa: Problem of Economic Growth and Development. Co-authored with
Professor Anirudha Gupta (Sterling Publishers).

Song Shuhua (China)

Born 19 June 1928, Chengdu, Sichuan Province, China.

Education

B.A. in sociology, Yenching University (1944-1946), China

M.A. in anthropology, University of Sydney (1947-1949), Australia

Employment

Lecturer, West China Union University, Chengdu, Sichuan, China (1949-1952)

Lecturer, Associate Professor and Professor, Central Institute of Nationalities, Beijing, China (1952-1991)

Vice-President, Central Institute of Nationalities (1980-1987)

Member, Academic Committee of the Institute for Nationality Studies, Chinese Academy of Social Sciences (1983-1988)

Member, United Nations Committee on the Elimination of Racial Discrimination (1984-1991)

Vice-Chairman, China-Latin America Friendship Association (1984-1991)

Member, Academic Degree Evaluation Sub-Committee, State Council's Academic Degree Committee (1985-1991)

Principal publications

Los Problemas de las Nacionalidades de China, Facultad de Ciencias Politicas y Sociales UNANM, 1981

Cihai (a comprehensive dictionary), Shanghai, 1979 (co-author)

China's Minority Nationalities, Beijing, 1981 (co-author)

The History of Primitive Society, Beijing, 1984 (co-author)

The Volume of Ethnic Groups, Encyclopedia Sinina, Vice-Editor in Chief of Ethnology, 1980

A Comprehensive Dictionary of Ethnic Groups, 1987, Vice-Editor in Chief and co-author

0059

Luis Valencia Rodríguez (Ecuador)

Born: Quito, Ecuador, 5 March 1926

Academic studies and qualifications

Higher studies at the Faculty of Law of the Central University of Ecuador (Quito)

Fifth Special Course for Government Legal Advisers, London (1968-1969)

Degree in Public and Social Sciences (Central University of Ecuador, Quito)

Qualified barrister in the Ecuadorian courts and Doctor of Jurisprudence at the Central University, Quito

Knowledge of foreign languages

English, French, Portuguese and Russian

Principal assignments in the Foreign Service of Ecuador

Head of the Political Section of the Ministry of Foreign Affairs (1951)

Director of the OAS (Organization of American States) Section (Ministry of Foreign Affairs) (1955)

Counsellor at the Permanent Mission of Ecuador to the United Nations (16 July 1959 - 30 October 1963)

Minister Plenipotentiary at the Permanent Mission of Ecuador to the United Nations (31 October 1963 - 8 March 1964)

Under-Secretary for Diplomatic and Political Affairs at the Ministry of Foreign Affairs (9 March 1964 - 16 March 1964)

Promoted to Ambassador on 25 August 1965

Acting Minister for Foreign Affairs (on various occasions between July and December 1965)

Minister for Foreign Affairs (two terms: 14 December 1965 - 31 March 1966 and 4 November 1981 - 9 August 1984)

Ambassador Extraordinary and Plenipotentiary of Ecuador to Argentina (1989-   )

A full list of positions held may be consulted in the files of the Secretariat.

Main official assignments

Head of delegation to the eighteenth session of the United Nations General Assembly (1963)

0060

Representative to the Fifth World Conference of the Society for International Development (New York, 1963)

Representative to the fifth session of the Inter-American Council of Jurists (San Salvador, 1965)

Head of delegation to the twenty-first regular session of the United Nations General Assembly (1966)

Member of the Ecuadorian delegation to the second session of the United Nations Conference on the Law of Treaties (Vienna, 1969)

Head of the Ecuadorian delegation to the thirtieth session of the United Nations General Assembly (1975)

Head of the Ecuadorian delegation to the eleventh, twelfth and thirteenth regular sessions of the General Assembly of the Organization of American States (OAS) (1981, 1982 and 1983)

Head of the Ecuadorian delegation to the thirty-seventh regular session of the United Nations General Assembly (1982)

A full list of participation in international conferences may be consulted in the files of the Secretariat.

Other posts and assignments

Member, in a personal capacity, of the United Nations Committee on the Elimination of Racial Discrimination (1970-1986). Two terms as Chairman of the Committee (1972-1974 and 1984-1986)

OAS Representative assigned to observe the elections in Grenada (December 1984)

A list of teaching assignments and lecturing activities may be consulted in the files of the Secretariat.

Official missions

As Ecuadorian Minister for Foreign Affairs or as a member of official Ecuadorian delegations, has travelled on official missions to Argentina, Austria, Barbados, Belgium, Bolivia, Brazil, Bulgaria, Chile, China, Colombia, Costa Rica, Czechoslovakia, the Dominican Republic, El Salvador, France, Germany, Italy, Japan, Panama, the Republic of Korea, St. Lucia, Spain, Switzerland, Trinidad and Tobago, the United Kingdom, the United States of America, Uruguay, the Vatican, Venezuela, the United Nations, the Organization of American States (OAS), the European Economic Community and the Latin American Integration Association.

A full list of official missions may be consulted in the files of the Secretariat.

Publications

Fundamentos y propósitos de las Naciones Unidas (Bases and purposes of the United Nations) (1970)

Principios de las Naciones Unidas (Principles of the United Nations) (1972)

Protección de los Derechos Humanos (Protection of human rights) (1972), sole prizewinner in an international competition organized by the World Peace through Law Centre

Los derechos humanos de los trabajadores migrantes (The human rights of migrant workers) (1975)

Cumplimiento del artículo 6 de la Convención Internacional sobre la Eliminación de Todas las Formas de Discriminación Racial (Compliance with article 6 of the International Convention on the Elimination of All Forms of Racial Discrimination) (1977)

Visión del Ecuador (A vision of Ecuador) (1982)

Various legal and literary studies

A full list of publications may be consulted in the files of the Secretariat.

Decorations and honours

Awarded the "Bien de la Patria" decoration by decision of the National Constituent Assembly of Ecuador in November 1966

Grand Cross of the "Al Mérito" National Order of Ecuador

Grand Cross of the "Al Mérito" National Order of Italy

Grand Cross of the "Cóndor de los Andes" Order of Bolivia

Grand Cross of the "Cruzeiro do Sul" Order of Brazil

Grand Cross of the "Rubén Darío" Order of Nicaragua

"Francisco de Miranda Primera Clase" decoration of Venezuela

Grand Cross of the "Boyacá" Order of Colombia

Grand Cross of the "Libertador San Martín" Order of Argentina

Grand Cross of the "Rio Branco" Order of Brazil

Grand Cordon of the "Libertador" Order of Venezuela

Grand Cross of the "Orden del Sol" of Peru

Grand Cross of the Gwanghwa Order of Merit for Diplomatic Service of Korea

Grand Cross of the "José Matías Delgado" Order of El Salvador

Grand Cross of the Order of Duarte, Sánchez and Mella of the Dominican Republic

Grand Cross of the "Ponche Verde" Order of Río Grande do Sul, Brazil

0062

Kazimir Vidas (Yugoslavia)

Born 21 March 1928, Rijeka.

Studied in Oslo, New York, Zagreb.

Graduated in 1955 from the University of Zagreb, Faculty of Economics.

In diplomatic service held posts in New York, Warsaw, Geneva and Paris.

Federal Under-Secretary for Finance (International Affairs) 1975-1978, Assistant Federal Secretary for Foreign Affairs (United Nations and multilateral relations) 1978-1982 and 1986-1989, Ambassador-Permanent Representative of Yugoslavia to the United Nations Office at Geneva 1982-1986, Special Adviser to the European Centre for Peace and Development in Belgrade of the United Nations University for Peace since 1989.

Participated in many sessions of the United Nations General Assembly, Summit Meetings in Cancún and of Non-Aligned Countries, conferences of United Nations human rights bodies, UNHCR, ILO, WHO, UNCTAD.

Published studies on social and human rights problems, racial discrimination, and international economic relations.

Awarded several Yugoslav and foreign decorations and the Legion d'Honneur of France.

Member of CERD 1988-1992, Vice-Chairman of CERD 1990-1991.

As a member of CERD and its Vice-Chairman, he has significantly contributed to the improvement of the functioning of the Committee.

Undertook many appreciated initiatives for better coordination with the States parties to the Convention and with other United Nations human rights bodies.

Served as country rapporteur on several periodic reports and as liaison for the Committee against Torture.

Participated in many national and international meetings dealing with problems of racial discrimination and human rights and published articles on racial discrimination.

0063

Mario Jorge Yutzis (Argentina)

Born in Buenos Aires, Argentina, 26 July 1936

Married to Teresita Grach Felkar, two children

Vicar of the United Lutheran Church in Argentina

Master of Theology, José C. Paz Lutheran Faculty of Theology, Buenos Aires, Argentina

Doctor of Religious Sciences, Faculty of Protestant Theology, University of Strasbourg, France

University studies in psychology and anthropology, Montevideo and Buenos Aires

Student Chaplain, Student Christian Movement of Argentina (1960)

Studies Secretary of the Latin American Executive Committee of the World Student Christian Federation (1973-1976)

Member of the Executive Committee of the World Student Christian Federation

Human Rights Adviser to the Lutheran World Federation (1978-1979)

Co-editor of the Newsletter "Human Rights Concern" of the Lutheran World Federation (1978-1979)

Professor of Philosophical Anthropology at the Buenos Aires Higher Evangelical Institute for Theological Education (ISEDET)

Professor of Contemporary Ideologies at ISEDET

Professor of Christian Ethics at the José C. Paz Lutheran Faculty of Theology, Buenos Aires (1963-1964)

Professor of Fundamental Psychology, Young Men's Christian Association of Argentina (1983-1986)

Visiting Professor, Hamma School of Theology, Springfield, Ohio (1969)

Visiting Professor, St. Paul Luther Seminary, St. Paul, Minnesota (1985)

Visiting Professor, Dayton University, Columbus, Ohio (1969)

Visiting Professor, Washington Ecumenical Consortium (1981)

Visiting Professor, School of Theology, Vancouver, Canada (1984)

Visiting Professor, Ecumenical Institute of Bossey (Céligny, Vaud, Switzerland) (1978-1979)

0064

Assistant Professor in the Adult Education Service of the University of Geneva, Switzerland (1978-1979)

Member of CERD (1984-1988)

Vice-Chairman of CERD (1986-1988).

Member of CERD (1988-1992)

Publications

La noción de la persona en la antropología de Unamuno (The notion of person in Unamuno's anthropology), Salamanca.

La construcción Social de la enfermedád (The social construction of illness), Buenos Aires.

Identidad nacional y democracia (National identity and democracy).

Derecho internacional, multilateralismo y la paz en el mundo (International law, multilateralism and world peace), Buenos Aires.

Derechos humanos y la hermenéutica de la fe cristiana (Human rights and the hermeneutics of Christian faith), Buenos Aires.

Ideología y cambio social (Ideology and social change), Geneva.

Algunas reflexiones en torno al lenguaje de la fe cristiana (Some reflections on the language of Christian faith), Buenos Aires.

0065

Téléfax: (022) 733 98 79
Télégrammes: UNATIONS, GENÈVE
Télex: 412 962 UNO CH
Téléphone: 734 60 11   731 02 11
RÉF. N°:   G/SO 237/2 (3)
(à rappeler dans la réponse)

Palais des Nations
CH-1211 GENÈVE 10

The Secretary-General of the United Nations presents his compliments to the Minister for Foreign Affairs of the Republic of Korea and has the honour to refer to his note G/SO 237/2 (3) of 30 August 1991 concerning the election of nine members of the Committee on the Elimination of Racial Discrimination, as provided for under article 8 of the International Convention on the Elimination of All Forms of Racial Discrimination.

The Secretary-General wishes to inform His Excellency's Government that the Fourteenth Meeting of the States Parties to the Convention to elect nine members of the Committee, as well as to discuss the provision of sufficient resources to ensure the effective functioning of the Committee, is scheduled to be held at United Nations Headquarters, New York, on Wednesday, 15 January 1992.

His Excellency's Government is hereby invited to be represented at the Meeting and to forward, if possible not less than one week before the Meeting, the credentials for its representative, issued either by the Head of State or Government, or by the Minister for Foreign Affairs, together with the names of the other members of its delegation.

The following documents for the Meeting are forwarded herewith:

(a) The provisional agenda (CERD/SP/41), based on the relevant provisions of the Convention and the decisions of the Meetings of the States Parties;

(b) The rules of procedure (CERD/SP/2/Rev.1), adopted at the First Meeting of the States Parties and revised at the Eleventh Meeting of the States Parties;

(c) A note by the Secretary-General (CERD/SP/42), concerning the election of the nine members of the Committee and containing a list, in alphabetical order, of all persons nominated for the election by the States Parties with an indication of the States Parties which have nominated them and including also, in an annex, the biographical data of persons nominated, as furnished by the States Parties concerned.

Any further nominations and biographical data which may be received by the Secretary-General before the Meeting will be circulated to the States Parties in addenda to document CERD/SP/42.

The report of the Secretary-General (CERD/SP/43) regarding provision of sufficient resources to ensure the effective functioning of the Committee, including information concerning the status of assessed contributions, the establishment of a "contingency reserve fund", and concerning the possibility of incorporating the financing of the Committee's activities into the regular budget of the United Nations, as proposed by Norway, will be forwarded to His Excellency's Government in due course.

0066

20 November 1991

주 소 대 사 관

주소정20276- 528   1991. 11. 13.

수신 : 국제기구국장

발신 : 주소대사

제목 : 인종차별 철폐에 관한 위원회 입후보 지지

연 : SVW-4316

연호 주재국 정부의 공한 및 입후보자 이력사항을 별첨하여 송부합니다.

첨부 : 공한 및 이력사항(노어본 및 한글번역본).   끝.

주 소 대

0067

2065862

Министерство Иностранных Дел СССР свидетельствует свое уважение Посольствам государств-участников Конвенции о ликвидации всех форм расовой дискриминации и имеет честь сообщить, что Правительство СССР приняло решение о выдвижении кандидатуры Чрезвычайного и Полномочного Посла СССР, начальника Управления по международному гуманитарному сотрудничеству и правам человека МИД СССР Ю.А.Решетова для переизбрания в Комитет по ликвидации расовой дискриминации.

Ю.А.Решетов - доктор юридических наук, кандидат философских наук имеет многолетний опыт работы в области международного сотрудничества по вопросам прав человека.

Правительство СССР придает большое значение работе упомянутого Комитета как одного из наиболее авторитетных международных механизмов защиты прав человека и было бы весьма признательно за поддержку кандидатуры Ю.А.Решетова во время выборов, которые состоятся в январе 1992 года в Нью-Йорке.

ПОСОЛЬСТВУ
РЕСПУБЛИКИ КОРЕИ

г.Москва

0068

К данной ноте прилагаются биографические данные Ю.А.Решетова.

Министерство Иностранных Дел СССР пользуется случаем, чтобы возобновить Посольствам государств-участников Конвенции о ликвидации всех форм расовой дискриминации уверения в своем весьма высоком уважении.

Москва, 24 октября 1991 года

0069

Юрий Александрович РЕШЕТОВ

Родился 10 января 1935 года в городе Горьком (Нижний Новгород).

Образование: в 1959 году окончил Московский государственный институт международных отношений, в 1971 году - Дипломатическую академию МИД СССР, доктор юридических наук, кандидат философских наук, владеет английским, французским, шведским, датским и исландским языками.

С 1959 г. по 1975 г. работал в Отделе скандинавских стран и Отделе международных экономических организаций МИД СССР, а также совпосольствах в Исландии и Дании, участвовал в женевском этапе (1974-1975 гг.)   Совещания по безопасности и сотрудничеству в Европе.

С 1975 г. по 1980 г. работал в Секретариате Отделения ООН в Женеве руководителем секции по предотвращению дискриминации и защите меньшинств в отделе прав человека и одновременно являлся секретарем Подкомиссии ООН по предупреждению дискриминации и защите меньшинств.

1980 г. по 1986 г. работал в Институте государства и права АН СССР.

Ю.А.Решетов - известный специалист в области международного права. Он является автором более 100 публикаций по вопросам прав человека, межнациональных отношений, роли ООН в области прав человека.

В 1987 г. он был назначен заместителем заведующего Отделом гуманитарных проблем МИД СССР. В круг его обязанностей входило

0070

разрешение различных гуманитарных проблем, а также приведение советского законодательства в соответствие с международными обязательствами Советского Союза.

С 1988 года Ю.А.Решетов - начальник Управления по международному гуманитарному сотрудничеству и правам человека МИД СССР. Возглавлял делегации СССР на Копенгагенском совещании конференции СБСЕ по человеческому измерению и 47-й сессии Комиссии ООН по правам человека.

0071

(비공식번역)

　　소련 외무성은 인종 차별 철폐에 관한 협약 당사국 대사관들에
존경을 표하면서, 소련 정부가 소련 외무성 국제인도협력 및 인권
국장인 유.아. 레쉐또브 대사를 인종차별 철폐위원회 위원으로
재입후보하도록 했음을 알리게 됨을 영광으로 생각합니다.

　　법학박사이며, 철학 박사 후보인 유.아. 레쉐또브는 인권문제에
관한 국제협조 분야에서 다년간 일해온 경험을 가지고 있읍니다.

　　소련 정부는 상기 위원회를 인권보호에 관한 가장 권위있는 국제
기구의 하나로서 인정하고 그 활동에 큰 의의를 부여하고 있는바,
귀 정부가 1992년 1월에 실시될 선거에서 유.아. 레쉐또브 후보를
지지해 주시면 대단히 감사하겠읍니다.　　유.아. 레쉐또브의 이력
사항을 동봉하였읍니다.

　　소련 외무성은 이 기회를 이용하여 인종차별 철폐에 관한 협약
당사국 대사관들에 다시한번 존경의 뜻을 표하는 바입니다.

1991. 10. 24
모스크바

0072

유리 알렉산드로위츠 레쉐또브 대사 이력사항

o 출생 : 1935년 1월 10일 고리키(니즈니 노브고로드) 시에서 출생

o 학력 :

- 1959년 모스크바 국제관계 국립대학 졸업
- 1971년 소련 외무성 외교아카데미 졸업, 법학박사, 철학박사 후보
          (영어, 프랑스어, 스웨덴어, 덴마크어, 아이스랜드어 구사)

o 경력 :

- 1959년-1975년간 소련 외무성 국제경제국과 스칸드나비아 담당국 근무,
   주아이스랜드 및 주덴마크 소련대사관 근무
- 1971년-1975년간 유럽안보협력에 관한 제네바 회의에 참가
- 1975년-1980년간 제네바 주재 유엔사무소 인권국 인종차별 방지 및
   소수민족 보호과장겸 유엔 인종차별 방지 및 소수민족 보호 소위원회
   서기로 근무
- 1980년-1986년간 소련 과학아카데미 산하 국가 및 법률연구소 근무
- 1987년 소련 외무성 인문문제국 부국장에 임명, 인도주의 및 소련법과
   국제법과의 관계 등 담당
- 1988년 소련 외무성 인도주의 협조 및 인권국 국장 재직, 인권에 관한
   CSCE 코펜하겐 회의 대표, 인권문제에 관한 제47차 유엔위원회 회의 대표

o 기타 :

- 유.아.레쉐또브는 국제법 분야의 전문가이며, 인권, 국제관계, 인권분야
   에서의 유엔 역할에 관해 100여편의 저작 발표

0073

외 무 부

종 별 :

번 호 : SVW-4316

일 시 : 91 1113 1430

수 신 : 장 관(연이,동구일)

발 신 : 주 쏘 대사

제 목 : 인종차별 철폐위원회 입후보 지지요청

1. 주재국 외무성은 1992 년 1 월에 실시될 인종차별 철폐에관한 위원회위원 선거에 재입후보 할 예정이라하면서 아국정부가 동 후보를지지하여 줄것을 요청하는 공한을 보내왔음. 후보는 현 소외무성 테쉐또브 국제인도협력및 인권국장임.

2. 상기 공한및 후보자 인적사항은 금 파편 송부 위계임.끝

(대사공로명-국장)

92.6.30

국기국   차관   1차보   구주국

PAGE 1

주 제 네 바 대 표 부

제네(정) 2031-1022   1991. 11. 27.

수신 : 장관

참조 : 국제기구국장

제목 : 자메이카의 인종차별 철폐위 위원 출마

91. 11. 29

표제관련 당지 자메이카대표부의 공한을 별첨 송부합니다.

첨부 : 상기 공한 사본 1부.   끝.

주 제 네 바 대 사

0075

Jamaica의
CERD 입후보
추천장면CABLES: JAGEN

PERMANENT MISSION OF JAMAICA
TO THE OFFICE OF THE UNITED NATIONS AT GENEVA

YOUR REF.:

OUR REF.: 500/121

42, RUE DE LAUSANNE
1201 GENEVA

The Permanent Mission of Jamaica to the United Nations
Office at Geneva and its Specialised Agencies presents its
compliments to the Secretary General of the United Nations
and with reference to the latter's Note No. GSO 237/2(3)
dated August 30, 1991, has the honour to inform that the
Government of Jamaica has decided to present the candidature
of Miss Florizelle A. O'Connor for election to the Committee
on the Elimination of Racial Discrimination at elections to
be held during the Meeting of States Parties to the
Convention in January, 1992 in New York.

The Government of Jamaica attaches great importance to
the work of the Committee on the Elimination of Racial
Discrimination, and to its role in protecting human rights
and fundamental freedoms.

In presenting the candidature of Miss Florizelle O'Connor,
the Government of Jamaica is confident in her ability to make
a substantial contribution to the Committee's effectiveness.
Miss O'Connor has had considerable experience in the field
of human rights, at both the national and international
levels and has paid special attention to the subject of racial
discrimination. A copy of Miss O'Connor's biographical
data is attached.

The Permanent Mission of Jamaica apologises for the late
submission of Miss O'Connor's candidature and avails itself
of this opportunity to renew to the Secretary General of
the United Nations the assurances of its highest consideration.

Geneva, 12th November, 1991

0076

S

BIOGRAPHICAL DATA

Miss Florizelle A. O'Connor

EDUCATION:

Attended Queen's High School, Kingston, Jamaica

GCE Ordinary ('O') and Advanced ('A') levels Certificates with distinction in English Language

Bachelor of Arts (B.A.), History (Honours) - University of the West Indies, Mona Campus

Certificate and Diploma in Mass Communication - University of the West Indies, Mona Campus

WORK EXPERIENCE:

Producer/Script Writer/News Reporter - Jamaica Broadcasting Corporation, Public Affairs Division

Produced both television and radio programmes with special emphasis on social themes for example the following:

Television programme entitled: 'The Verdict is Yours' - a discussion programme on current issues.

'Roundabout' - an investigative programme on the lives of ordinary Jamaican citizens.

Magazine type radio programmes

1981 to date: Coordinator - Jamaica Council for Human Rights

Responsible for the administration of Council's Office and implementation of policies

Represented Jamaica at a number of International Human Rights Conferences, including African National Congress (ANC) Peoples of the World Congress held in Arusha, Tanzania.

The Council is the only Human Rights Organisation in Jamaica and the oldest in the Caribbean

During the last five (5) years, the Council has broken new ground in the area of hearings before Their Lordships of the Judicial Committee of the Privy Council in London and at present receives assistance from over thirty law firms in London which handle legal matters on a voluntary basis on the Council's behalf.

0077

The Council carries out a Public Education Programme centered mainly on the issue of apartheid, in response to the call made by the United Nations to intensify attempts to dismantle the inhuman system of apartheid.

This Programme involves cultural concerts, using Mandela's birthdate as a focus each year, organises seminars, as well as lectures to churches, teachers, students, clubs and civil association groups on the subject which has resulted in a general heightening of consciousness of the issue of apartheid in particular on the wider issue of racial discrimination in the world

The Council has been pivotal in arranging for visits by International Missions to Jamaica to analyse the human rights situation, e.g. 'Americas Watch' which deals with police excesses, and Amnesty International which deals with capital punishment.

The Human Rights Council is responsible for making contact with international organizations on a wide range of human rights issues, i.e. both United Nations and other related organisations and works very closely with the United Nations Human Rights Committee and also United Nations Centre Against Apartheid, Council for Namibia, ANC.

Miss O'Connor has represented Jamaica at several conferences sponsored by the United Nations Centre Against Apartheid, UNESCO, and the Council for Namibia and several other international organisations.

OTHER RELATED ACTIVITIES:

1973-1980:   Public Relations Officer - People's National
             Party

Member of Press Team accompanying Prime Minister Michael Manley to Non-Aligned Conference in Algiers

Also toured African Continent, visited Cuba with Prime Minister.

0078

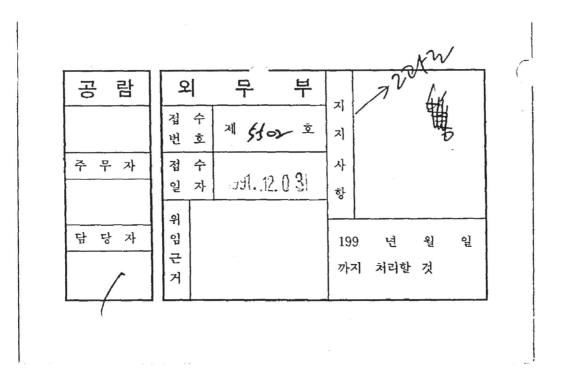

공 람	외 무 부		지지사항	
	접수번호	제 5502 호		
주 무 자	접수일자	'91. 12. 0 3		
	위임근거		199 년 월 일	
담 당 자			까지 처리할 것	

24.

M/35

        The Embassy of Peru presents its compliments to the Ministry of Foreign Affairs and regarding to its note No. M/29 dated 15 October, 1991, about the candidacy of Dr. Eduardo Ferrero for the Committee on the Elimination of Racial Discrimination of the United Nations, has the honor to inform that the Peruvian candidacy has been endorsed by the Latin American and Caribbean Group (GRULAC) in order to support it as a Regional candidacy.

        The Peruvian government will appreciate very much the Korean support to this aspiration which has received already the regional endorsement.

        The Embassy of Peru avails itself of this opportunity to renew to the Ministry of Foreign Affairs the assurances of its highest consideration.

                Seoul, 28 November 1991

TO
THE MINISTRY OF FOREIGN AFFAIRS
S E O U L

0080

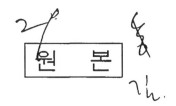

관리 번호	91 -215

외 무 부

종 별 :

번 호 : COW-0546　　　　　　　　　일 시 : 91 1211 1715

수 신 : 장 관(연일,미중)

발 신 : 주 코스타리카 대사

제 목 : 주재국대표 유엔총회 인종차별철폐위 위원 입후보

　　1. 주재국 정부는 당관앞 외무성공한으로 92.1.15 일 선출될 유엔총회 직속기구(협약기구)인 인종차별 철폐위원회(CERD)위원직에 주재국 정부의 DR. JORGE RHENAN SEGURA 위원을 재입후보키로 결정하였다면서 아국정부의 지지를 요청하여 왔음. 주재국은 민주주의 100 여년의 역사에 긍지를 가지고 유엔의 인권위, CERD 등 각종 인권관계 위원회에 적극참여하고 인권문제에 지대한 관심을 가져왔으며, 따라서 금번 입후보도 매우 중요시하고 있음.

　　2. DR. RHENAN SEGURA 의 주요약력 아래와 같음

0 생년원일:56.10.6(산호세 출생)

0 주요경력

- 현 유엔 군축회의자대사, 유엔 OFICINA EUROPEA 교체대표(대사), CERD 위원

- 전 유엔 인권위 교체대표(대사)

- 외교관, 교수로 많은 활동을 함(많은 국제회의 참가, 저서, 논문 다수)

　　4. 동 공한 파편 송부위계임.끝.

(대사 김창근-국장)

예고: 92.6.30 까자 대 대고문대 의거 인반문서로 재분류됨

국기국　　차관　　1차보　　미주국　　외정실　　분석관　　청와대　　안기부

PAGE 1　　　　　　　　　　　　　　　　　　91.12.12　10:33

　　　　　　　　　　　　　　　　　　　　외신 2과 통제관 BS

　　　　　　　　　　　　　　　　　　　　　　　0081

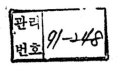관리번호 91-148

신뢰받는 정부되고 받쳐주는 국민되자

주 코 스 타 리 카 대 사 관

코스타(정)20312-57   1991. 12. 11

수 신 : 장관

참 조 : 국제기구국장, 미주국장

제 목 : 주재국 대표 유엔총회 인종차별 위원회 위원 입후보

        연 : COW-0546

        연호 주재국 대표의 유엔총회 인종차별위원회 재입후보 지지를 요청하는 외무성
공한 사본을 별첨 송부합니다.

        첨 부 : 동 공한 사본 1부. 끝.

                        예고 : 92. 6. 30까지

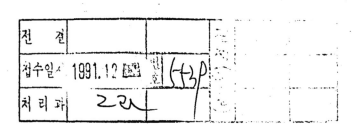

전 결			
접수일시 1991.12			
처 리 과			

주 코 스 타 리 카 대 사

                                                        0082

REPUBLICA DE COSTA RICA
MINISTERIO DE RELACIONES EXTERIORES Y CULTO

No.1667-91-DCC

San José, 29 de noviembre de 1991

Excelencia:

Tengo el agrado de dirigirme a Vuestra Exclencia, en ocasión de hacer de Vuestro Conocimiento que el Gobierno de Costa Rica ha decidido presentar la candidatura del Dr. Jorge Rhenán Segura para su reelección como Miembro del Comité para la Eliminación de todas las Formas de Discriminación Racial, C.E.R.D., en la elección que tendrá lugar durante la próxima reunión de Estados Partes de la Convención a realizarse el 15 de enero de 1992 en Nueva York, Estados Unidos de América.

La República de Costa Rica otorga gran importancia a la institucionalización de la protección de los derechos humanos en su compromiso con la promoción y vigencia efectiva de estos derechos. En este sentido, fue uno de los primeros Estados en ratificar la Convención Internacional para la Eliminación de todas las Formas de Discriminación Racial, como una muestra más de su compromiso con la igualdad de todos lo hombres.

Excelentísimo Sr.
Chang Keun Kim
Embajador de la República
de Corea
Ciudad.-

0083

Como es del digno conocimiento de Vuestra Excelencia, Costa Rica mantiene un interés permanente en los foros especializados sobre Derechos Humanos del sistema internacional e interamericano, en los cuales expertos costarricenses formados en el contexto de la tradición de los derechos humanos y de profundas convicciones humanitarias, han tenido una valiosa participación en diversos comités especializados, tales como la Subcomisión para la Prevención de la Discriminación y Protección a las Minorías, el Comité de Derechos Humanos y el Comité sobre la Eliminación de todas las Formas de Discriminación Racial.

Al solicitar el apoyo de ese Ilustrado Gobierno para la reelección del Dr. Rhenán Segura, el Gobierno de Costa Rica desea destacar sus altos méritos, los cuales habrán de permitirle continuar brindando un valioso aporte en los trabajos del referido Comité si resultase honrado con esa distinción.

El Dr. Segura ha sido reconocido como experto internacional en el campo de los Derechos Humanos. Cuenta con una amplia formación y experiencia sobre los problemas de discriminación, así como sobre los diferentes procedimientos y órganos del sistema de Naciones Unidas encargados de controlar las actividades de los Estados Partes de la Convención sobre la materia. Ha participado en varias reuniones, seminarios, coloquios y mesas redondas sobre Derechos Humanos y Política Internacional organizados en las Universidades de Costa Rica,

-2-

0084

La Sorbona, Sevilla y San Marcos de Lima. Es autor de varios libros sobre Política Internacional y Derecho Internacional, así como de varias decenas de artículos sobre estos temas en revistas especializadas. Adjunto encontrará su curriculum vitae.

En virtud de lo anteriormente expuesto, me valgo del digno conducto de Vuestra Excelencia para manifestar el interés del Gobierno de Costa Rica en obtener el valioso apoyo de Vuestro Ilustrado Gobierno para la anterior candidatura.

Hago propicia la oportunidad para reiterar a Vuestra Excelencia los testimonios de mi más distinguida consideración.

Hernán R. Castro H.
Ministro a.i.

-3-

0085

Curriculum Vitae
de
Embajador Jorge Rhenán Segura

Apellidos: Rhenán Segura

Nombre: Jorge

Fecha y lugar de Nacimiento: 6 de octubre de 1956. San José de
Costa Rica

Estudios Superiores :

UNIVERSIDAD DE LA SORBONNA.

- Doctor en Ciencias Políticas (Summa Cum Laude)

- DEA (Master) del Instituto de Estudios de América
  Latina. Paris III

UNIVERSIDAD DE GINEBRA

- DEA (Master) del Instituto de Estudios Europeos

- Estudios en Derechos Humanos y Humanitario

UNIVERSIDAD DE COSTA RICA

- Licenciatura en Derecho Público
- Licenciatura en Ciencias Políticas
- Master en Historia de las Rel. Internacionales
- Notario Público

UNIVERSIDAD AUTONOMA DE CENTRO AMERICA

- Licenciatura en Periodismo

Cargo actual

- Diplomático de carrera del Servicio Exterior de
  Costa Rica. Actualmente con rango de Embajador.

- Embajador. Representante Permanente Alterno de Costa
  Rica ante la Oficina Europea de Naciones Unidas.

- Embajador ante la Conferencia de Desarme.

- Miembro del Comité de Discriminación Racial.

- Miembro de la Comisión Académica (Com. sobre
  Migración) del Institut de Droit Humanitaire de
  Sanremo, Italia,(1990).

- Profesor con permiso Universidad de Costa Rica
  (actualmente dirige trabajos de graduación, en la
  Esc. de Ciencias Políticas, U.C.R.).

TRABAJOS REALIZADOS   0086

-Profesor en Esc. Relaciones Internacionales (Derecho
Internacional y Económico Int.) Universidad Nacional
(1979-1982)

-Director de la Oficina de Asuntos Internacionales
(Esc. Rel. Internacionales, U. Nacional de Costa Rica.
(1981)

-Consejero Jurídico (Programa P.N.U.D) -Ministerio de
Planificación y Política Económica (1981).

-Consejero Jurídico de la Misión Permanente de Costa
Rica ante los Org. especializados de Nac. Unidas.
(1982-1987).

-Encargado de Negocios de la Misión Permanente de
Costa Rica ante Naciones Unidas (1987-1988).

-Ministro-Consejero de la Misión Permanente de
Costa Rica ante Nac. Unidas (1988-1990).

-Miembro Adjunto de la Subcomisión de Prevención y
Protección a las Minorías de O.N.U. (1988- 1990).

-Miembro Experto del Grupo de Trabajo de Naciones
Unidas sobre los territorios no autónomos del
Pacífico y el Océano Indíco (1988-)-

ACTIVIDADES DIPLOMATICAS

-Embajador. Representante Permanente Alterno de Costa
Rica ante la Comisión de Derechos Humanos (1983-1991)

-Consejero Técnico a las Conferencias Internacionales
de Trabajo (1983-88). y Jefe Alterno de la LXXV y
LXXVI Confs. Internacional de Trabajo (1990-91).

-Jefe de Delegación al Consejo de Administración de la
O.I.T (1990-91) y Coordinador del Grupo Gubernamental
en la O.I.T. (1990-)

-Consejero Jurídico ante el Alto Comisionado para los
Refugiados, Comité Intergubernamental de Migraciones
y la Cruz Roja (1983-1990).

-Representante Alterno de la segunda Conferencia Int.
sobre la situación Palestina (1983).

0087

-Representante de Costa Rica en la segunda Conferencia Internacional contra la Discriminación Racial (1983).

-Representante de Costa Rica a las sesiones del Consejo Económico y Social (ECOSCC) (1983-1991).

-Representante de Costa Rica a la VII UNCTAD. Ginebra. (1987).

-Consejero Jurídico sobre la Adhesión de Costa Rica al Acuerdo General (GATT) (1987-1989).

-Vice-presidente de la segunda Conferencia para el examen de la Convención de Armas Biológicas (1986).

-Representante Especial de Costa Rica, Jefe de Delegación ante la Conferencia Internacional de Paris sobre la Prohibición de Armas Químicas. Protocolo de Ginebra. Enero de 1989.

-Jefe Alterno de Costa Rica, 43 Asamblea General de las Naciones Unidas, 1988.

-Jefe de Delegación, 42 y 43 Conf. Int. de Educación. Ginebra, (1989) - (1990).

-Representante de Costa Rica en la Conferencia Int. sobre Refugiados Indochinos, Ginebra, Junio de 1989.

-Jefe de la Delegación del Gob. de Costa Rica encargado de presentar el II Informe Periódico al Comité de Derechos Económicos Sociales y Culturales (Dic. 1990) y de la Delegación encargada de presentar el III Informe ante el Comité de Derechos Civiles y Políticos (Abril. 1990).

-Representante del Gob. de Costa Rica en las reuniones especiales del Grupo de Trabajo encargado de la redacción de la Convención sobre Derechos del Niño (1983-1989).

-Rep. del Gob. de Costa Rica ante el Grupo de trabajo Encargado de elaborar un programa int. eficaz en materia de delincuencia y justicia penal (Viena, Agosto de 1991)

PARTICIPACION EN ASOCIACIONES Y DIVERSOS

-Miembro del Colegio de Abogados de Costa Rica.

-Miembro del Colegio de Ciencias Políticas de Costa Rica.

-Miembro de la Asociación de Autores de Obras Científicas y Literarias de Costa Rica

-Ex-Miembro del Comité del Consejo Consultativo Int. de la Asociación Internacional contra la Tortura.

0088

-Miembro del Comité de Expertos para la Prevención de la Tortura en las Américas, C.E.P.T.A.

-Colaborador del Diario La Nación de Costa Rica (Política Internacional y Problemas Económicos).

-Ha participado en varias reuniones, seminarios, coloquios y mesas redondas sobre los Derechos Humanos y política Internacional organizados en las Universidades de Costa Rica, Ginebra, La Sorbonna, Sevilla, y San Marcos de Lima.

-Profesor en el Instituto de Derecho Humanitario de San Remo, Italia, en los cursos de Discriminación Racial, y el papel de la policía y los derechos Humanos (1988).

-Profesor en el Instituto Interamericano de Derechos Humanos, en el curso sobre Discriminación Racial (1989).

-Ha dirigido en la Esc. de Ciencias Políticas (UCR) trabajos finales (tesis) de investigación a estudiantes. (1988-1990)

-Asesor del Presidente Arias para la Cumbre Hemisférica de Presidentes Americanos (Octubre de 1989)

-Jefe 'de delegación al Seminario Regional sobre Migración y cooperación internacional de la O.I.M (La Paz, Bolivia, 1990)

El Dr. Rhenán-Segura es autor de varios libros sobre política Internacional y derecho internacional, y autor de varias decenas de artículos sobre derechos humanos y política internacional en revistas especializadas.

0089

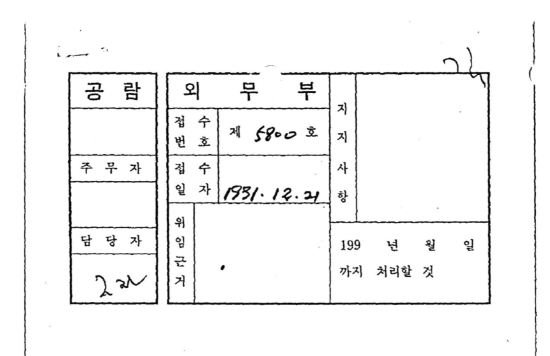

공 람	외 무 부		지지사항	
	접수번호	제 5800 호		
주 무 자	접수일자	1981. 12. 24		
담 당 자	위임근거	·	199 년 월 일 까지 처리할 것	
2 か				

0090

EMBASSY OF INDIA
C. P. O. BOX 3466, SEOUL
TEL : 798-4257, 798-4268
TELEX: K24641 INDEMB
FAX : 796-9534

भारतीय राजदूतावास
सिओल

No. SEO/162/1/91   December 17, 1991

        The Embassy of India presents its compliments to the
Ministry of Foreign Affairs of the Government of the Republic
of Korea and has the honour to state that based on the adoption
of the International Convention on the Elimination of all forms
of Racial Discrimination by the United Nations General Assembly
in 1965 and entered into force in 1969, the convention provides
for the establishment of a Committee on the Elimination of
Racial Discrimination (ERD) which is to consist of 18 experts
of high moral standaing and acknowledged impartiality. These
experts are to be elected by parties to the convention and
serve in their personal capacity. The Committee is required
to report annually to the Assembly on its activities and may
make suggestions and recommendations based on its examination
of the reports and information provided by state parties.

2.   The States Parties to the Convention will hold a meeting
in New York in January, 1992 to elect 9 Members of Convention
on the Elimination of all forms of Racial Discrimination to
replace those whose terms are due to expire. The Government of
India have nominated Mrs. Shanti Sadiq Ali, an eminent social
worker and Human Rights expert who has served with great distinction in the Committee on the Elimination of Racial Discrimination.
She was an active participant in India's freedom struggle and
has great experience and expertise in the themes and issues
which are the concern of the Committee.

3.   The Embassy of India would appreciate if the Government
of the Republic of Korea's invaluable support is extended to
the candidature of Mrs. Shanti Sadiq Ali as a Member of CERD
and the decision in this matter is conveyed to the Embassy of
India as soon as possible.

                                             0091

4.   The Embassy of India avails itself of this opportunity
to renew to the Ministry of Foreign Affairs of the Government
of the Republic of Korea, the assurances of its highest consideration.

Ministry of Foreign Affairs,
Government of the Republic of Korea,
Seoul

0092

주 국 련 대 표 부

주국련20314211- **1032**   1991. 12 . 18 .

수신 장관

참조 국제기구국장

제목 인종차별 철폐위 위원

1. 당지 소련대표부는 별첨 공한을 통하여 92.1.15 당지개최 인종차별 철폐협약
    당사국 회의에서 선출예정인 인종차별 철폐위원회 위원으로 자국인 Yuri A.
    Reshetov의 지지를 요청하여 온바, 동 공한 사본을 별첨 송부합니다.

2. 동 회의 참가예 필요한 자료등은 가급적 1.10까지 송부하여 주시기 바랍니다.

첨 부 : 상기공한 사본 1부. 끝.

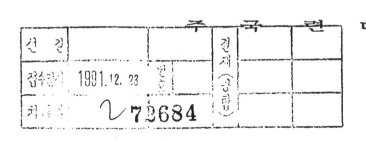

0093

ПОСТОЯННОЕ ПРЕДСТАВИТЕЛЬСТВО
СОЮЗА СОВЕТСКИХ СОЦИАЛИСТИЧЕСКИХ
РЕСПУБЛИК
ПРИ
ОРГАНИЗАЦИИ ОБЪЕДИНЕННЫХ НАЦИЙ

1058/μ

PERMANENT MISSION
OF THE UNION OF SOVIET SOCIALIST
REPUBLICS
TO THE UNITED NATIONS
136 East 67th Street
New York, N. Y. 10021

The Permanent Mission of the Union of Soviet Socialist Republics to the United Nations presents its compliments to the Permanent Missions of the States Parties to the International Convention on the Elimination of All Forms of Racial Discrimination and has the honor to inform that the Government of the Union of Soviet Socialist Republics has decided to nominate Mr. **Yuri A.Reshetov** for re.-election to the Committee on the Elimination of Racial Discrimination at the elections to be held during forthcoming Meeting of the States Parties to the International Convention on the Elimination of All Forms of Racial Discrimination in January 1992.

The Soviet Government is confident that Mr. Reshetov, being an internationally acknowledged expert in the protection of human rights, is capable of making a substantial contribution to the efficient work of this Committee.

The Permanent Mission of the USSR would be most grateful for the valuable support of Mr. Reshetov's candidature.

Enclosed herewith please find the Curriculum Vitae of Mr. Yuri A.Reshetov.

The Permanent Mission of the USSR to the United Nations avails itself of this opportunity to renew to the Permanent Missions of the States Parties to the International Convention on the Elimination of All Forms of Racial Discrimination the assurances of its highest consideration.

New York, December *12,* 1991

Permanent Missions of the
States Parties to the
International Convention
on the Elimination of All Forms
of Racial Discrimination

0094

Yuri Alexandrovich RESHETOV (USSR)

Born on 10 January 1935, in the city of Gorky (Nizhny Novgorod).

Graduated from the Moscow State Institute of International Relations in 1959 and from the Diplomatic Academy in 1971. Ph.D. in philosophy, Doctor of Law, speaks English, French, German, Swedish, Danish and Icelandic.

From 1959 to 1975 worked in the Scandinavian Countries Department and in the International Economic Organizations Department of the Ministry of Foreign Affairs of the USSR, and also in the Soviet Embassies in Iceland and Denmark. Participated in the proceedings of the European Conference on Security and Co-operation during the Geneva round in 1974-1975.

From 1975 to 1980 headed the Prevention of Discrimination and Protection of Minorities Unit of the Human Rights Department of the UNOG Secretariat, worked as a Secretary of the Sub-Commission on Prevention of Discrimination and Protection of Minorities.

From 1980 to 1986 worked in the Institute of State and Law of the USSR Academy of Sciences. Y.Reshetov is a prominent expert in the field of international law. He is the author of more than 100 publications on human rights issues, on relations between nationalities, on international crimes, on the United Nations role in the field of human rights, etc.

Since 1986 Y.Reshetov has been Deputy Chief of the Division for Humanitarian issues of the Ministry of Foreign Affairs of the USSR. His duties concern mainly the solution of humanitarian problems, and especially the perfection of the Soviet legislation.

Since 1988 Y.Reshetov heads the Directorate on International Humanitarian Cooperation and Human Rights of the Ministry of Foreign Affairs of the USSR. He headed the USSR Delegations at the CSCE meeting in Copenhagen and at the 47th session of the UN Commission on Human Rights.

0095

발 신 전 보

	분류번호	보존기간

번 호 : WUN-4329   911219 1429   WG 종별 : 암호통신

수 신 : 주   유엔   대사. ♣♣♣♣♣

발 신 : 장 관 (연이)

제 목 : 인종차별철폐위(CERD) 당사국 회의

92.1.15. 유엔본부에서 개최예정인 제14차 CERD 당사국 회의

우리대표단에 포함할 귀관 직원을 보고바람. 끝.

(국제기구국장   문동석)

	보 안 통 제	^윤

앙고재	91년12월19일	유엔2과	기안자 성명 김종술		과 장	심의관	국 장		차 관	장 관	

		외신과통제

0096

148 한국 인권문제 민주화 관련 기타 자료 3

발 신 전 보

분류번호	보존기간

번   호 : WGV-1860   911219 1429 WG   종별 : _____

수   신 : 주   제네바   대사. 🍀🍀🍀🍀

발   신 : 장 관 (연이)

제   목 : 인종차별철폐위(CERD) 위원 입후보 현황

      CERD 위원 선출을 위한 CERD 당사국 회의가 92.1.15.

유엔본부에서 개최될 예정인바, 동 입후보 현황을 파악,

보고바람. 끝.

                              (국제기구국장   문동석)

보 안 통 제	로

앙 고 재	91년 12월 19일	유엔 2 과	기안자 성명 강정훈		과 장 홍	심의관	국 장 정권	차 관	장 관	외신과통제

0097

외 무 부

종 별 :

번 호 : UNW-4434   일 시 : 91 1219 1900

수 신 : 장 관(연이)

발 신 : 주 유엔 대사

제 목 : 인종차별 철폐협약 당사국회의

　　대:WUN-4329

　　1. 대호 대표단 구성을 아래와같이 건의함.

　　0. 수석대표: 신기복 차석대사

　　0. 대표: 최종무 참사관

　　2. 당관에서는 상금회의문서등을 접수치 못하였는바, 확인후 추보예정임.끝.

　　(대사 노창희-국장)

국기국

외 무 부

종 별 :

번 호 : GVW-2790   일 시 : 91 1220 1930

수 신 : 장관(연이)

발 신 : 주제네바대사

제 목 : 인종차별 철폐위 위원 입후보 현황

대: WGV-1860

1. 대호 입후보 현황 아래 보고함.

MR. THEODOOR CORNELIS VAN BOVEN(NETHERLANDS)

MR. ION DIACONU (ROMANIA)

MR. EDUARDO FERRERO COSTA(PERU)

MR. IVAN GARVALOV (BULGARIA)

MR. YURI A. RHENAN SEGURA (COSTA RICA)MRS. SHANTI SADIQ ALI (INDIA)MR. SONGSHUHUA (CHINA)

MR. LUIS VALENCIA RODRIGUEZ (ECUADOR)

MR. KASIMIR VIDAS (YUGOSLAVIA)

MR. MARIO JORGE YUTZIS (ARGENTINA)

MR. OUSMAN DIAO BALDE (GUINEA)

MISS FLORIZELLE A. O'CONNOR (JAMAICA)

2. 92.1.19 자로 임기 만료되는 위원 명단은 다음과 같음

MR. EDUARDO FERRERO COSTA (PURU)

MR. ISI FOIGHEL (DENMARK)

MR. IVAN GARVALOV (BULGARIA)

MR. YURI A.RECHETOV (UNION OF SOVIET SOCIALIST REPUBLICS)

MR. JORGE RHENAN SEGURA (COSTA RICA)

MRS. SHANIT SADIQ ALI (INDIA)

MR. SONG SHUHUA (CHINA)

MR. KASIMIR VIDAS (YUGOSLAVIA)

국기국

PAGE 1   91.12.24   09:06 DQ

외신 1과 통제관

0099

MR. MARIO JORGE YUTZIS (ARGENTINA)끝
(대사 박수길-국장)

외 무 부

110-760 서울 종로구 세종로 77번지 / (02) 723-8934 / (02) 723-3505

문서번호 연이 20314-

시행일자 1991.12.26.

(경유)

수신 건 의

참조

취급		차 관	장 관
보존		전결	
국 장		제1차관보	
심의관		아주국장	
과 장		미주국장	
기안	김종훈	구주국장	협조

제목 인종차별철폐위 위원 입후보 지지

1. 92.1.15. 유엔본부에서 개최되는 제14차 인종차별철폐협약 당사국회의에서는
   동협약산하 인종차별철폐위원회 위원 총 18명중 9명에 대한 선거가 있을
   예정입니다.

2. 상기 선거에는 총 13개국에서 입후보하였으며, 이들중 8개국에서 아국에 대해
   지지요청을 하였는바, 동 선거관련, 아국입장을 아래와 같이 건의합니다.

- 아   래 -

/ 계속 /

0101

첨부 : 1. 입후보 지지요청 현황

2. 인종차별철폐위원회 현황. 끝.

0102

공 란

인종차별철폐위원회 개요

o 설치근거

　　- 인종차별 철폐협약(CERD) 제8조의 규정에 의하여 설치

o 구　　성

　　- 당사국 회의에서 선출하는 임기 4년의 18명의 전문가로 구성

　　　* 91.12월 현재 당사국 :　129개국

o 위원선출 절차

　　- 당사국 회의(정족수 2/3)의 비밀투표에서 출석, 투표한 국가의 최대
　　　다수표 및 절대다수표를 얻은 후보자가 위원으로 당선

　　- 당사국은 자국국민중에서 후보자 1명을 지명할수 있음.

o 위원회의 임무

　　- 각 당사국이 2년마다 제출하는 정기보고서를 심의

　　- 당사국이 제출한 각종 보고와 정보를 검토, 이를 근거로 제의와
　　　일반적인 권고를 하며, 위원회 활동사항을 매년 유엔총회에 보고

o 위원의 활동

　　- 위원은 개인자격으로 활동

　　- 위원들이 위원회의 제반임무를 수행하는 동안의 경비는 체약국들이
　　　부담

0104

공 란

공　　　　란

외 무 부

110-760 서울 종로구 세종로 77번지 / (02) 723-8934 / (02) 723-3505

문서번호 연이 20314

시행일자 1992.1.4.

(경유)

수신 건 의

참조

취급		차 관	장 관
보존			
국 장			
심의관		제1차관보	
과 장			
기안	김종훈		협조

제목 제14차 "인종차별 철폐에 관한 국제협약" 당사국 회의

우리나라가 가입하고 있는 "모든 형태의 인종차별 철폐에 관한 국제협약" (International Convention on the Elimination of All Forms of Racial Discrimination) 제14차 당사국 회의가 1992.1.15. 유엔본부에서 개최예정인바, 동 회의에 참가할 대표단을 아래와 같이 임명하고, 동 대표단에 대한 장관님 명의 신임장을 별첨과 같이 제출할것을 건의하오니 재가하여 주시기 바랍니다.

- 아   래 -

가 . 회의의제

  ㅇ 인종차별철폐위 위원 선거

    - 총 18명중 9명 선출

  ㅇ 인종차별철폐위 예산 확보 문제

나 . 대 표 단

  ㅇ 수석대표 : 주유엔대표부 차석대사 신기복

  ㅇ 대 표 : 주유엔대표부 참사관 최종무

/ 계속 /

0107

첨부 : 1. 아국대표단 신임장 1부.

2. 인종차별철폐에 관한 국제협약 개요 1부.

3. 인종차별철폐위원회 개요 1부. 끝.

0108

Seoul,

Excellency :

I have the honour to inform you that the following persons have been appointed to represent the Government of the Republic of Korea at "the Fourteenth Meeting of the States Parties to the International Convention on the Elimination of All Forms of Racial Discrimination" to be held at the United Nations Headquarters, New York, on Wednesday 15 January 1992:

Representative   : Mr. SHIN Kee Bock
                                    Ambassador and Deputy Permanent
                                    Representative
                                    Permanent Mission of
                                    the Republic of Korea
                                    to the United Nations

Alternate Representative   : Mr. CHOI Jong Moo
                                    Counsellor
                                    Permanent Mission of
                                    the Republic of Korea
                                    to the United Nations

Accept, Excellency, the assurances of my highest consideration.

                                    LEE Sang-Ock
                                    Minister of Foreign Affairs

His Excellency
  Boutros Boutros Ghali
  Secretary-General
  United Nations
  New York

0109

인종차별철폐에 관한 국제협약 개요

o 채택경위

  - 65.12.21. 제20차 유엔총회 결의(2106 A)에 의해 채택

  - 69.1.4. 협정 발효

o 당 사 국

  - 91.12.31.현재 129개국

  - 미국, 일본은 가입하지 않고 있음.

  - 북한도 미가입

o 아국과의 관계

  - 78.8.8. 협약 서명

  - 78.12.5. 유엔 사무총장에게 비준서 기탁

  - 79.1.4. 아국에 대해 발효

  - 80년 이래 인종차별 철폐위에 6차의 정기보고서 제출

0110

인종차별철폐위원회 개요

o 설치근거

  - 인종차별 철폐협약(CERD) 제8조의 규정에 의하여 설치

o 구   성

  - 당사국 회의에서 선출하는 임기 4년의 18명의 전문가로 구성

    * 91.12월 현재 당사국 : 129개국

o 위원선출 절차

  - 당사국 회의(정족수 2/3)의 비밀투표에서 출석, 투표한 국가의 최대
    다수표 및 절대다수표를 얻은 후보자가 위원으로 당선

  - 당사국은 자국국민중에서 후보자 1명을 지명할수 있음.

o 위원회의 임무

  - 각 당사국이 2년마다 제출하는 정기보고서를 심의

  - 당사국이 제출한 각종 보고와 정보를 검토, 이를 근거로 제의와
    일반적인 권고를 하며, 위원회 활동사항을 매년 유엔총회에 보고

o 위원의 활동

  - 위원은 개인자격으로 활동

  - 위원들이 위원회의 제반임무를 수행하는 동안의 경비는 체약국들이
    부담

0111

공 란

공   란

공 란

공 란

공 란

공   란

공　　　　　란

공   란

공 란

주 아 르 헨 티 나 대 사 관

7೬.

문서번호 : 아르헨(정)20200—/246   1992. 1 . 6 .
수   신 : 외무부장관
참   조 : 국제기구국장
제   목 : 여성차별철폐위 입후보 지지 요청

          연 : ARW - 1105

   연호 주재국 외무부 공한 및 LILIANA GURDALICH 상원의원의 이력사항을
별첨 송부합니다.

   첨   부 : 상기공한. 끝.

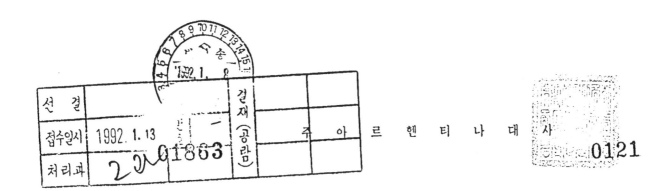

Ministerio de Relaciones Exteriores y Culto

Letra: DIOIN
No.: 11.597/91

EL Ministerio de Relaciones Exteriores y Culto -Dirección de Organismos Internacionales- presenta sus atentos saludos a la Embajada de la República de Corea y tiene el honor de solicitar apoyo a la candidatura de la Senadora Nacional Liliana Gurdulich de Correa para su elección como experta del Comité Para la Eliminación de la Discriminación contra la Mujer (CEDAW), en las elecciones que tendrán lugar en la Reunión de Estados Partes de la Convención Para la Eliminación de todas las Formas de Discriminación contra la Mujer, a efectuarse en la Sede de las Naciones Unidas en la Ciudad de Nueva York el día 4 de febrero de 1992.

Se adjunta curriculum vitae de la Senadora Nacional Liliana Gurdulich de Correa.

El Ministerio de Relaciones Exteriores y Culto -Dirección de Organismos Internacionales- encuentra propicia la oportunidad para renovar a la Embajada de la República de Corea las expresiones de su más alta y distinguida consideración

AGREGADOS: lo mencionado.

BUENOS AIRES,11 de noviembre de 1991.-

A LA EMBAJADA DE LA
REPUBLICA DE COREA
BUENOS AIRES

0122

OGY 92- 02

The Ministry of Foreign Affairs of the Republic of Korea presents its compliments to the Embassy of the Republic of Bulgaria and has the honour to refer to the latter's Note No. 290 dated September 3, 1991 concerning the candidature of Mr. Ivan Garvalov for membership of the Committee on the Elimination of Racial Discrimination(CERD) at the election to be held in New York on January 15, 1992.

The Ministry is pleased to inform the Embassy that the Government of Republic of Korea has decided to support the above-mentioned candidature.

It is being requested, in reciprocity, that the Government of the Republic of Bulgaria would extend its invaluable support to the Korean candidature for membership of the United Nations Commission on Human Rights at the election during a organizational session of the Economic and Social Council in April 1992.

The Ministry of Foreign Affairs avails itself of this opportunity to renew to the Embassy of the Republic of Bulgaria the assurances of its highest consideration.

Seoul, 6 January 1992

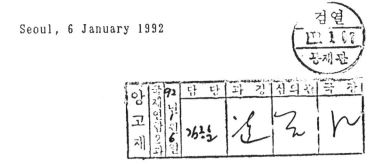

0123

OGY 92- 02

The Ministry of Foreign Affairs of the Republic of Korea presents its compliments to the Embassy of the Republic of Bulgaria and has the honour to refer to the latter's Note No. 290 dated September 3, 1991 concerning the candidature of Mr. Ivan Garvalov for membership of the Committee on the Elimination of Racial Discrimination(CERD) at the election to be held in New York on January 15, 1992.

The Ministry is pleased to inform the Embassy that the Government of Republic of Korea has decided to support the above-mentioned candidature.

It is being requested, in reciprocity, that the Government of the Republic of Bulgaria would extend its invaluable support to the Korean candidature for membership of the United Nations Commission on Human Rights at the election during a organizational session of the Economic and Social Council in April 1992.

The Ministry of Foreign Affairs avails itself of this opportunity to renew to the Embassy of the Republic of Bulgaria the assurances of its highest consideration.

Seoul, 6 January 1992

0124

MINISTRY OF FOREIGN AFFAIRS
REPUBLIC OF KOREA

7 January 1992

Excellency :

I have the honour to inform you that the following persons have been appointed to represent the Government of the Republic of Korea at "the Fourteenth Meeting of the State Parties to the International Convention on the Elimination of All Forms of Racial Discrimination" to be held at the United Nations Headquarters, New York, on Wednesday 15 January 1992 :

Representative   : Mr. SHIN Kee Bock
                               Ambassador and Deputy Permanent
                               Representative
                               Permanent Mission of
                               the Republic of Korea
                               to the United Nations

Alternate Representative   : Mr. CHOI Jong Moo
                               Counsellor
                               Permanent Mission of
                               the Republic of Korea
                               to the United Nations

Accept, Excellency, the assurances of my highest consideration.

LEE Sang-Ock
Minister of Foreign Affairs

His Excellency
  Boutros Boutros Ghali
  Secretary-General
  United Nations
  New York

0125

공 란

외 무 부

110-760 서울 종로구 세종로 77번지   /   (02) 723-8934   /   (02) 723-3505

문서번호 연이 20314-

시행일자 1992.1.8.

01794

(경유)

수신 주유엔대사

참조

취급		장 관
보존		
국 장	전결	
심의관		
과 장		
기안	김종훈	협조

제목 제14차 인종차별철폐협약 당사국 회의

　　　92.1.15. 개최되는 표제회의에 참가할 아국 대표단에 대한 본직명의

신임장을 별첨과 같이 송부합니다.

　　첨부 : 동 신임장 원본 1부 및 사본 2부.

0127

MINISTRY OF FOREIGN AFFAIRS
REPUBLIC OF KOREA

7 January 1992

Excellency :

I have the honour to inform you that the following persons have been appointed to represent the Government of the Republic of Korea at "the Fourteenth Meeting of the State Parties to the International Convention on the Elimination of All Forms of Racial Discrimination" to be held at the United Nations Headquarters, New York, on Wednesday 15 January 1992 :

Representative	: Mr. SHIN Kee Bock Ambassador and Deputy Permanent Representative Permanent Mission of the Republic of Korea to the United Nations
Alternate Representative	: Mr. CHOI Jong Moo Counsellor Permanent Mission of the Republic of Korea to the United Nations

Accept, Excellency, the assurances of my highest consideration.

LEE Sang-Ock
Minister of Foreign Affairs

His Excellency
Boutros Boutros Ghali
Secretary-General
United Nations
New York

0128

발 신 전 보

WUN-0051   920108 1726 ED   종별 :

번 호 :

수 신 : 주   유엔   대사. ♣♣♣♣   (사본 : 주제네바대사)

발 신 : 장 관 (연이)

제 목 : 제14차 인종차별철폐협약 당사국 회의

　　　　연 : WUN-0014

1. 표제회의 아국 대표단을 아래와 같이 임명하였으니 회의참석토록
　　조치바람.

　　- 수석대표 : 신기복 차석대사

　　- 대　　표 : 최종무 참사관

2. 본직명의 대표단 신임장은 정파편 송부함.

　　　　　　　　　　　　　　　　　　　　　끝.

　　　　　　　　　　　　　　　　　　(국제기구국장   문동석)

보안통제	[서명]

앙고재	92년 1월 8일	유엔 2과	기안자성명 76철	과 장 [서명]	십의관 [서명]	국 장 자결	차 관	장 관 [서명]	외신과통제

0129

공　　　란

관리 번호	92 ~ 19

외 무 부

종 별 : 지 급

번 호 : GVW-0039 　　　　　　　　일 시 : 92 0109 1630

수 신 : 장관(연이) 사본: 주유엔대사(본부중계필)

발 신 : 주 제네바 대사

제 목 : 인종차별 철폐위 선거

　　대: WGV-0022

　　대호 표제 선거 관련 당지 화란대표부로부터 자국의 TH.C.VAN BOVEN 위원의지지를 요청하는 1.7 자 공한을 접수하였음을 보고함. 끝

　　(차석대사 김삼훈-국장)

예고:92.6.30 까지에 예고문에
의거 일반문서로 재분류됨

국기국　　중계

PAGE 1 　　　　　　　　　　　　　　　　　　92.01.10　　04:03

주 국 련 대 표 부

주국련2031- 028   1992. 1. 10.

수신 장관

참조 국제기구국장

제목 '92 CERD 분담금

        사무국은 별첨과 같이 아국 '92 CERD 분담금이 $1504임을 통보하여
왔음을 참고바랍니다.

        첨 부 : 동 사무국 문서. 끝.

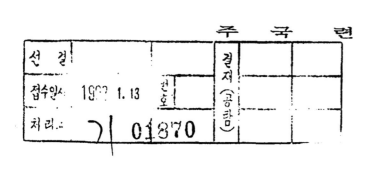

0132

REFERENCE The Secretary-General of the United Nations presents his compliments to
the Permanent Representative of the Republic of Korea to the United Nations
and has the honour to refer to article 8, paragraph 6, of the International
Convention on the Elimination of All Forms of Racial Discrimination (General
Assembly resolution 2106 A (XX)), according to which, States parties "shall be
responsible for the expenses of the members of the Committee while they are in
performance of Committee duties". The expenses of the members of the
Committee on the Elimination of Racial Discrimination for the year 1992
(twenty-third financial year) are estimated at $248,920. The amount assessed
His Excellency's Government is shown below:

	$
Gross assessment for 1992	2,405
Less:	
Adjustment due to surplus in 1990	901
Net assessment payable	1,504

In addition, an amount of $736 remains due in respect of the 1991
assessment for the Committee.

Since funds are urgently needed to meet the expenses of the Committee
which is scheduled to convene from 2-20 March 1992, it would be greatly
appreciated if the above amounts could be made available at an early date.
Payment may be made by cheque payable to the United Nations, or by deposit to
the following bank account, with an indication in each case of the purpose of
the payment:

United Nations General Trust Funds Account
No. 015-004473
Chemical Bank
United Nations Branch
New York, N.Y. 10017

The Secretary-General avails himself of this opportunity to renew to the
Permanent Representative the assurances of his highest consideration.

31 December 1991

0133

공　　　란

공   란

공   란

외 무 부

종 별 :

번 호 : UNW-0131   일   시 : 92 0115 1930

수 신 : 장 관(연이)

발 신 : 주 유엔 대사

제 목 : 인종차별 철폐협약 당사국회의

1. 표제 14차 회의가 금 1.15 유엔본부에서 119 개국대표가 참석한 가운데 개최되어 별첨의제를 심의하였음. (당관 최종무 참사관및 최종문서기관 참석)

2. 금일 회의에서는 의장으로 노르웨이 HUSLID대사를 선출하였으며 이어 금번 개선되는 위원선거가 시행되었는바 결과는 아래와같음.

(괄호내는 득표수)

화란(107), 에쿠아돌 (107), 페루(106), 인도 (104),중국(103), 러시아 (92), 알젠텐(91), 불가리아(83), 루마니아 (63), 루완다 (53), 예멘 (49),기네(48)

3. 의제 6

재정문제관련, 예산사정으로 협약위원회 개최가 취소될 형편임에 비추어 각국에 미 납분담금을 조속 납부하여 줄것을 촉구하였음.

4. 또한 동회의는 의제7관련 동협약 8조 PARA 6개정을 골자로한 결의안 CERD/SP/1992/L.1 을 투표없이 채택하였는바 (46/428 과 동일한 내용으로 A/46/72/P110 참조), 동결의가 47차총회에서 통과될 경우 CERD 경비는 유엔정규예산에서 충당케됨.

5. 관련문서 파편 송부예정임.

첨부:의제: UNW(F)-50 끝

(대사 노창희-국장)

국기국   1차보   외정실   분석관   청와대   안기부

PAGE 1   92.01.16   09:55 WG

외신 1과 통제관
0137

UNW(F)-50 20115 1P7
몽 104

**UNITED
NATIONS**

CERD

International Convention
on the Elimination of all Forms
of Racial Discrimination

Distr.
GENERAL

CERD/SP/41/Rev.1
30 December 1991

ORIGINAL: ENGLISH

MEETING OF THE STATES PARTIES
Fourteenth Meeting
New York, 15 January 1992

PROVISIONAL AGENDA

Submitted by the Secretary-General

1. Opening of the Meeting by the representative of the Secretary-General.

2. Election of the Chairman.

3. Adoption of the agenda.

4. Election of other officers of the Meeting.

5. Election of nine members of the Committee on the Elimination of Racial
    Discrimination to replace those whose terms of office will expire on
    19 January 1992, in accordance with article 8, paragraphs 1 to 5, of the
    Convention (CERD/SP/42).

6. Provision of sufficient resources to ensure the effective functioning of
    the Committee on the Elimination of Racial Discrimination (CERD/SP/43).

7. Consideration of a proposed amendment to article 8, paragraph 6, of the
    Convention (General Assembly decision 46/428).

8. Other matters.

UNW-0131
첨부

/—/

91-42504 2957e (E)

0138

외 무 부

관리번호 72 -47

종   별 : 지 급

번   호 : RMW-0026   일   시 : 92 0118 1610

수   신 : 장관(국기)

발   신 : 주 루마니아 대사

제   목 : 유엔 인권차별철폐위원 입후보

1. 주재국 외무부는 1.19 부터 시작되는 유엔 인권차별철폐위원회의 MANDATE중의 하나로 ION DIACON 주재국 외무부 법무조약국장이 입후보하였다고 아국정부의 지원을 요청하는 공한을 1.17 당관에 전달하여 왔음.

3. 동인의 주요약력 아래와 같음.

- 1938 년생(54 세), 부카레스트 법과대학 졸업

-1971 제네바 대학교에서 정치학 박사

-1960-80 루마니아 외무부 조약국 근무

-1980-81 주벨기에 대사관 참사관

1981-86 주유엔대표부(뉴욕) 공사,1983 년도 제 6 위원회 부의장 및 실무그룹 의장 역임

-1986-90 루마니아 외무부 대외경제 및 조약, 국제기구국 부국장

-1990 이후 법무 및 조약국장, 부카레스트 대학 국제법 교수

1962-91 CSCE, UNESCO, CMS 등 각종 유엔기구 회의에 루마니아 대표로 참석(인권문제 전문가 회의 등)

1988-91 소수민족차별철폐 및 보호 소위원회 위원

1990 이후 국제사법재판소 위원.끝.

(대사 이현홍-국장)

예고:92.6.30 까지 대고 대고문

국기국   구주국   외정실   분석관

주 국 련 대 표 부

주국련2031- **041**   1992. 1 . 17.

수신 장관

참조 국제기구국장

제목 인종차별 철폐 협약 당사국회의

         연 : UNW - 0131

      연호, 92.1.15 개최된 표제회의 관련문서를 별첨 송부합니다.

   첨 부 : CERD/SP/41/Rev.1, 43, 44

             CERD/SP/1992/L.1. 끝.

주   국   련   대   표   사

선 결			결재 (총괄)	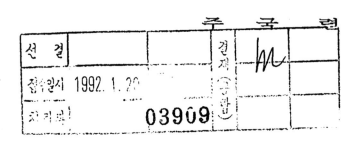	
접수일시 1992. 1. 20					
처리과	03909				

0140

주 제 네 바 대 표 부   乙 김

20, Route de Pre-Bois, POB 566   /   (022) 791-0111   /   (022) 791-0525(FAX)
▨▨

문서번호 제네(정) 2031 - 1014

시행일자 1992. 11. 19.

수신 장관

참조 국제기구국장

선결			지시		
접수	일자시간		결재		
	번호	66346			
	처리과		공람		
	담당자				

제목 제 14차 인종차별 철폐 협약 당사국 회의

92. 11. 20

    92. 1. 개최된 표제회의 결의 문서를 별첨 송부합니다.

첨부 : 문서 1부. (CERD/SP/45) 끝.

주 제 네 바 대

0141

INTERNATIONAL CONVENTION
ON THE ELIMINATION
OF ALL FORMS
OF RACIAL DISCRIMINATION

OFFICIAL RECORDS:
FOURTEENTH MEETING OF STATES PARTIES

15 January 1992

DECISIONS

UNITED NATIONS

0142

INTERNATIONAL CONVENTION
ON THE ELIMINATION
OF ALL FORMS
OF RACIAL DISCRIMINATION

OFFICIAL RECORDS:
FOURTEENTH MEETING OF STATES PARTIES

15 January 1992

DECISIONS

UNITED NATIONS
New York, 1992

0143

NOTE

Symbols of United Nations documents are composed of capital letters combined with figures. Mention of such a symbol indicates a reference to a United Nations document.

CERD/SP/45

(0144

CONTENTS

iii

0145

AGENDA

1. Opening of the Meeting by the representative of the Secretary-General.
2. Election of the Chairman.
3. Adoption of the agenda.
4. Election of other officers of the Meeting.
5. Election of the nine members of the Committee on the Elimination of Racial Discrimination to replace those whose terms of office will expire on 19 January 1992, in accordance with article 8, paragraphs 1 to 5, of the Convention.
6. Provision of sufficient resources to ensure the effective functioning of the Committee on the Elimination of Racial Discrimination.
7. Consideration of a proposed amendment to article 8, paragraph 6, of the Convention.
8. Other matters.

iv

DECISIONS OF THE FOURTEENTH MEETING OF STATES PARTIES

Adoption of the agenda

The Fourteenth Meeting of States parties to the International Convention on the Elimination of All Forms of Racial Discrimination adopted the provisional agenda submitted by the Secretary-General.

Election of nine members of the Committee on the Elimination of Racial Discrimination

In accordance with article 8 of the Convention, the States parties elected nine members of the Committee on the Elimination of Racial Discrimination to replace those whose terms of office were to expire on 19 January 1992. The following members were elected by secret ballot for a term of four years, beginning 20 January 1992:

Mr. Theodoor VAN BOVEN (Netherlands);

Mr. Ion DIACONU (Romania);

Mr. Eduardo FERRERO COSTA (Peru);

Mr. Ivan GARVALOV (Bulgaria);

Mr. Yuri A. RECHETOV (Russian Federation);

Mrs. Shanti SADIQ ALI (India);

Mr. SONG Shuhua (China);

Mr. Luis VALENCIA RODRÍGUEZ (Ecuador);

Mr. Mario Jorge YUTZIS (Argentina).

Provision of sufficient resources to ensure the effective functioning of the Committee on the Elimination of Racial Discrimination

The Meeting of States parties took note of the report of the Secretary-General (CERD/SP/43) concerning the responsibilities of the States parties for the expenses of the members of the Committee under article 8, paragraph 6, of the Convention, and requested the Secretary-General to continue to report to the Meeting of States parties on the Committee's financial status.

Consideration of a proposed amendment to article 8, paragraph 6, of the Convention

(a) The Meeting of States parties considered the note of the Secretary-General (CERD/SP/44) concerning draft resolution CERD/SP/1992/L.1 proposing an amendment to article 8, paragraph 6, of the Convention.

(b) The Meeting adopted draft resolution CERD/SP/1992/L.1 without a vote (see annex).

0147

1

STATES PARTIES TO THE CONVENTION AS AT 15 JANUARY 1992

Afghanistan
Algeria
Antigua and Barbuda
Argentina
Australia
Austria
Bahamas
Bangladesh
Barbados
Belarus
Belgium
Bolivia
Botswana
Brazil
Bulgaria
Burkina Faso
Burundi
Cambodia
Cameroon
Canada
Cape Verde
Central African Repubic
Chad
Chile
China
Colombia
Congo
Costa Rica
Côte d'Ivoire
Cuba
Cyprus
Czech and Slovak Federal
    Republic
Denmark
Dominican Republic
Ecuador
Egypt
El Salvador
Ethiopia
Fiji
Finland
France
Gabon
Gambia

Germany
Ghana
Greece
Guatemala
Guinea
Guyana
Haiti
Holy See
Hungary
Iceland
India
Iran (Islamic Republic of)
Iraq
Israel
Italy
Jamaica
Jordan
Kuwait
Lao People's
    Democratic Republic
Lebanon
Lesotho
Liberia
Libyan Arab Jamahiriya
Luxembourg
Madagascar
Maldives
Mali
Malta
Mauritania
Mauritius
Mexico
Mongolia
Morocco
Mozambique
Namibia
Nepal
Netherlands
New Zealand
Nicaragua
Niger
Nigeria
Norway
Pakistan

Panama
Papua New Guinea
Peru
Philippines
Poland
Portugal
Qatar
Republic of Korea
Romania
Russian Federation
Rwanda
Saint Lucia
Saint Vincent and
    the Grenadines
Senegal
Seychelles
Sierra Leone
Solomon Islands
Somalia
Spain
Sri Lanka
Sudan
Suriname
Swaziland
Sweden
Syrian Arab Republic
Togo
Tonga
Trinidad and Tobago
Tunisia
Uganda
Ukraine
United Arab Emirates
United Kingdom of
    Great Britain
    and Northern Ireland
United Republic of Tanzania
Uruguay
Venezuela
Viet Nam
Yemen
Yugoslavia
Zaire
Zambia
Zimbabwe

2

0148

OFFICERS OF THE FOURTEENTH MEETING

Chairman: Mr. Martin Johannes HUSLID (Norway).

Vice-Chairmen: Mr. Anatoliy T. OLIYNYK (Ukraine);

                      Ms. Marjorie THORPE (Trinidad and Tobago);

                      Mr. Nouhad MAHMOUD (Lebanon);

                      Mr. Balla Moussa CAMARA (Guinea).

LIST OF DOCUMENTS ISSUED FOR THE FOURTEENTH MEETING
OF STATES PARTIES

Document No.	Title
CERD/SP/41 and Rev.1	Provisional agenda of the Fourteenth Meeting of the States parties
CERD/SP/42 and Add.1, Add.2, Add.3, Add.4, Add.5 and Add.6	Election of nine members of the Committee on the Elimination of Racial Discrimination to replace those whose terms will expire on 19 January 1992, in accordance with the provisions of article 8 of the Convention: note by the Secretary-General
CERD/SP/43	Responsibilities of the States parties for the expenses of the members of the Committee under article 8, paragraph 6, of the International Convention on the Elimination of All Forms of Racial Discrimination: Report of the Secretary-General
CERD/SP/44	Consideration of the request for revision of article 8, paragraph 6, of the International Convention on the Elimination of All Forms of Racial Discrimination
CERD/SP/1992/L.1	Proposed amendment to article 8, paragraph 6, of the International Convention on the Elimination of All Forms of Racial Discrimination on arrangements for meeting the expenses of members of the Committee on the Elimination of Racial Discrimination while in performance of their duties
CERD/SP/SR.22	Summary records of the twenty-second meeting
CERD/SP/45	Official Records of the International Convention on the Elimination of All Forms of Racial Discrimination: Thirteenth Meeting of States parties, Decisions

4

0150

ANNEX

Decision to amend article 8, paragraph 6, of the Convention on the Elimination of All Forms of Racial Discrimination on arrangements for meeting the expenses of members of the Committee on the Elimination of Racial Discrimination while in performance of their duties

The States parties to the International Convention on the Elimination of All Forms of Racial Discrimination,

Reiterating the importance of the International Convention on the Elimination of All Forms of Racial Discrimination, which is the most widely accepted human rights convention adopted under the auspices of the United Nations, as well as the contribution of the Committee on the Elimination of Racial Discrimination to the United Nations efforts to combat racism and all other forms of discrimination based on race, colour, descent or national or ethnic origin,

Concerned that the financial arrangements for meeting the expenses of members of the Committee on the Elimination of Racial Discrimination, in conformity with article 8, paragraph 6, of the Convention, have not proved sufficient to ensure that the Committee can discharge its mandate effectively,

Recalling the decisions adopted by the Eleventh, Twelfth and Thirteenth Meetings of States parties appealing to all States parties to meet in full their financial obligations under article 8, paragraph 6,

Recalling also the decisions of the Committee on the serious impediment to its work resulting from the financial situation, including the cancellation and shortening of meetings,[1]

Noting the concern expressed by the Chairman of the Committee about the continuing financial problems in his letter of 14 November 1989,[2]

Aware that the General Assembly has, in its resolutions 41/105, 42/57, 43/96, 44/68 and 45/88, expressed grave concern at the continuing deterioration of the proper functioning of the Committee as a result of interruptions to its meeting schedule and has made reiterated appeals to all States parties to fulfil their financial obligations without delay,

Noting also that the General Assembly has endorsed the recommendations of the 1988 and 1990 meetings of the chairpersons of human rights treaty monitoring bodies on the need to ensure adequate financing and adequate staffing resources for the operations of the treaty bodies, and in particular that the General Assembly in its resolution 46/111 endorsed the recommendation of the 1990 meeting of chairpersons that the General Assembly take appropriate measures to ensure the financing of each of the monitoring committees from the regular budget of the United Nations,

Taking note of the General Assembly's request in the resolution 46/83 and 46/111 that the States parties to the Convention consider, as a matter of priority, all possibilities of establishing a more secure basis for the future financing of all the costs of the Committee, including possible amendment to the funding provisions of the treaty,

Noting the proposed amendment to article 8, paragraph 6, put forward by the Government of Australia[3] in accordance with article 23, paragraph 1, of the Convention,

Taking note further of General Assembly decision 46/428 in accordance with article 23, paragraph 2, of the Convention, requesting that the current meeting of States parties consider the proposed amendment and to limit the scope of any revision of the Convention to the question of arrangements for meeting the expenses of Committee members while in performance of their duties,

1. *Decide* to replace paragraph 6 of article 8 of the Convention with the paragraph "The Secretary-General of the United Nations shall provide the necessary staff and facilities for the effective performance of the functions of the Committee under the Convention.";

2. *Decide* to add a new paragraph, as article 8, paragraph 7, "The members of the Committee established under the present Convention shall, with the approval of the General Assembly, receive emoluments from United Nations resources on such terms and conditions as the General Assembly may decide.";

3. *Recommend* that the General Assembly approve these amendments at its forty-seventh session;

4. *Decide* that the amendment shall enter into force when it has been approved by the General Assembly and accepted by a two thirds majority of States parties which shall have so notified the Secretary-General as depositary;

5. *Urge* all States parties to meet their financial obligations under the existing article 8, paragraph 6, in full until such time as the amendment in paragraph 1 above enters into force;

---

[1] CERD 1989 (XXXVII) I, 1988 (XXXVI) I, 1987 (XXXIV) II, (XXXV) I.

[2] CERD/SP/39.

[3] C.N.285.1991.TREATIES-4 of 20 December 1991.

5

0151

6. *Strongly ap*——*to all States parties in arrears in making the contribu*||||||| *required by the existing provisions of the Convention to meet those payments in full;*

7. *Emphasize* that the entry into force of the amendments cannot in any way be interpreted as relinquishing the obligation of States parties to meet in full any arrears in payments of their assessed contributions.

22nd Meeting
15 January 1992

0152

Printed at United Nations, Geneva
GE.92-17691
October 1992–1,800

United Nations publication

0153

공 란

정 리 보 존 문 서 목 록					
기록물종류	일반공문서철	등록번호	2021020008	등록일자	2021-02-02
분류번호	734.29	국가코드		보존기간	30년
명 칭	각국의 인권보장기구 현황 조사, 1992				
생 산 과	국제연합2과	생산년도	1992~1992	당당그룹	
내용목차					

0001

분류번호	보존기간

발 신 전 보

번 호 : ~~WUS-2468~~ 외 별지참조   종별 : _____

WUS-2468 920526 1647 EG

수 신 : 주 수신처 참조 대사. ~~총영사~~

발 신 : WCN장0549관 WUK -~~0421~~-이UFR -1082 WGE -0703 WAV -0806

제 목 : ~~WHO 인권보장관련1과 내부WDY-0519~~ WRF -1548 WHG -0264 WHC -116, WNR-145 WSD-313,

WCZ -0304 WAU -0469 WJA -2357 WPH -0489 WMX -0341

WCS -0191 WAR -0326

인권관련 업무에 참고하고자 하니 주재국 인권보장 관련 기구

현황에 대하여 아래사항 조사 보고바람.(관계자료는 파편 송부)

1. 인권보장기구의 성격, 기능 및 주요활동

   - 정부기구 또는 독립기구 여부 등 기구의 성격

   - 인권관련 주요문제 발생시 활동내용

   - 인권관계 입법활동에의 참여 정도

2. 외무부내 인권업무 담당부서의 업무내용

3. 기타 정부부처내 인권업무 담당부서 업무내용

   - 우리나라의 경우 법무부 법무실 인권과가 있음. 끝.

(국제기구국장대리 금정호)

수신처 : 주미, 주카나다, 주영, 주불, 주독, 주오지리, 주화란,

주노르웨이, 주스웨덴, 주러시아, 주헝가리, 주체코, 주호주,

주일, 주필리핀, 주멕시코, 주칠레, 주알젠틴 대사

	보 안 통 제	

앙 고 재	92 년 5 월 26 일	유 인 2 과	기안자 성 명 가홍율		과 장	심의관 대결	국 장		차 관	장 관		외신과통제

0002

외 무 부

종   별 :

번   호 : PHW-0598   일   시 : 92 0527 1450

수   신 : 장 관(연이, 아동)

발   신 : 주 필리핀 대사

제   목 : 인권보장관련 국내 기구

대:WPH-489

1. 주재국은 헌법기관으로서 인권 위원회를 설치하여 인권보호 업무를 담당하고 있는바, (헌법 제 17 조 내지 19 조) 동기구 현황은 아래와 같음.

가. 성격

헌법상 독립 기구임(의장 및 4 명의 위원으로 구성됨)

나. 활동내용

1) 인권침해 상황조사 (인권침해 호소시 또는 기구 자발적으로)

2) 내부 규칙 제정

3) 국내외 필리핀 국적 보유자의 인권 보호를 위한 법적 구제조치, 인권 피보호 대상자에 대한 인권침해 예방조치

4) 구치소, 형무소등에 대한 방문

5) 인권 신장을 위한 연구, 교육, 홍보

6) 의회에 대하여 인권 침해자에 대한 적절한 보상조치 마련 촉구

7) 정부의 인권관련 국제 규약 준수여부 감시

8) 인권 침해 사실 조사에 협조한 증인 보호

9) 정부 각기관에 대하여 인권보호 활동에 필요한 협조 요구

10) 자체 인사 조직

11) 기타 법률로 규정된 사항

2. 주재국 외무부 유엔 6 과는 유엔의 인권관련 업무를 담당함.

3. 기타 정부내 별도 인권 담당 부서는 없음. 끝.

(대사 노정기-국장)

예고:92.12.31. 까지

───────────────────────────────

국기국   아주국

검토 필(1992. 6 .30 .)

92.05.27   16:41

외신 2과   통제관 BS

0003

원 본

외 무 부

종 별 :

번 호 : GEW-1088

일 시 : 92 0528 1730

수 신 : 장관(연이)

발 신 : 주 독 대사

제 목 : 인권보장 관련 국내기구 조사

대:WGE-0703

대호관련, 5.29. 당관 권세영 서기관이 외무부 유엔. 경제사회기구 담당 SEEGER 담당관을 면담, 파악한 바를 아래 보고함

1. 인권보장기구의 성격, 기능 및 주요활동

0 주재국내 주요인권보장기구로는 민간단체인 인권문제 국제기구(INTERNATIONALE GESELLSCHAFT FUER MENSCHENRECHTE)가 프랑크프르트에 설립 되어 있음

0 동 단체는 1972 년 설립된 사단법인으로서, 현재 미, 영, 불, 오스트리아, 스위스 등 국가에 지부가 있으며, 동 단체는 독립기구로는 기부금과 회원회비로서 운영되고 있음

0 동 단체는 연례 보고서 발간, 주요 인권문제 발생시 사법당국에 제소하는등의 활동을 하고 있으며, 언론자유 등 개별 인권문제와 관련한 책자발간 등으로 홍보및 교육활동을 하고 있음

0 동단체는 또한 총 42 개국에서 인권을 향상시키기 위한 개발지원 프로젝트에 종사하고 있음

0 인권관계 입법과 관련, 동 단체는 하원에서의 법안의결에 앞서 개최되는 청문회에 참석하여 의견을 개진하고 있으며, 또한 정치일선에서 활동하는 다수 정당인들이 동단체 회원으로 활동하고 있으므로 인권문제 관련 정당에도 영향력을 행사 한다함.

2. 외무부내 인권업무 담당부서 업무 내용

0 외무부는 유엔담당 국장을 인권문제 조정관(KOORINATOR DER MENSCHENRECHTSFRAGEN)으로 지정하여, 정부 부.처내 인권문제 관련 협의및 조정업무를 담당하고 있음

국기국   구주국

O 유엔담당 국장 관장하에 유엔의 경제. 사회기구 담당과에서 인권문제 관련실무를 담당하고 있는 바, 동 실무는 주로 해외의 인권문제를 다룬다고 함. 즉 해외주재 대사가 보고하는 주재국 인권보고를 접수, 필요한 훈령을 하달함(이에 있어 주재국 단독으로 혹은 여타 EC 회원국과의 상호협의를 거침)

O 기타 CSCE 및 COUNCIL OF EUROPE 의 테두리 내에서도 구라파내 인권문제를 취급하며, 특히 구주안보협력회의 체제(CSCE PROCESS)내의 인권문제를 다루는업무는 CSCE 담당과에서 다루고 있음

O 또한 인도적 지원, 외국의+ 긴급재난및 난민지원을 담당하는 1 개과도 운영하고 있음

3. 기타 정부 부.처내 인권업무 담당부서

O 내무부에 인권문제를 담당하는 1 개과를 설치, 헌법내 보장된 인권문제를 다루고 있음

O 법무부 내에는 공법담당 국장을 인권문제 담당 수임자로 지정하고, 산하 1개과에서 인권문제를 담당하고 있음

O ODA 를 담당하고 있는 경제협력부에서도 개발원조 프로젝트 지원을 통하여 외국의 인권문제에 깊이 관여하고 있음. 끝

(대사-국장)

예고:92.12.31. 까지

검 토 필(1992. 6 .30 .) /Hum/

2 72

관리 (2
번호 -405

주 필 리 핀 대 사 관

주비정 700 - **0452**   1992. 5. 29.

수 신 : 장관

참 조 : 국제기구국장

제 목 : 자료송부

            연 : PHW - 0598

            연호 관련, 자료를 별첨 송부합니다.

별 첨 : 상기 자료 1부.   끝.

(예고: 92.12.31까지(일반))

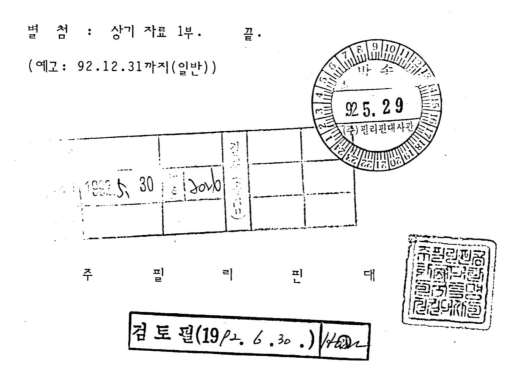

발 송
92 5. 29
(주) 필리핀대사관

1992. 5. 30 2006

주   필   리   핀   대

검 토 필(19/2. 6. 30 .)

0006

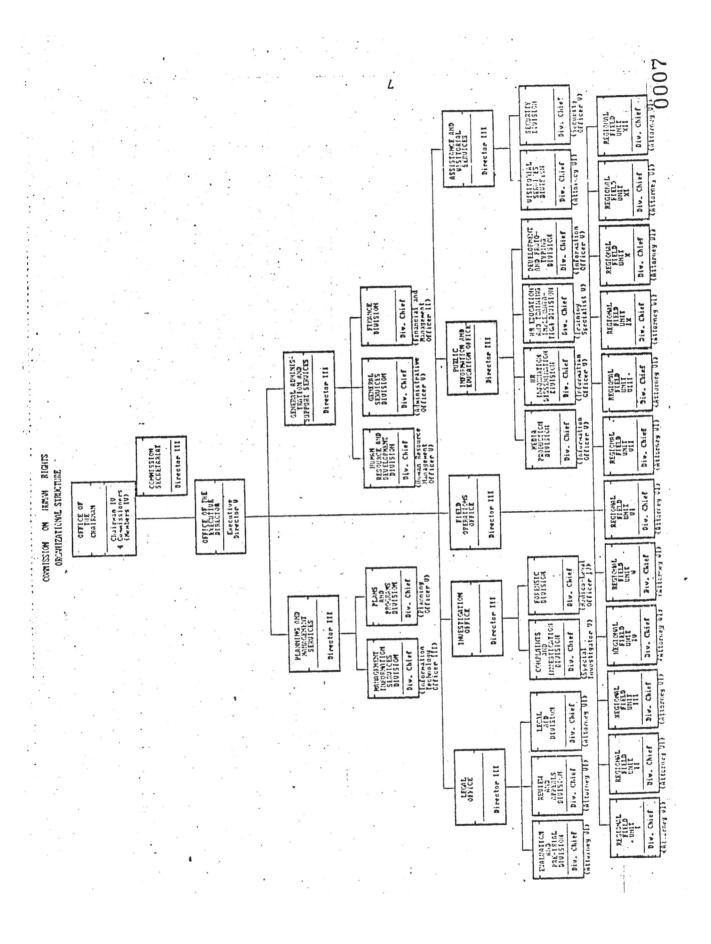

COMMISSION ON HUMAN RIGHTS
ORGANIZATIONAL STRUCTURE

주 캐 나 다 대 사 관

2 7ㄴ

캐나다(정) 720 - 458   92. 6. 2.

수 신 : 외무부장관

참 조 : 국제기구국장

제 목 : 인권보장 관련기구

        대 : WCN - 0549

        연 : CNW - 0037

연호 캐나다의 인권보장 관련 기구자료를 별첨 송부합니다.

첨부 : 1. Department of Multiculturalism and Citizenship 관련자료 1부.

     2. 외무부 인권과 주요 업무현황 1부.

     3. OAU의 인권위원회 제출 보고서 1부.

     4. 인권관련 민간기구 현황 1부.

     5. Canadian Human Rights Commission 연례보고서 1부.

     6. 기타 관련자료 7부. 끝.

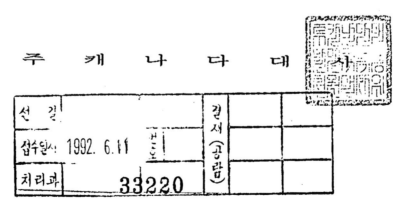

주 캐 나 다 대

선 결			결재 (공람)		
접수일: 1992. 6. 11					
처리과	33220				

0008

관리 번호	PL -418

외 무 부

종 별 :

번 호 : UKW-0945   일 시 : 92 0602 1830

수 신 : 장관(연이,구일)

발 신 : 주 영 대사

제 목 : 인권보장 관련기구 조사

대: WUK-0921

1. 대호 주재국 인권보장 관련기구에 관해 아래 보고함.

가. 정부기구

-주재국 정부는 외무성 유.엔과내 인권정책부서 (HUMAN RIGHTS POLICY UNIT)를 두고있으며, 동 부서는 개별 외국 국가의 인권문제 및 국제인권협약 가입등외교정책에 있어서 인권업무를 총괄 조정함.

-국내 인권문제담당 정부기구는 별도로 설치되어 있지않고 있으며 내무성의 형사사건 및 헌정과 (THE CRIMINAL JUSTICE AND CONSTITUTIONAL DEPARTMENT) 의 A DIVISION 에서 업무의 일부로 제반 인권문제 관련사항을 총괄 조정하고 있음.

-인권관련 주요문제 발생시 외무성의 경우 각국 인권문제에 대한 외교정책 수립이 주요활동이며, 내무성의 경우 개별 인권문제를 담당할 부서를 지정하는등업무분장 및 조정의 역할을 함에 그치며, 실제 지정부서에서 동 업무를 담당하게됨.

-주재국 의회내 초당적 인권보장기구인 PARLIAMENTARAY HUMAN RIGHTS GROUP이 있음.

나. 비정부기구

-주재국내 인권보장관련 주요 비정부기구는 하기와 같으며, 동 기구들에 제반 인권문제에 대한 일반의 관심환기 및 정부기관에 대하여 인권침해 제도개선, 인권보장 입법요구등 압력단체로 활동하고 있음.

.AMNESTY INTERNATIONAL .MINORITY RIGHTS GROUP

.CATHOLIC INSTITUTE FOR INTERNATIONAL RELATIONS

.EDUCATION IN HUMAN RIGHTS NETWORK

.ARTICLE 19

국기국   구주국

.INDEX

.INTERNATIONAL ALERT

.INTERNATIONAL COMMISSION OF JURISTS

.INTERNATIONAL PEN

.INTERRIGHTS

2. 상기 인권보장기구에 대한 관련자료는 파편 송부 예정임.끝

(대사 이홍구-국장)

예고: 92.12.31 까지

검 토 필(1992. 6 .30 .)

외 무 부

관리
번호 ~428

종 별 :

번 호 : USW-2791

일 시 : 92 0602 1700

수 신 : 장 관 (연이)

발 신 : 주 미 대사

제 목 : 인권보장 기구 조사

대: WUS-2468

1. 대호 관련, 인권 (HUMAN RIGHTS) 보장을 위한 미국내 별도 정부 독립기구는 없으며, 국무부내 인권및 인도적 업무담당국 (BUREAU OF HUMAN RIGHTS AND HUMANITARIAN AFFAIRS)에서 (1) 전세계적인 차원에서의 인권준수와 관련한 미국정책의 형성, 발전, 집행업무 (2) 유엔회원국 및 미국원조 수혜국에 대한 인권조사 보고서 작성 업무 (3) 외국인의 정치적 망명과 관련한 정책 조언 업무등을 수행하고 있음.

2. 민권 (CIVIL RIGHTS)에 관해서는 민권위원회 (COMMISSION ON CIVIL RIGHTS)라는 독립기구가 있어서, 동 기구는 인종, 피부색, 종교, 성, 연령에 따른 차별에 관한 여러 정보들을 수집하여, 동 사실 및 개선 건의안 (RECOMMENDATIONS)을 대통령과 의회에 보고하는 역할을 수행하고 있으며, 법무부내에도 민권국(CIVIL RIGHT DIVISION) 이있어서 상기와같은 차별 사건에 대한 연방차원의 민권보호법을 적용하는 역할을 수행하고있음.

3. 상기 국무부내 인권부서의 구체적 업무내용에 관해서는 6.4(목) 국무부 관계관을 면담예정인바 추보예정임.끝

(대사 현홍주-국장)

예고: 92.1231 까지

접 수 (1992. 6 .30.)

국기국

관리
번호 | *12 - 431*

원 본

외 무 부

종 별 :

번 호 : CNW-0637

수 신 : 장관(연이,미일)

발 신 : 주 캐나다대사

제 목 : 인권보장 관련기구

일 시 : 92 0602 1600

대:WCN-0549

표제관련 당관 백참사관이 6.1. 주재국 외무부 인권사회관(UNMAN RIGHTS AND SOCIAL AFFAIRS DIVISION) 과장 IAN FERGUSON 및 MARCEL CLOUTIER 담당관을 면담 파악한 내용 아래 보고함.

1. 주재국 인권 관련 기관

0 카정부로부터 보조금을 지급 받는 준정부 기관으로서 캐나다 인권위원회,공식언어 위원회 및 프라이버시 위원등 5 개 위원회가 있으며, 민간기관으로 100 여 이상의 단체가 있음.

0 정부 보조금을 받는 기관도 정부 간섭 없이 독자적으로 활동

2. 외무부 인권사회과 주요업무

0 카 외교정책에 인권문제 포함증진

0 외무부와 인권관련 비정부기관과의 협조 관계 증진,0 카 인권 현황에 대한 국제적 인식 제고등

3. 여타 정부부처내 인권 업무 담당부서

0 중앙부서로 DEPARTMENT OF MULTICULTURALISM AND CITIZENSHIP 이 인권관련조정업무 담당

- 1 년에 2 회에 걸쳐 인권관련 부처회의 개최

0 법무부 및 보건사회부내에 인권과가 있고, 노동부에서는 국제기구과가 인권업무 담당

0 기타 부서 및 주정부도 인권관련 전담부서는 없으나 인권관련 업무 수행

4. 주재국 종교단체도 인권담당부서를 두고, 인권문제에 있어 70 년대부터 카정부에 막장한 영향력을 행사하고 있음 참고 바람.

국기국   미주국

5. 관계자료는 파편 송부 예정임.

(대사 박건우-국장)

예고: 92.12.31. 까지

점토필(1992. 6.30.) /Kim

원 본

외 무 부

번 호 : USW-2861   일 시 : 92 0604 1832

수 신 : 장관(연이,미일)

발 신 : 주 미 대사

제 목 : 국무부 인권국 업무

연: USW-2791

1. 연호 관련, 당관 김홍균 서기관은 금 6.4 PATRICK HOTZE 국무부 인권국 양자업무과 동아시아 담당관을 면담, 인권국 업무내용등에 대해 파악한 바, 주요내용을 하기 보고함..(PEG WILLINGHAM 인권국 다자업무과 담당관 동석)

가. 개관

. 국무부 인권 및 인도적 업무담당국은 차관보 산하에 1 명의 수석부차관보와 2 명의 부차관보를 두고 있는 바, 각 부차관보는 (1) 양자 및 다자업무(BILATERAL AND MULTILATERAL AFFAIRS) 와 (2) 정책 및 프로그램(POLICY AND PROGRAMS) 업무를 각기 맡고 있음.

. 그러나 인권국의 주축은 양자 및 다자업무 부서이며, 정책 및 프로그램 부서는 인도주의적 업무를 담당하면서 주로 외국인의 정치적 망명과 관련하여 법무부 이민국(IMMIGRATION AND NATURALIZATION SERVICE)에 정책적 조언을 하고 있다고 함.

나. 양자업무과(OFFICE OF BILATERAL AFFAIRS)

. 동 부서는 과장산하에 부과장 1 명과 지역별로 유럽, 중남미, 아프리카, 아시아. 태평양, 중동.남아시아 5 개 지역으로 구분, 각각 담당관을 두고 있음.

. 동 부서는 미국과 타국과의 양자관계에 있어서 인권문제가 필수요소(AN INTEGRAL PART)가 되며, 올바로 정립되도록(PROPERLY MANAGED), 국무부내 해당지역국등과 정책을 조정해 나가면서, 특정국의 인권상황 개선을 위해 경제 및 군사원조, 비난성명, 정치적 압력등 제수단의 사용 필요성을 검토, 제시함.

. 동 부서는 특정국가의 인권상황등과 관련하여 미국내 및 국제적 비정부인권기구(NGO)들과 상호정보를 교환하며, 의회와의 관계에 있어서는 각의원 사무실을 통해 접수되는 각국 인권침해 사례등에 대한 업무처리 및 정보제공도

국기국   장관   차관   1차보   미주국   분석관   정와대   안기부

외신 2과 통제관 BX

0014

담당하고 있음.(김서기관이 동 비정부 인권기구들의 수준 및 동 기구들이 소유한 정보의 질등에 대한 평가를 문의한 바, HOTZE 담당관은 자신은 ASIA WATCH, PUEBLA INSTITUTE 정도의 기구들이 비교적 정확한 정보와 균형된 시각을 갖고 있다고 생각하며, AMNESTY INTERNATIONAL 경우 아시아 지역 정보가 런던에서 수집되는등 정보의 제한성을 갖고 있고, 케네디 인권센타 경우는 충분한 정보나 균형된시각을 갖추지 못한 것으로 생각하고 있다는 견해를 보임.)

. 또한, 양자업무과는 유엔회원국 및 미국원조(AID) 수혜국을 대상으로 매년 작성되는 인권고서(COUNTRY REPORTS ON HUMAN RIGHTS PRACTICES)에 포함될 내용을 검토, 해당지역국과 협의, 최종 확정하고 이듬해 2.1 까지 의회에 제출함.

- 상기 인권보고서는 각국 주재 미국대사관에 의해서 초안(DRAFT)이 작성되며, 이 초안은 매년 10.1 까지 국무부 지역과에 제출되어 검토를 거친후 인권국에 제출됨. 인권국은 동 초안을 검토, 수정이 필요하다고 생각되는 경우 해당 지역과와 협의를 거치게 되며, 동 수정안은 다시 해당국 주재 미국대사관에 보내져의견을 수렴한 후 인권국에 의해 최종 확정된다고 함.

다. 다자업무과(OFFICE OF MULTIALTERAL AFFAIRS)

. 동 부서는 과장산하에 부과장 1 명과 UN, CSCE, OAS, 국제적십자사, 다자개발은행(MULTI-DEVELOPMENT BANKS) 별로 각 담당관을 두고 있음.

. WILLINGHAM 담당관은 대유엔 업무와 관련하여, 동 부서가 국제기구국내 인권.여성과(HUMAN RIGHTS AND WOMEN'S AFFAIRS OFFICE) 등과 협조, 유엔 인권위원회(UN COMMISSION ON HUMAN RIGHTS) 활동을 모니터하면서, 매년 2-3 월 (93 년도 49 차 회의는 1.25-3.5 간 개최 예정) GENEVA 에서 개최되는 회의에서의 부표지침(VOTING GUIDANCE) 과 같은 미대표단 활동지침을 마련한다고 설명함.

. 동 담당관은 아국이 금년도에 최초로 유엔 인권위원회 이사국으로 선임되어 95 년까지 활동하게 된 것을 환영한다고 하면서, 각국 인권상황 토의나 인권관련 각종 규범 작성과정에 있어서 한. 미 양국간 긴밀한 협조체제를 구축해 나가길 바란다고 언급함.

2. 면담 말미에 김서기관이 92.3 RICHARD SCHIFTER 차관보의 갑작스런 사임으로 현재 공석중인 동 차관보의 후임에 대한 진전이 있는지 문의한 바, HOTZE 담당관은 아직 후임자 임명은 없는 것으로 알고 있으며, 언론보도등에 의하면 현재 장거리전화회사인 US SPRINT 의 COPORATE LAWYER 로 있는 PATRICIA DIAZ-DINNIS 라는

PAGE 2

0015

인물이 유력하다는 애기도 있다고 소개하였음.
  (대사 현홍주-국장)
  92.12.31 까지

접 르 민(1992. 6. 30.) Ham

외 무 부

종 별 :

번 호 : SDW-0528   일 시 : 92 0605 1600

수 신 : 장관(연의)

발 신 : 주 스웨덴 대사

제 목 : 인권보장 관련기구

대:WSD-0213

대호 주재국 인권보장 관련기구 현황을 아래와 같이 조소, 보고함.

- 아 래 -

1. 일반현황

0 주재국은 인권이 헌법 및 관련법 (PRESS FREEDOM ACT, EXPRESSION FREEDOMACT, SUCCESSION ACT, THE INSTRUMENT OF GOVERNMENT 등)에 명시 보장되어 있으며, 인권관련 문제도 일반법원에서 통상적인 절차에 의해 처리됨.

0 이에따라, 인권업무를 별도로 담당하는 정부기구 또는 독립기구는 없으며, 법무부를 포함한 정부기관내에 인권업무를 전담하는 부서는 없음.

2. 외무부내 인권업무 담당부서

0 91.10. 출범한 보수계 신정부는 대외정책의 3 대원칙으로 자유민주주의, 시장경제 및 인권을 추진중에 있으므로 주재국 외교정책에 있어서 인권무내의 중요성이 더욱 강조되고 있으며, 특히 인권문제를 대외원조와 연계시키고 있음.

0 외무부내 대외원조를 담당하는 국제협력처 장관(주재국 외무부에는 외무부, 외무부 대외통상처, 외무부 국제협력처 등 3 개의 부처가 있으며 모두 각료급 장관임)의 공식명칭은 MINISTER FOR INTERNATIONAL DEVELOPMENT COOPERATION AND HUMAN RIGHTS ISSUES 인바, 동처의 지역담당관들은 담당국의 인권상황과 원조를 연계, 검토하며 장관급 직원 1 명이 인권문제를 총괄함.

0 또한 외무부 정무담당 지역과는 담당국가의 인권상황을 파악 및 필요조치실행 (성명서 발표등), 상기 국제협력처 지역담당관과 협조하고, 정부 7 국(국제기구담당)내에 AMNEUS 대사가 정무국내 인권문제를 총괄담당하며(직원 1 명보조)동인은 UN COMMISSION ON HUMANS 를 겸하고 있음. 한편, 외무부 법율 4

국기국   구주국

국내에서는 직원 4 명이 COUNCIL OF EUROPE, CSCE 및 UN 의 인권관련 CONVENTIONS 등의 인권관련 업무를 담당하고있음.

　　(대사 최동진-국장)

　　예고: 92.12.31 일반

접 토 편(1992. 6. 30 .) /Ham

113 Empire Circuit, Yarralumla A.C.T. 2600   /(06)273 3044   /(06)273 4839

문서번호 호주(정) 20352- 71

시행일자 1992. 6. 5. (   )

선 결	.		지 시	
접	일자 시간		결 재	
수	번호	**33531**	공	
처 리 과			람	
담 당 자				

수신 장 관

참조 국제기구국장

제목 인권보장관련 국내기구 조사

 대 : WAU-0469

 대호 관련사항을 아래와 같이 보고합니다.

1. 주재국 인권보장관련 기구 현황

   - 현   황 : 주요 인권관련 기구 9개(별첨 명단 참조)

   - 성   격 : 민간기구

   - 활동내용 : 인권문제에 관한 감시(monitor), 대화(dialogue),

     자문(consultation)

   - 입법활동 참여 : 자문의 범위내에서 참여

2. 주재국 외무부내 인권업무 담당부서

   - 명   칭 : Human Rights Section

     International Organizaton and Legal Division

     (외무부내 국제기구국 인권과)

   - 업무내용 : 인권상황의 감시(monitor), 양자간 문제제기(representation),

     다자간 협의(multiletateral participation)

     (별첨 활동보고서 참조)

                                                계   속 ...

                                                    0019

3. 기타 정부부처내 인권업무담당부서

   - 명   칭 : Hunman Rights Branch

             Civil Law Division

             Attorney General's Department

             (법무성내 인권과)

   - 업무내용 : 국내 인권관련 업무 총괄

첨 부 : 1. 주요 인권관련 민간기구 명단.

         2. 외무성 인권업무활동 보고서.

         3. 인권관련 홍보책자(Every Right). 끝.

주   호   주   대

0020

(첨부1)

① Mr David Bitel
  Secretary General
  International Commission
   of Jurists-Australian Section
  GPO Box 173
  SYDNEY NSW 2001
  ph. (02) 233 1100
     (02) 283 1333(w)

② Ms Elsa Atkin
  Director
  H.V. Evatt Memorial Foundation
  Level 3
  750A George St
  SYDNEY NSW 2000
  ph. (02) 281 8677

③ Mr Jim Dunn
  Human Rights Council
       of Australia
  13 Percy Davis Drive
  MORUYA NSW 2537
  ph. (044) 74 3484

④ Ms Margaret Piper
  Executive Director
  Refugee Council of Australia
  Locked Bag No 15
  PO CAMPERDOWN NSW 2050
  ph. (02) 565 9111

⑤ Mr John Launder
  Secretary
  Australian Human Rights Society
  PO Box 5127
  HUGHESDALE VIC 3166
  ph. (03) 568 2523

⑥ Mr Keith O'Neill
  Australian Catholic Social
       Justice Council
  19 MacKenzie St
  NORTH SYDNEY NSW 2060
  ph. (02) 956 5811

⑦ Mr Russell Rollason
  Executive Director
  Australian Council for
       Overseas Aid
  PO Box 1562
  CANBERRA ACT 2601
  ph. 247 4822

0021

⑧ Mr Harris van Beek
National Director
Amnesty International
Private Bag 23
BROADWAY NSW 2007
ph. (02) 211 3566

⑨ Mr Nicholas Cowdery QC
Chairman
Human Rights Committee
Law Council of Australia
GPO Box 1989
CANBERRA ACT 2601

0022

SUBMISSION BY THE DEPARTMENT OF FOREIGN AFFAIRS AND TRADE ON THE AUSTRALIAN GOVERNMENT'S INTERNATIONAL HUMAN RIGHTS POLICY AND ACTIVITIES

SECTION A: POLICY STATEMENT

General

The Australian Government accords a high priority to the promotion and protection of human rights internationally. This position is based on the belief that the universal observance of the rights and principles contained in the Universal Declaration of Human Rights (and other major international human rights instruments) would result in a more just international order, from which the security and prosperity of all nations and individuals would benefit.

2.   In taking a leading role in international human rights, the Government is also conscious of its moral obligation to reflect in its foreign policy the democratic and individual values of Australian society. This amounts to translating good citizenship to the international arena. Care is taken to ensure close contact is maintained between the Government and the community, through regular consultative processes.

3.   The Government considers that the standards set out in the Universal Declaration have an application which transcends national borders, and hence human rights constitute a legitimate subject for international scrutiny and concern. The Government does not accept that the treatment of human rights constitutes an "internal affair" for any country.

4.   The Government has been careful to ensure that its policies take account of the major changes in the observation of human and democratic rights taking place within the USSR and central Europe. It has done so through an emphasis on dialogue and co-operation, aimed at not only encouraging wider adherence to fundamental human rights, but lessening East-West tensions in the human rights field.

5.   Similarly, the Government is anxious to develop closer contact and dialogue with developing countries, particularly in the Asia-Pacific region, and to help diminish North-South differences over human rights perspectives and issues, which have threatened to emerge as a new focus in the aftermath of the Cold War.

6.   The Government appreciates that there are varying perspectives on human rights, and that cultural, social and historic influences should be taken into account in addressing human rights situations. Nevertheless, it is important to understand that there is no society which does not value human dignity nor recognise the fundamental nature of the principles set out in the Universal Declaration.

7.   The Government also accepts that for many regional and other developing countries, economic rights are seen as especially important, and

agrees on the need to address the underlying causes of human rights abuse. We do not consider, however, that economic rights should be accorded priority over civil and political freedoms - the two are not mutually exclusive. A society which respects and promotes individual rights (with the physical and intellectual mobility and flexibility they involve) is more likely than not to enjoy economic growth. Australia rejects the hypothesis that a State may determine that the pursuit of the collective economic well-being of its citizens can justify the suppression of individual and democratic freedoms.

8.   The bottom line objective of the Government in its pursuit of improved standards of human rights is to better the situation of the individual human rights victim. To this end, Government policy is to adopt the most constructive approach possible in a given situation.

9.   Experience has shown that confrontation does not bring positive results for the victims of human rights abuse; rather it is more productive to engage in rational and open dialogue on human rights issues and cases of concern.

10.   There are additional aspects which the Australian Government considers important to the credibility of its international human rights policy. It is essential that Australia be demonstrably consistent and non-discriminatory in raising human rights matters; there must be no selectivity in approaches to other countries. It is also necessary to ensure that in raising human rights concerns any approach is based on accurate information - in many instances, the initial steps in looking into human rights allegations involve careful enquiry rather than accusation.

11.   A result-oriented approach to human rights also calls for flexibility and judgement. In raising human rights concerns the Government employs a variety of approaches which are designed to be most effective in the circumstances of the case or issue in question; thus, it is usually considered that bilateral representations should remain on a confidential government-to-government basis, to avoid possible charges of grandstanding, though there are occasions when a public statement is judged a more effective form of pressure. The channels for representations may also vary according to the requirement to register an effective demarche.

12.   Judgements are also required on the question of what actions might be employed in support of representations and appeals on human rights cases and issues. The Australian Government takes a case-by-case approach to such questions as sanctions or aid embargoes; however, it is generally felt that punitive measures against a regime guilty of human rights violations are more likely to adversely affect the human rights victims themselves than the perpetrators of abuse. Exceptions can arise, particularly where there is strong support amongst the international community, and when there are few other available means of persuasion.

13.   The Government is conscious that it must itself subscribe to the principles and rights it seeks to uphold. There can be no denying that Australia's record has been far from perfect, in particular in respect to the treatment of Aboriginal and Torres Strait Islander people. We do not shy away from acknowledging this fact, though we point out at the same time that positive steps are being taken to redress past injustices and Government policy is to eliminate racial and other discrimination from Australian society. The Government takes an active part in the international promotion of indigenous peoples' rights.

14.   Australia is also aware of the need to uphold vigorously the principle of international accountability by itself adhering to the major human rights

instruments, and responding accurately and fully to enquiries raised as a consequence of the monitoring processes.

The Multilateral Arena

15. Australia strongly encourages all countries to adhere to international human rights instruments. Australia is itself a Party to nineteen of the twenty-four international instruments, including all the major conventions (see *Table 1*).

16. Australia attaches considerable importance to the effective operation of these international instruments, which, with the Universal Declaration, form the basis of international human rights law. The Government has been active in advocating reform measures to rationalise the functioning of the monitoring bodies, and has nominated candidates to serve (in their personal capacity) on two of these bodies - the Economic, Social and Cultural Rights Committee, and the Committee on the Elimination of Discrimination Against Women.

17. Australia has also recently become a Party to the First Optional Protocol to the ICCPR, thus recognising the competence of the Convention's monitoring body (the Human Rights Committee) to receive communications from persons within Australia concerning Australia's compliance with the Convention. Australia is a Party to the Second Optional Protocol, against Capital Punishment.

18. The Government is a strong supporter of the United Nations' human rights role, including its standard-setting and monitoring activities. Australia is currently serving a three year term as a Member of the UN Commission on Human Rights, the main international forum for the promotion and protection of human rights. Australia also actively pursues human rights goals at the United Nations General Assembly.

19. The Government seeks to promote adherence to international standards through the operations of these forums. It therefore supports such mechanisms as special country rapporteurs, working groups and thematic studies.

20. Given the international composition of the UN bodies, the Government accepts that progress often requires negotiation, dialogue and consensus. As a country of Western traditions located in a developing region of the world, Australia is keen to play a role in promoting contacts and dialogue between regional groups at multilateral forums. With a history of support for developing countries' perspectives in such areas as economic rights, and our focus on the Asia-Pacific region, the Government has developed a record of active involvement in multilateral consensus procedures.

Bilateral Approaches

21. Australia has been active in raising individual human rights cases and situations with other countries. It is the Government's policy to take up all individual human rights cases which are brought to its attention when it is satisfied that there are valid grounds for enquiry. A large proportion of these cases are initially referred to the Government by the Australian Parliamentary Group of Amnesty International. Information is also drawn from Australia's overseas diplomatic network, and from groups and individuals within Australia. (Details of this activity appear in the second part of this Report.)

22. It is the Government's practice first to investigate the accuracy of any such allegations of human rights abuse, through its relevant diplomatic missions, before raising a case with the authorities of another country. The basic format

0025

Table 1

LIST OF INTERNATIONAL HUMAN RIGHTS INSTRUMENTS TO WHICH AUSTRALIA IS A PARTY

- The International Covenant on Civil and Political Rights (ICCPR).

- The (First) Optional Protocol to the ICCPR.

- The Second Optional Protocol to the ICCPR aiming at the abolition of the death penalty.

- The International Covenant on Economic, Social and Cultural Rights (ICESCR).

- The Convention on the Elimination of All Forms of Racial Discrimination (CERD).

- The Convention against Torture and other Cruel, Inhuman or Degrading Forms of Punishment (CAT).

- The Convention on the Elimination of All Forms of Discrimination against Women (CEDAW).

- The Convention on the Rights of the Child.

- The Convention on the Prevention and Punishment of the Crime of Genocide.

- The Convention on the Political Rights of Women.

- The Convention on the Nationality of Married Women.

- The Slavery Convention of 1926.

- The 1953 Protocol amending the 1926 Convention.

- The Slavery Convention of 1926 as amended.

- The Supplementary Convention on the Abolition of Slavery, the Slave Trade, and Institutions and Practices Similar to Slavery.

- The Convention on the Reduction of Statelessness.

- The Convention relating to the Status of Stateless Persons.

- The Convention relating to the Status of Refugees.

- The Protocol relating to the Status of Refugees.

0026

of approaches to other·governments in cases where it is considered action is warranted is first to seek clarification of the reported abuse in a non-confrontational manner; the receiving authority is informed that, if the allegation were correct, it would be a matter of concern to the Australian Government. The Government is careful not to initiate action in cases where it judges that to do so would not be beneficial to the individual(s) concerned.

23.   Representations are normally made through the Australian diplomatic mission in, or accredited to, the country concerned as this is considered the most effective channel to register Australian views with the relevant authorities. In exceptional cases, representations are made by the Department of Foreign Affairs and Trade to diplomatic representatives in Canberra. Both the Minister for Foreign Affairs and Trade, Senator Gareth Evans, and the Minister for Trade Negotiations, Dr Neal Blewett, frequently raise individual cases and wider human rights concerns in their meetings with senior foreign government representatives abroad and in Australia.

24.   The Government is well aware that this is an area of great sensitivity in the field of bilateral relations. However, it considers that with skilful handling, human rights issues can be managed without significant adverse impact upon other areas of bilateral relationships.

25.   Australia is particularly conscious of the differing cultural and social perspectives on human rights amongst our Asian-Pacific regional neighbours. The Government considers that the best prospect for improving human rights situations within the region will usually lie in a non-confrontational approach and the development of mutual understanding. The Government's policy is to achieve the observance of internationally-accepted standards through common agreement based on dialogue and co-operation, without compromising on fundamental human rights principles.

26.   The recent Australian Human Rights Delegation to China constitutes a relevant example of the application of rational and open discussion in advancing Australian human rights goals. The Delegation carried out a constructive and non-confrontational dialogue, to the satisfaction of both sides, in the course of which Australian Government concerns on a range of human rights issues and on individual cases of prisoners of conscience were clearly conveyed. At the same time, the Delegation listened carefully to Chinese perspectives on human rights, and gathered much useful information on the Chinese legal, judicial and penal systems. Moreover, in accepting the visit the Chinese Government implicitly accepted the legitimate place of human rights on the international agenda as a proper subject for bilateral discourse. The Delegation visit also, importantly, provided the opportunity to contribute to a better understanding on the part of the Chinese authorities that there are alternative approaches to human rights, and that there are advantages in adopting a more open and humane attitude. This exemplifies the direction of Australia's international human rights policy.

0027

SECTION B: ACTIVITIES DURING FINANCIAL YEAR 1990/91

Representations

The Department of Foreign Affairs and Trade maintains a register of Australia's bilateral human rights representations. This shows that during the period 1 July 1990 to 30 June 1991, the Australian Government made 428 representations to the government authorities of 78 different countries over individual human rights cases or situations. In addition, there was on-going activity on cases raised prior to 1 July 1990. (In the period from 1 July 1987, when statistics were first maintained, to 30 June 1991, the Government has made a total of 1657 representations to 122 different countries.)

2.   These figures do not constitute the actual number of individual cases raised, as any one representation may include more than one person - some, for example, have involved as many as eighty individuals.

3.   The chart at *Table 2* shows a regional breakdown of representations made in the period under review. This does not constitute an relative index of human rights abuse in various parts of the world, but does provide an indication of the level of activity of the Australian Government in making human rights representations.

4.   While it is difficult to precisely assess the results of specific representations, responses were received in approximately 20 to 25% of these cases, of which some 15% can be considered positive. Such responses could take the form of information on the health or whereabouts of the person concerned, advice that a prisoner had been released, or an assurance that the individual's human rights were being protected. Of course, it is not always possible to know whether a representation has produced a result, nor to suggest that an outcome is the sole result of any one representation.

Monitoring

5.   The Department of Foreign Affairs and Trade takes care to monitor closely human rights situations worldwide, utilising its network of diplomatic missions. Evaluation and formulation of policy responses to such situations are the responsibility of the Department's Human Rights Section.

6.   The Section also ensures that assessments on human rights situations and cases are regularly made to Ministers, Parliamentarians and senior officials.

Dialogue

7.   Following the conclusion of the Australia-USSR Human Contacts Agreement in 1989, the Soviet Foreign Ministry proposed that a framework be established for holding bilateral human rights consultations. The first such discussions were held, at officials level, in Moscow in January 1991. As well as reviewing the operation of the Human Contacts Agreement, the consultations included discussion of issues of mutual interest on the agenda of the 47th Session of the Commission on Human Rights and human rights issues of concern within each country. In respect of the last item, the Australian side raised a number of individual human rights cases, the incidence of capital punishment in the Soviet Union, the lack of an alternative to military service for conscientious objectors, nationalities and minority issues and on-going problems for Soviet Jews. Considerable attention was given to the situation in the Baltic Republics.

0028

Table 2

Australian Government Human Rights Representations: New Cases 1990/91

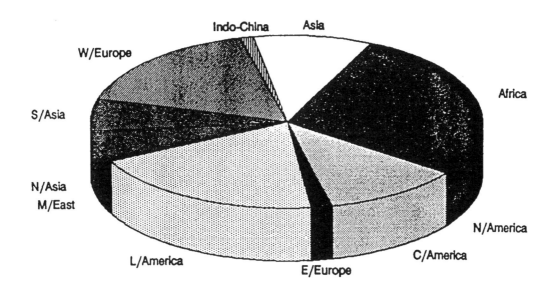

Regional Distribution (new cases)

Asia	42
Africa	114
N/America	6
C/America	49
E/Europe	7
L/America	84
M/East	23
N/Asia	3
S/Asia	24
W/Europe	72
Indo-China	4
TOTAL	**428**

0029

8.   A number of bilateral consultations were also held between the Australian Delegation and Asian Delegations at the Commission on Human Rights in Geneva in January/February 1991. Discussion focussed mainly on issues of mutual interest before the Commission, including human rights in Burma, and Sri Lanka.

9.   One country with which such consultations were held was Indonesia, which had joined CHR for the first time in 1991. It was agreed between Delegations that the idea of bilateral consultations be explored further, and in May 1991 the subject was again raised in the course of annual senior officials talks held in Canberra. It was then agreed that there would be merit in a round of human rights discussions prior to the 1992 Session of CHR.

10.   In April 1991, the Minister for Foreign Affairs and Trade, Senator Gareth Evans, during a visit to Beijing reached agreement with his Chinese counterpart, Qian Qichen, on details of an Australian delegation to examine and discuss the human rights situation in China and related matters. It was agreed that the objectives of the delegation would include:

.   to commence a constructive and serious dialogue on human rights issues of concern, or of interest, to either side;

.   to obtain information on Chinese laws and policies affecting human rights, including on

-     formal and constitutional rights

-     the Chinese legal, judicial and penal systems

-     how laws and policies are observed and implemented in practice, particularly in relation to the protection of the rights of individuals;

.   to hold discussions with, and convey Australian views on human rights issues to, relevant Chinese organisations, officials and others involved in human rights matters;

.   to seek information and make representations about particular cases, and to pursue the establishment of a satisfactory mechanism for conveying such representations in the future; and

.   to respond to Chinese interest in human rights issues in Australia.

11.   It was agreed that the Delegation would consist of Parliamentarians, academics and officials and would visit Beijing, Tibet and other regions. It was also agreed that Australia would host a reciprocal delegation should that be sought at any time by the Chinese Government.

12.   The agreement to send a human rights delegation to China provided the opportunity to develop a constructive dialogue on human rights with an important regional country. This was seen by the Australian Government to:

(a)   enable Australia to encourage the Chinese Government to respect internationally-accepted standards of human rights and improve its overall human rights situation

0030

- and urge Chinese ratification of the International Covenants on Civil and Political Rights and on Economic, Social and Cultural Rights;

(b)   persuade the Chinese that human rights constitute an important element in international affairs - affecting a wide range of relationships - and are a legitimate subject of international enquiry;

(c)   demonstrate Australia's willingness to listen to differing cultural and social perspectives on Human Rights issues; and

(d)   enable Australia to raise specific human rights cases of concern, and seek improvements in conditions of individual prisoners of conscience.

13.   In May, Senator Evans selected a Delegation, led by Senator Chris Schacht, Chairman of the Parliamentary Joint Committee on Foreign Affairs, Defence and Trade. The Delegation departed for China for a two week visit in mid- July, and its Report was tabled in Parliament by Senator Evans on 9 September 1991.

Multilateral

14.   In May 1990, Australia was elected for a three-year term as a Member of the UN Commission on Human Rights (CHR), commencing in January 1991. Australia therefore participated as a full Member at the 47th Session of CHR from 28 January to 8 March 1991. The Australian Delegation played an active role in the consideration of issues before the Commission, making 13 statements (see Section C), and participating in several working and drafting groups. Consideration of country human rights situations under Agenda Item 12 was of particular interest and a major statement of Australian concerns was delivered under this Item. Australia also took an active part in the review of country situations under the Confidential Procedures Item, giving close attention to the situation in Burma.

15.   CHR 47 proved to be a productive Session, with the appointment of three new Special Rapporteurs (Iraq, Occupied Kuwait and Cuba) and a new Working Group on Arbitrary Detention. The existing mandates of Rapporteurs on Iran, Romania, Afghanistan, and El Salvador were renewed, and consideration was given to the need for a Rapporteur on Guatemala. Continuation of CHR scrutiny of Burma was also maintained. For the first time, a Permanent Member of the Security Council was the subject of formal action by the Commission when a Chairman's Statement was delivered on the situation in the Baltic Republics of the USSR. In the area of standard-setting, the Commission decided to set up a Working Group to examine a draft Declaration on the Protection of Persons from Enforced or Involuntary Disappearances.

16.   Australia also played an active role on the question of national and regional human rights institutions, indigenous peoples' rights, and preparations for the 1993 World Conference on Human Rights.

17.   The Australian Delegation took the opportunity to develop contacts with representatives of Asian-Pacific countries, and to promote wherever possible non-confrontational and consensus solutions to issues facing the Commission.

18.   Immediately prior to CHR 47, Australia chaired a session of an on-going UN Working Group drafting a Declaration on the Protection of Human Rights Defenders (formally known as the Declaration on the Right and Responsibility of Individuals, Groups and Organs of Society to Promote and Protect Universally

0031

Recognised Human Rights and Fundamental Freedoms). Australia also participated in two sessions of the UN Working Group preparing Principles for the Protection of Persons with Mental Illness and for the Improvement of Mental Health Care.

19. At the 45th Session of the United Nations General Assembly (September to December 1990), Australia was also active in supporting UN scrutiny of major international human rights problems, including country situations and standard-setting exercises. Included in Section C are Australia's statements on human rights delivered in the Third Committee.

20. In August 1990, Australia attended in an observer capacity the annual meeting of the United Nations Sub-Commission (of CHR) on the Prevention of Discrimination and the Protection of Minorities.

21. Australia signed the international Convention on the Rights of the Child on 22 August 1990, and ratified it, thereby becoming a full Party, on 17 December 1990. This followed active participation by Australia over a period of 10 years in a UN Working Group which prepared the text of the Convention, and extensive consultation between Australian Federal, State and Territory Governments and with community groups concerning the Convention. This international instrument sets minimum standards for the protection of children's rights.

22. On 30 September 1990, the Minister for Foreign Affairs and Trade attended the World Summit for Children and endorsed the World Declaration on the Survival, Protection and Development of Children. The Declaration identifies the most critical disadvantages faced by children throughout the world, and includes a ten-point program of commitment by Governments to give priority to measures to assist children.

23. On 2 October 1990, Australia deposited its instrument of accession to the Second Optional Protocol (against capital punishment) to the International Covenant on Civil and Political Rights. The Protocol states that no-one within the jurisdiction of States Parties shall be executed. Accession followed an active international campaign, in which Australia played a prominent role, to progress this human rights instrument. Accession is consistent with the Government's strong and universal opposition to the death penalty.

24. Australia participated in the Eighth Session of the UN Working Group on Indigenous Populations in Geneva in July 1990, delivering a major statement on developments relating to Aboriginal and Torres Strait Islander Australians, and working actively in the preparation of an Universal Declaration on the Rights of Indigenous Peoples.

25. The Government also submitted in June 1991, in compliance with its obligations as a Party to the Convention on the Elimination of All Forms of Racial Discrimination (CERD), Reports covering the period January 1987 to December 1990 on measures taken to give effect to the provisions of the Convention. These Reports, together with the Report for the period October 1984 to December 1986, were heard by the CERD Committee (the body of independent experts monitoring the Convention) on 6 and 7 August 1991.

Indigenous Peoples Issues

26. International interest in the treatment and rights of indigenous peoples and minority groups is increasing. Under the auspices of the UN Working Group on Indigenous Populations, work has begun on a draft Universal

0032

Declaration on the Rights of Indigenous Peoples. Australia has played a prominent role in the progression of this exercise in recent years (see also above), in keeping with the Government's conviction that the special needs of indigenous peoples should be recognised and addressed.

27. The Australian Government is also conscious of its particular need to promote and protect the rights of Aboriginal and Torres Strait Islander Australians. The Department of Foreign Affairs and Trade continues to play a role in relating international interest and human rights standards to measures being taken domestically to remedy discrimination and mistreatment based on grounds of race - including for example the governmental response to the Royal Commission into Aboriginal Deaths in Custody.

Human Rights Fund

28. The Department of Foreign Affairs and Trade administers, through its International Organisations Branch and Human Rights Section, a Human Rights Fund, totalling annually $40,000. The purpose of the Fund is to provide assistance directly to organisations and individuals, in other countries, who are involved in the promotion and protection of human rights.

29. During the period under review, the following disbursements were made from the Fund:

. $10,000 to the Commonwealth Secretariat to assist in the holding of a South Pacific Human Rights Workshop, focussed on the importance of international human rights instruments;

. $20,000 to the United Nations Voluntary Fund for Advisory Services in the field of human rights (Australia's first contribution for several years to this Fund, which provides valuable services to countries in need of expert advice on the implementation of human rights policies);

. $11,410 to the Guatemala Human Rights Ombudsman, for the printing of a report on human rights to the Guatemala Congress.

30. In previous years, the Fund has been used for such projects as the printing of a booklet on "Women and the Law" in Pakistan, administrative assistance to the Sri Lanka Bar Association in habeas corpus cases, and to assist community groups opposed to apartheid in South Africa. A project already approved for 1991/92 is to provide training in human rights for police and military personnel through the Philippines Human Rights Commission ($10,7000).

Community Consultations

31. The Department of Foreign Affairs and Trade conducts regular consultations (usually three times a year) with representatives of Australian human rights NGOs on issues of current interest in the field of human rights. The agenda for these talks is set by the Department and NGO representatives jointly. Subjects discussed during 1990/91 included UNGA 45, CHR 47, human rights in Indonesia and Australian defence exports. Senator Evans attended the consultation held on 14 September 1990.

32. The Department liaises on a regular, on-going basis with Parliamentary representatives, particularly with the Parliamentary Group of Amnesty International, and with NGOs and individuals on human rights issues and cases of interest to the Australian community.

0033

Public Statements

33.   The Minister for Foreign Affairs and Trade delivered 47 public and parliamentary statements on Australia's international human rights policy during the period under review.   Section C of this Report includes speeches dealing with, inter alia, human rights, relevant press releases and major parliamentary statements on human rights issues by Senator Evans.

34.   Statements presented by Australian representatives at the 45th United Nations General Assembly and the 47th Session of the Commission on Human Rights are also attached.

35.   Although not delivered in the period under review, speeches by the Minister for Foreign Affairs and Trade on 26 August 1991 (to Amnesty International in Sydney) and on 26 September 1991 (to the Asia Society in New York) are attached, as these provide a clear and comprehensive outline of Australia's current international human rights policies.

0034

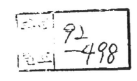

주 일 대 사 관

주일(정)700-*438*   92. 6. 8.

수신 : 장관

참조 : 국제기구국장

제목 : 인권보장관련 기구 조사

         대 : WJA-2357

         대호, 일본의 인권보장기구는 정부부서로서는 「외무성
인권난민과」「법무성 인권옹호국」이 설치되어 있으며, 기타 민간
차원의 인권옹호활동을 촉진하기 위한 「인권옹호위원」이 설치되어
있는바, 관련사항 하기 보고함.(상세는 별첨 참고자료 참조)

1. 인권옹호위원

  가) 목적

     o 인권문제는 정부기구(법무성, 외무성등)만으로는 충분한
        대응이 불가능하므로, 일반국민중에서 인권옹호문제에
        깊은관심과 이해를 갖고있는 인사들을 선정하여, 정부의
        인권문제 추진에 대한 협조를 제공토록함.(일본의 독특한
        제도)

  나) 설치근거

     o 1948.7 인권옹호위원령 제정
     o 1949.5 인권옹호위원법 제정(동년 6월시행)

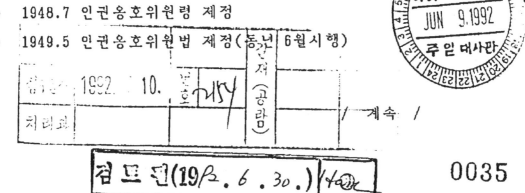

0035

다) 위원수

   ㅇ 1989년 현재 11,640명(여성위원 1,754명 포합)
   ㅇ 정수는 12,548명

라) 위촉절차

   ㅇ 법무대신이 각지방 자치단체장에게 후보추천의뢰
   ㅇ 각지방자치단체장의 추천에 의해 법무대신이 위촉

마) 임기

   ㅇ 3년(재위촉가능)

바) 직무내용

   ㅇ 자유인권사상에 관한 계몽, 선전활동
   ㅇ 민간의 인권옹호 운동의 조장
   ㅇ 인권 침해사건에 대해 조사하여 법무대신 및 관계 기관에
      보고 및 권고
   ㅇ 빈곤자에 대하여 소송원조등 인권옹호를 위한 구제수단 강구
   ㅇ 기타 인권옹호 일반에 관할 활동

마) 신분 및 보수

   ㅇ 각위원은 비상근 국가공무원(법무대신이 지휘감독)
   ㅇ 무보수원칙이나, 교통비등 직무집행을 위한 실비지급 가능

/ 계속 /

0036

바) 구조

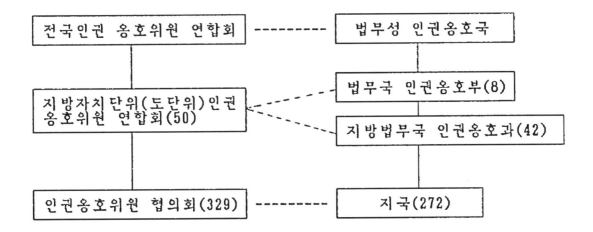

```
┌─────────────────────────┐          ┌──────────────────────┐
│  전국인권 옹호위원 연합회  │---------- │  법무성 인권옹호국      │
└─────────────────────────┘          └──────────────────────┘
            │                                    │
            │                         ┌──────────────────────┐
┌─────────────────────────┐          │  법무국 인권옹호부(8)   │
│ 지방자치단위(도단위)인권   │          └──────────────────────┘
│ 옹호위원 연합회(50)       │          ┌──────────────────────┐
└─────────────────────────┘          │ 지방법무국 인권옹호과(42)│
            │                         └──────────────────────┘
            │                                    │
┌─────────────────────────┐          ┌──────────────────────┐
│  인권옹호위원 협의회(329)  │-------- │      지국(272)         │
└─────────────────────────┘          └──────────────────────┘
```

2. 법무성 인권옹호국

  가) 설치

    ο 1948년
    ο 미국연방 정부 사법성 형사부의 Civil Rights Section(현재는
      Civil Rights Division)을 참고

  나) 소관업무

    ο 인권 침해사건의 조사 및 정보수집에 관한사항
    ο 민간의 인권옹호운동 조장에 관한사항
    ο 인권옹호위원(상기1항 참조)에 관한사항
    ο 빈곤자의 소송원조등 인권옹호에 관한사항

  다) 구성(정원 23명)

    ο 총무과
    ο 조사과(인권침해사건의 조사 및 정보수집)
    ο 인권옹호관리관(자유인권사상의 계몽활동 및 빈곤자의
      소송원조등)   / 계속 /

0037

라) 지방기구

   o 법무국 인권옹호부(동경, 오오사카등 8개 주요도시)
   o 지방법무국 인권옹호과(상기이외 지방도시 42개소)

3. 외무성 국제연합국 인권난민과

   가) 설치

      o 1982년

   나) 소관업무

      o 인권 및 난민 분야의 유엔 활동에 관한사항
      o 인권 및 난민에 관한 다자조약 및 기타 국제 약속의 체결
         준비 및 체결후의 실시에 관한사항
      o 인권 및 난민에 관한 국제회의 참가

   다) 인원수 : 19명

첨부 : 일본의 인권옹호기관 및 법률 부조제도   1부.   끝.
예고 : 92.12.31 일반

주   일   대

0038

원 본

외 무 부

종 별 :

번 호 : CSW-0426   일 시 : 92 0608 1530

수 신 : 장관(연이,미남)

발 신 : 주 칠레 대사

제 목 : 인권보장 관련 기구 조사

　　　대:WCS-0191

　　　대호 주재국 인권보장관련 기구 현황 아래 보고함.

　　　1. 인권보장 기구의 성격, 기능및 주요활동

　　　0 칠레 인권위원회(COMISION CHILENA DE DERECHOS HUMANOS)

　　　-비정부독립 민간기구로 유엔인권 헌장 및 기타 인권관련 국제조약 정신에 따라 칠레에서의 제반 인권(정치적, 민법적, 문화적, 사회적, 경제적 제반 민권)존중, 보호, 증진을 목적으로 78.12. 설립되었는바, 유엔인권위 및 미주인권위등국제인권관련 기구에 대한 칠레 인권상황 자료제공, 인권위반 감시, 인권구조,인권보호, 타국 인권기구와의 연대활동, 인권관련 홍보 및 교육활동을 주요 활동으로함.

　　　-과거 군정시에는 인권구조, 보호활동(진상조사, 사실보도, 변호활동, 국제기구등과 연대하의 대정부 압력행사)을 위주로 활동하였으나 90.3. 민정 이양후에는 형법, 형사소송법등 각종 법규의 민주적 보완, 개선과 여성, 어린이, 원주민(INDIOS), 장애자 인권증진, 소비자보호운동 및 인권관련 교육, 홍보활동에 역점을 두고 있으며 정부(법무장관실, 외무부 인권문제 담당관실)의 자문에도 응하고 있음.

　　　-상. 하원인권위 및 정부의 자문에 수시로 응하고 인권관련 법안에 의견을 제출하는등 입법활동에 기여하고 있음.

　　　0 정의, 평화, 연대위원회(VICARIA DE LA SOLIDARIDAD, SERVICIO DE PAZ Y JUSTICIA)

　　　-비정부 칠레 카토릭교회 소속 인권보호 및 구조를 목적으로 하는 기구이나민정복귀후 활동이 미미해져가고 있음.

국기국　　　미주국

O 대중 인권보호위원회(COMITE DE DEFENSA DE LOS DERECHOS DEL PUEBLO)

-인권침해를 당한 사람에게 사법적 구조를 제공하는 비정부 민간 단체로 민정복귀후 활동 및 중요성이 퇴색되어 가고 있음.

2. 외무부내 인권업무 담당부서 업무 내용

-외무부 차관실 직속 인권문제 담당관실(ASESORIA DE DERECHOS HUMANOS)에서 인권관련 대외정책및 외교적 사안을 취급하고 있음.

3. 기타 정부 부처내 인권업무 전담부서는 없음.

4. 주재국내 가장 중요한 인권기구인 상기 칠레인권위원회 관련자료 파편 송부 하겠음. 끝

(대사 문창화-국장)

예고:92.12.31. 까지

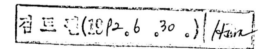

주 영 대 사 관

영국(정) 723- 648   1992. 6. 9.

수신 : 장관

참조 : 국제기구국장(연이)

제목 : 인권보장관련기구

        대 : WUK-0921

        연 : UKW-0945

        연호 하기 주재국 인권보장기구 관련자료를 별첨 송부합니다.

        1. Amnesty International

        2. Minority Rights Group

        3. Education in Human Rights Network

        4. Index

        5. Justice (International Commission of Jurists)

        6. International PEN

        7. Interights

    첨부 : 상기자료. 끝.

                        주   영   대

0041

주 멕 시 코 대 사 관

멕정 700 - 223   1992. 6. 9.

수 신 : 외무부장관

참 조 : 국제기구국장

제 목 : 인권보장관련 국내기구조사

　　　　대 : WMX - 0341

　　　　대호 주재국 인권보장 관련기구 현황자료를 별첨 보고합니다.

첨부 : 　1. 멕시코 인권기관 개요

　　　　2. 멕시코국가 인권위자료 (규정, 활동 관계보고서, 기타 인권보호를

　　　　　　위한 각종 홍보전단 견본)

　　　　3. 기타 정당 (야당-PRD당) 인권위 보고.　　끝.

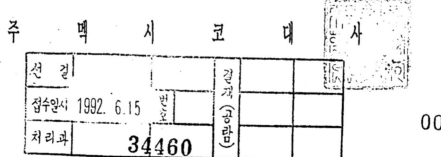

0042

멕시코 인권기관 개요

1. 멕시코국가 인권위 (정부기구)

국가인권위

내무성 산하 외청(독립기관)으로 멕시코헌법 및 멕시코가 승인 비준한 국제법규가 보장하는 인권옹호 규정의 준수 여부를 감시하는 책임기관으로 사회기관이며 사회를 보호하는 역활

권능

o 공공기관의 개인 또는 단체에 대한 범죄행위 악행, (부정행위) 처벌등 행정법상의 위반

o 면책특권이 있는 사법경찰이 범한 범죄, 소송상의 악행 및 행정법 위반행위 (부정행위)

개입권능의 한계 (개입 불가능 분야)

o 사법상의 문제

o 노동쟁의등 사법상의 문제 (단, 행정당국과 관련있는 경우 개입가능)

o 선거등 사법적문제 (단, 헌법상 보장된 개인인권 침해경우 개입가능)

인권위의 역활

o 인권수호정책 입안, 제의기능

o 국내외 관련 기관과의 협력

o 국제문제에 있어 외무성과의 협력

o 관련조약, 협정체결 수행을 위한 계획수립 및 조치제의

인사

o 위원장은 대통령이 임명

o 관련업무 지휘, 감독

o 인권위기능 및 업무관련 사항 대통령에 보고 (매 6개월)

0043

<u>위원임명</u>

o 명예직 10명 (위원은 대통령이 임명)

o 사무총장 (위원장 임명)

o 위원임기 3년 (재임명 가능)

<u>인권보호 대상</u>

o 내국인 (해외거주 포함)

o 국내거주 외국인

<u>인권위 기구</u>

o 총무국 (행정관리)

o 통신문서국

o 홍보훈련국

o 국제국

o 지도, 이의신청, 처리국

o 소송, 심판, 의결국

2. 각정당 인권위 (독자기관)

예) PRD (민주혁명당)당 인권위

: 정부 (여당)산하 국가인권위 기능에 불만, 인권실태 보고서 발행등

별도활동

0044

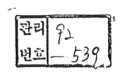

駐 칠 레 大 使 館

칠레(정) 20700-39   1992. 6. 12.

수 신 : 장 관

참 조 : 국제기구국장, 미주국장

제 목 : 인권보장기구 조사

　　　　　대 : WCS - 0191

　　　　　연 : CSW - 0426

　　1. 연호, 칠레 인권위원회(Chilean Human Rights Commission)소개자료 및
동 위원회 발간자료를 별첨 송부합니다.

　　2. 주재국 인권상황 관련, 90. 3 민정이양후 주재국 정부는 국민적 화해,
통합을 이루기 위해 1973-90년간 군정하의 인권위반 사례를 조사할 목적으로 90. 5.9
"진실·화해 위원회(Truth & Reconciliation National Commission)"를 91. 2.28.
까지의 한시적 기구로 설치, 보고서를 제출케 하였는바, 칠레 인권위원회는 외무성의
후원하에 대국민 인권홍보를 위해 92. 5. 상기 진실, 화해 위원회의 보고서를 요약,
발간하였기 별첨 송부하니 참고 바랍니다.

　　3. 한편 주재국 정부는 상기 진실·화해위원회의 건의에 따라 과거 군정시
인권피해자에 대한 치유, 위무, 보상을 위한 공공기관으로"보상·화해공사(National
Corporation for Reparation & Reconciliation)"을 92. 1. 31자로 설립하였는바,
동 "보상 및 화해공사"법을 별첨 송부하니 참고바랍니다.

첨 부 : 1. 칠레 인권위원회 소개 팜프렛 1부.

　　　　　2. 동 위원회발간 인권보고서등 자료 5부.

　　　　　3. 진실·화해위원회 보고서 요약 보고서 2부.

　　　　　4. 보상 및 화해 공사법 2부.
　　　　　(이상 첨부물 국제기구국으로 송부). 끝.

예 고 : 1992. 12. 31. 까지

駐　　칠　　레　　大　　使

검토필(1992. 6. 30.)

0045

관리
번호 **-548**

외 무 부

종 별 :

번 호 : HGW-0412   일 시 : 92 0619 1500

수 신 : 장관(연이,동구이)

발 신 : 주 헝가리 대사

제 목 : 인권보장 관련 국제기구 조사

대: WHG-0264

표제건 다음 보고함.

1. 인권보장기구

가. 국회의 인권, 소수민족 및 종교위원회(현재 27 명의 국회의원으로 구성)

0 국회 상임위원회의 하나로서, 인권관련 주요문제 발생시 국회에서 결의를채택하거나, 인권관련 입법활동을 적극적으로 추진

나. 헝가리 인권센타

0 과학원산하의 비정부기구의 성격으로, 국제인권관련 의무와 국내법과의 조화문제를 연구하고 국제회의를 개최하거나 참가하는 동시에, 인권관련 잡지를 발간

2. 외무부내의 인권 업무

가. 담당부서: 국제기구국 인권과(HUMAN RIGHT DESK, 직원 3 명)

나. 업무내용: 유엔총회와 경제사회이사회, 제네바소재의 인권과 소수민족 보호위원회 활동과 관련, 인권관련 STATEMENT, DRAFT RESOLUTION 등에 관하여 훈령하거나, 개별국가의 인권문제(특히 미얀마, 이란, 이락, 루마니아, 엘살바돌, 아프카니스탄)에 관한 업무를 담당

3. 기타 정부부처내 인권업무를 전적으로 다루는 부서는 없음. 끝

(대사 박영우-국장)

92.12.31. 까지

검 토 필(19 92. 6 . 30 .)

─────────────────────────

국기국   구주국   분석관

주 노 르 웨 이 대 사 관

Inkognitogaten 3, 0244 Oslo 2   / 55 20 18   / FAX. 56 14 11

문서번호 노 (정) 760-182
시행일자 1992. 6. 23.

수신 장 관
참조 국제기구국장

선결			지시	
접수	일자시간	92.6.26	결제	
	번호	2402	공람	
처리과				
담당자				

제목 인권보장 관련 국내기구 조사

대 : WNR - 0145

대호, 노르웨이의 인권보장 관련기구 현황 관련, 주재국의 인권 보장은 사법제도에 의하여 보호되고 있으며 주재국내 인권문제는 별로 없으므로 인권보호를 위한 특별한 기구는 없으며, 주재국은 인권의 국제적 보호에 커다란 관심을 갖고 있는 바, 주재국 인권 관련기구를 아래와 같이 보고합니다.

- 아   래 -

1. 노르웨이 인권연구소 (Norwegian Institute of Human Rights)

   가. 설립목적

      o 국제적으로 인정된 인권의 실현에 기여

      o 인권에 관한 연구 및 교육

      o 각국의 인권연구기관과 협력

계속....

0047

나. 연구분야

　　o 국제적 인권제도 및 각국의 인권 연구

　　o 유럽의 인권, 특히 동구, 구소련의 인권 문제

　　o 개발도상국의 인권 및 남북관계에 있어서 인권 문제

　　o 국제적 인권과 각 문화 및 규범에 따른 갈등

다. 조직

　　o 직원 : 약 20여명

　　o Board of Directors : The Norwegian Research Council for Science and
　　　　the Humanities, 오슬로대학, 민간 인권 관련기구 및 외무부 대표로 구성

라. 설립연도, 성격 및 재정

　　o 1987년에 설립, 정부재정지원의 독립 민간단체

　　o 동기구는 년간 교육부에서 약 4백만 크로나 (미불 62.5만 상당), 외무부
　　　에서 약 100만 코로나 (미불 15.6만 상당)지원을 받음.

마. 간행물

　　o Nordic Journal on Human Rights (노르웨이어, 계간)

2. 평화문제 연구소 (약칭 : PRIO)

　가. 설립목적 및 기능

　　o 국가단체간 평화 분쟁 문제에 대한 학술 연구

　　o 국가 및 국제간 연구 협력 조장, 교육 및 수련담당, 학술세미나 및 회의
　　　개최, 각종연구 보고서 작성 배포

　나. 연구분야

　　o 군비, 군축, 군사정책, 평화와 전쟁에 관한 문제

　　o 인권

　　o 국가 및 국제발전과 사회 분쟁 문제등

　다. 조직

　　o 직원 (연구원 포함) : 35명 (상임 연구원은 5명, 비상임 연구원은 4명)

　　o 인권문제는 상임 연구원이 AsBjorn Eide가 담당

계속....

라. 설립년도 및 성격 : 1959년 사회과학원의 일부로서 설립된 정부 재정지원의
　　 민간단체였으나 1966년 독립 연구기관이 됨.

마. 간행물

　　 o Journal of Peace Research (계간)

　　 o Bulletin of Peace Problems(계간)

　　 o PRIO report : 프로젝트논문, 논문보고

　　 o PRIO Inform : 평화연구보고

3. 정부기관

가. 법무부

　　 - 법무부내 인권침해에 대한 사법제도를 Division of Legistration Affairs
　　　 에서 담당

나. 외무부

　　 o Department of Political Affairs에 인권관계 Special adviser를 두어
　　　 국제인권문제를 담당

　　 o Department of Legal Affairs의 제 1법무과에서 인권관련 국제법을 담당

첨부 : Norwegian Institute of Human Rights보고서 1부. 끝.

검 토 필(1992. 6. 30.) 사인

주 노 르 웨 이 대 사

0049

<table>
<tr><td>관리
번호</td><td>ρ
-570</td></tr>
</table>

외 무 부

종 별 :

번 호 : RFW-2547

일 시 : 92 0624 1910

수 신 : 장 관(연이,동구일)

발 신 : 주 러 대사

제 목 : 인권보장관련 기구조사

대:WRF-1548

표제관련 박노벽 서기관이 주재국 외무성등 관계기관과 접촉 파악한 바를 아래 보고함.

1. 주재국의 인권정책

가. 주재국은 인권보장및 존중을 새로운 주요정책 목표로 세워 과거 소련체제 하에서 와는 달리 인권이 국제적 수준에서 보장될 수 있도록 노력하고 있음. 이러한 인권정책 방침은 북한유학생(김명세)의 망명 사건에서 명백히 보여준 바 있음.

또한 러시아정부와 최고회의는 51 년 난민협약및 동의정서 가입문제를 검토하고 있으며 소련체제하에 억압된 소수민족의 명예회복을 위한 방안도 강구중에 있음.

나. 한편 소련해체 이후 러시아외의 CIS 에 거주하고 있는 러시아인의 인권보호 문제도 새로운 과제로 등장하고 있는바 CIS 구성국간 긴밀한 협의를 통한 해결을 도모하고 있음.

다. 다만 현 주재국의 경제사정이 어렵기 때문에 동인권보장은 재정적 부담문제를 염두에 두고 신중히 처리하고 있음.

2. 인권담당 부서및 단체

가. 인권문제는 사안에따라 외무성내 인권 문화국및 해당지역국, 내무성및 법무성등 관계부서에서 해당 분야별로 검토하며 대통령실 산하에 신설된 공민권 위원회가 필요시 중요결정을 내리게 됨.

나. 최고회의(입법부)내에도 인권위원회가 설치되어 인권관련 입법조치 및 정책 심의를하고 있음.

다. 또한 헬싱키 그룹, 난민권 보고위원회등 민간차원의 인권단체도 활동하고 있음. 끝

국기국   구주국

92.06.25   02:38

외신 2과 통제관 BZ

0050

(대사홍순영-국장)
92.12.31 까지

검 트 필(1992. 6. 30 .) Haim

PAGE 2

0051

각국의 인권보장기구 현황 조사, 1992   257

외 무 부

종 별 :

번 호 : FRW-1349

일 시 : 92 0630 1130

수 신 : 장관(연이,구일)

발 신 : 주 불 대사

제 목 : 인권보장 관련 기구

대:WFR-1082

NICOLAS METTRA 외무성 인권 부국장이 언급한 주재국 인권보장 관련기구 현황 아래 보고함.

1. 성격 및 주요 활동

0 대부분이 정부 기구로서, 법무성을 중심으로 인권 보장 업무를 관장하고 있으며, 각종 인권 문제 발생시 의견 제시를 위주로하는 민간 차원의 인권 협의 위원회 (CNCDH: COMMISSION NATIONALE CONSULTATIVE DES DROITS DE L'HOMME)가 있음 (70 명으로 구성)

0 정부기구는 인권 문제 발생시, MEMOIRE 작성, 변호인 선임을 비롯, 유엔 인권문제 보고서 작성등을 전담하고 있음.

0 인권관계 입법활동에는 전적으로 법무성에서 참여 하고 있으며, 국제협약의 경우에는 외무성도 일부 관여함.

2. 외무부내 인권 업무 담당부서

0 GEORGES KIEJMAN 외교문제 담당장관(MINISTRE DELEGUE)에게 외무부내 인권 업무를 총괄 지휘하는 임무 부여(보좌관 2 명)

0 유엔국

- 유엔국 산하에 인권부국을 두어 (부국장 및 직원 2 명) 유엔 및 EC 차원의 인권 문제 전담.

0 정무국

- 정무국내에 CSCE 전담반 설치 (직원 4 명), CSCE 제 3BASKET 범주내에서의 인권 문제 담당

0 법무국

국기국   구주국

- 법무국 산하에 <u>인권부국</u>을 두어 (부국장 및 직원 3 명) 국제협약등 법적 측면의 업무와 함께 BOUR EUROPEEN DE JUSTICE DE STRASBOURG 관련 업무 관장

3. 기타 인권 업무 담당부서

0 <u>법무성</u> 산하에 인권실(BUREAU DES DROITS DE L'HOMME) 을 설치, 인권 문제를 담당하고 있으며, 인권 문제에 관한 최종적인 보장기관(GARANT) 은 법무성이 됨.

0 <u>수상 비서실</u>

수상 비서실내에 인권 문제 담당 보좌관 1 명 배치, 국내외 인권 문제관장

0 <u>내무성</u>

내무성 산하에 인권국(DERECTION DE LA LIBERTE PUBLIQUE)을 설치, 주로 국내 인권문제 담당

4. 상기 1 항 관련 <u>CNCDH 발행 91 년도 활동 보고서</u> 파편 송부함. 끝

(대사 노영찬- 국장)

예고: 92.12.31 까지

검 토 필(19△. 7. 10.)

주 아 르 헨 티 나 대 사 관

Av. Libertador 2257 (1425) Cap.Fed. Bs. As. Argentina 전화 (802-6897,9665,8865)

문서번호 주아르헨(정) 20400 - 3/3

시행일자 1992. 7. 6. (   )

(경유)

수신 장관

참조 국제기구국장

선결			지시		
접수	일자시간		결재·공람		
	번호	**40050**			
	처리과				
	담당자				

제목 인권보장관련 국내기구조사

　　　대 : WAR - 0327

　　　대호 주재국의 인권보장관련 기구현황을 별첨 보고합니다.

　　첨부 : 아르헨티나 인권보장관련 기구현황.　끝.

주 아 르 헨 티 나 대

0054

아르헨티나 인권보장관련 기구현황

1. 인권보장만을 위한 독립기구 : 없음.

2. 정부내 부서

   가. 외무부 인권 및 여성국 (아국의 차관보 해당)

   1) 명   칭 : DIRECCION GENERAL DE DERECHOS HUMANOS Y DE LA MUJER

   2) 조직구조 : DIRECCION GENERAL 에는 DIRECCION DE DERECHOS HUMANOS 와
                여성국이 있음.

   3) 기   능 : - UN 및 OAS 인권위원회등과의 협력, 협조요청사항등 업무

                  - 인권관련 각국정부, 각국대사관과의 관련업무

                  - 여타 인권관련 국제기구와의 협조 협력문제

                  - 내무부 인권국과 협조 법령입안등을 하고있으나 입법활동에
                    특별간여등 특기사항은 없음.

                  ※ 동국업무중 90%정도가 UN 및 OAS 인권위원회와 관계되는
                    업무라고함. (인권국장 언급)

   나. 내무부 인권국

   1) 명   칭 : DIRECCION NACIONAL DE DERECHOS HUMANOS, MINISTERIO DE
                INTERIOR

   2) 조직구조 : 1개국으로 되어있음.

   3) 기   능 : - 인권문제관련 내국인, 내국기관등과의 관련업무

                  - 내국인으로부터 인권관련 항의 소원등 민원등에 대한처리

                  - 기타 인권관련 국내관련사항 일체

0055

다. 브에노스 아이레스 주정부 인권국

    1) 명   칭 : DIRECCION DE DERECHO HUMANO

    2) 조직구조 : 브에노스 아이레스주 법무차관보 산하 기구로 되어있음.

    3) 기   능 : BUENOS AIRES 주내 인권관련 모든 문제

라. 상기 기구와는 별도로 인디안의 인권을 담당하는 기구로서 NUEVO DERCHOS
    DEL HOMBRE 가 있으며, 동 기구는 인디안 인권보호문제를 담당하는 기구로서
    통상 인권담당기구와는 다름.

마. 참   조 : 국회 (상.하원)에는 인권위원등 별도의 인권담당위원회나 부서가
           없음.

3. 민간기구 : 3개의 기구가 있으며, 각각 인권관련 활동을 하고있음.

   - ASAMBLEA PERMANENTE POR LOS DERECHOS HUMANOS

   - MADRES DE PLAZA DE MAYO

   - ABUELAS DE PLAZA DE MAYO

4. 아르헨티나 주재국 국제기구

   - SERVICIO DE PAZ Y JUSTICIA PARA AMERICA LATINA

   - MOVIMIENTO ECUMENICO POR LOS DERECHOS HUMANOS

   - CENTRO DE ESTUDIOS LEGALES Y SOCIALES

0056

"소득은 정당하게, 소비는 알뜰하게"

주 화 란 대 사 관

화란(정)20352 - *113*   1992. 7. 9.

수신 : 장관

참조 : 국제기구국장

제목 : 인권보장 관련기구

　　　　대 : WHO - 0116

　　　주재국 민간 및 정부 인권보장 관련기구 자료를 별첨 송부합니다.

첨부 : 상기자료 1부. 끝.

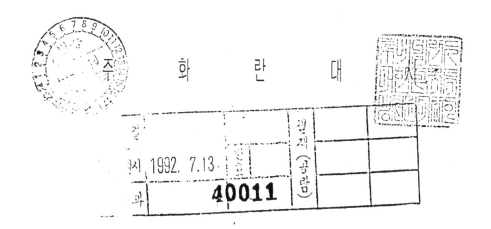

0057

HUMAN RIGHTS ORGANISATIONS IN THE NETHERLANDS.

NON-GOVERNMENTAL

Amnesty International

address: Keizersgracht 620, 1017 ER Amsterdam.
telephone: 020-6264436
telefax: 020-6240889

Purpose:Observance of the conditions of the Universal Declaration of the Rights of Man.

Publication: "Wordt Vervolgd" (Means literally "will be followed up")

General Information: Activities:
-working for the release of persons in prison because of their political or religious convictions;
-working for a fair trial within a reasonable length of time for all political prisoners;
-opposing the death penalty, torture and other cruel, inhuman and degrading forms of treatment of prisoners. The organisation is not affiliated to any regime, political party or ideology; its working territory encompasses the whole world.

Anti-Diskriminatie Overleg (ADO)

address: Drieharingstraat 35, Postbus 596, 3500 AN   Utrecht.
telephone: 030-341264
Management: Drs. H.Th.Wentholt : L.H. Sandberg.
Director: C. Serkei
Purpose: The avoidance, recognition and struggle against race discrimination.
General Information: the ADO is an organisation which cooperates with a number of national social organisations. ADO developes projects and conducts investigation in the area of mentality influence and conciousness regarding racism. Priority areas are media, education and discrimination on the work floor.

Azania Komittee

address: Postbus 5607, 3008 AP Rotterdam.
telephone: 010-4193494
Management: M. Boelsma: R. Grijzen

0058

Purpose: Support for the freedom struggle of the black majority in South Africa (Azania).

Commissie Justitia et Pax - Nederland
(Justice & Peace Commission, Netherlands)

address: Rhijngeesterstraatweg 40, Postbus 1031, 2340 BA Oegstgeest.
telephone: 071-175901
telefax: 071-175391
Management: Dr. H. van Munster : Drs. V.M. Scheffers
Purpose: Conciousness-raising within the Roman Catholic community with regard to peace
and justice, in particular, human rights.
Publication organ: Bulletin

Humanistisch Overleg Mensenrechten (HOM).

address: Oudkerkhof 11, Postbus 114, 3500 AC Utrecht.
tel: 030 318145
Management: A. Eikenaar: P.van Veenen
Purpose: Promoting an initiating an active human rights policy, political-citizen as well as
social-economic.
Publications: HOM Nieuwsbrief
General Information: HOM wants to increase public concern for human rights via
information provision and the organisation of meetings. HOM exercises pressure against
violation of human rights.

Johannes Wier Stichting(JWS).
Organisation for human rights and health care

address: Postbus 17425, 2502 CK The Hague.
tel: (070) 3554582
fax: (070) 3554530
Management: A.van Es. Mrs.N. Gevers Leuven-Lachinsky.
Directorate: Mrs. H.G. van der Graaf-Roossink.
Purpose: Through (writing)actions, missions, research and publications to:
            oppose medical involvement in human rights violations, torture,
            life sentence and death penalty:
            solidarity with colleagues who come into difficulties through supporting
            human rights:
            research, education and publications over specific subjects which are relevant

0059

to the protection of human rights.

Committee Zuidelijk Afrika (KZA)
Southern Africa Committee)

address: O.Z. Achterburgwal 173, Postbus 16879,1001 RJ Amsterdam.
telephone: 020 6270801
fax: 020 6270441
Purpose: To provide information about and support to the freedom struggle in Southern
Africa.
Publications: Amandla: Weerwerk: Facts and Reports
General Information: The KZA was set up as an action committee to focus attention on the
decolonisation struggle in Angola and has developed into a solidarity organisation for the
whole of southern Africa. Via actions and demonstrations, help to weaken the apartheid
regime and support the freedom movement.

Landelijk Bureau Racismebestrijding (LBR)
(National Office Against Racism)

address: Postbus 517, 3500 AM Utrecht.
telephone: 030 331421
Management: Mrs. L.Y. Gonçalves-Ho Kang You.
Purpose: Preventing and resisting race discrimination by judicial means.

Liga voor de Rechten van de Mens.
(Human Rights League).

address: Da Costastraat 71-bel.1053 ZG Amsterdam.
telephone: 020 6120974
Purpose: To circulate propaganda in the Netherlands for all human rights recognised by the
United Nations: preventing and resisting violations and disregard of human rights.
Publication: Nieuwsbrief
General Information: There are Leagues with the same purpose in 45 other countries.
Together they form the FIDH, Féderation Internationale des Droits de l'Homme
(International Federation for the Rights of Man).

0060

Stichting Anti-Apartheids Beweging Nederland (AABN).
(Anti-Apartheid Movement Netherlands.)

address: Lauriergracht 116, Postbus 10500, 1001 EM Amsterdam
telephone: 020 6267525
fax: 020 6237335
Management: Conny Braam. Fons Geerlings.
Director: Peter Hermes
Purpose: Organisation and solidarity with the anti-apartheid struggle in South Africa:
lending concrete political and material support to the anti-apartheid movement African
National Congress (ANC).
Publication: De Anti-Apartheid Krant (anti-apartheid newspaper).

Stichting Bestrijding Antisemitisme (STIBA).
(Anti-Semitism Foundation).

address: Postbus 2009, 3000 CA Rotterdam.
no telephone number stated
Management: Richard A. Stein: Nathan H. Wijnperle.
Publication: Overzicht van Aktiviteiten (Overview of Activities)
General Information: The foundation is active in the area of jurisprudence and law
application and of education and welfare aspects. Many readings and lectures are given at
home and abroad and anti-semitic occurences and abuses reported to the media. The
foundation strives for a better understanding of Judaism and an improved understanding
between Jew and non-Jew.

Stichting Comité Vladimir Boekovski.
(Vladimir Boekovski Committee).

address: Rosmarijnsteeg 10, Postbus 3754, 1001 AN Amsterdam.
telephone: 020 6279491
fax: 020 6208116
Management: J. Bax
Purpose: the promotion and confirmation of the Universal Declaration of the Rights of Man
in the (former) Soviet Union and Eastern Europe.

0061

Studie en Informatiecentrum Mensenrechten (SIM)
(Human Rights Study and Information Centre).

address: Janskerkhof 16, 3512 BM Utrecht.
telephone: 030 394033
fax: 030 393028
Management: Professor Mr. P. van Dijk: Professor Mr. G.J.H. van Hoof.
Director: Professor Dr. P.R. Bachr.
Purpose: The promoting and carrying out of studies and the collecting and spreading of
            information, national as well as international, about the promotion and
            protection of human rights.
Publication: Netherlands Quarterly of Human Rights.
General Information: The SIM has a documentation centre accessible to the public, with
around 10.000 documents in English. Summaries of these documents are to be found in a
databank and available via a "free text" system.

Werkgroep Betaald Antwoord.
(Paid Answer Workgroup)

address: Postbus 180, 3970 AD Driebergen.
telephone: 085 818264/03405-67387
Purpose: Support of the World Council of Churches programme against racism.
Publication: Bericht (Report).

Werkgroep Kairos
(Kairos Work Group).

address: Kromme Nieuwegracht 10, 3512 HG Utrecht.
telephone: 030 319714
fax: 030 316518
Purpose: Spreading of information over developments in Southern Africa, especially in an
ecumenical area, and the carrying out of actions opposing apartheid politics.

Young Women's Christian Association (YWCA)
Section Netherlands

address: F.C. Dondersstraat 23, 3572 JB Utrecht.
telephone: 030 715525

0062

Management: Mrs. A.E. Zanen-van Eeghen.

Purpose: From an ecumenical standpoint/community the YWCA Nederland works nationally and internationally in connection with the Rights of Man declaration, in which improvement of the position of women has a central theme.

Publication: Contour

Nederlands Juristen Comité voor de Mensenrechten (NJCM).
(Netherlands Jurists Committee for Human Rights).
Netherlands Section of the International Commission of Jurists in Geneva.

address: Hugo de Grootstraat 27, 2311 XK Leiden.
telephone: 071 277748
fax: 071 277600
Management: Drs. R.A. Lawson
Purpose: Lobbying for observance of the fundamental rights of man.
Publication: NJCM Bulletin
General Information: Activities include: giving advice of a judicial nature, addressing and taking up scientific investigation and giving policy information in the area of human rights. Membership is open to lawyers, law students and any other interested parties.

Association Internationale Défence des Artistes (AIDA)
(International Association for the Defence of Artists)
Section Nederland.

address: Van Ostadestraat 49a, 1072 SN Amsterdam.
telephone: 020 6713786
fax: 020 6732306
Purpose: Supporting colleagues who, because of their work, are censored, banned, tortured, detained, "disappeared" or otherwise suppressed. AIDA works with volunteers, such as artists and others.
Publication: AIDA Nederland
General Information: The organisation out cultural events, exhibitions and publications of censored work and investigates the position of suppressed artists, for which it attempts to gain attention from the media, the public and governments.

GOVERNMENTAL

Nationale Ombudsman.

address: Stadhoudersplantsoen 2, (Postbus 29729, 2502 LS) The Hague.
telephone: (070) 3563563
fax: (070) 3607572
Budget for 1992: ƒ6.272.000
Personnel strength: 63
Purpose: Investigation of (usually on request) alleged abuses or violations by police, judicial bodies and civil servants. Complaint must first be made to the person or organisation concerned, so that they have a chance to reply. After the investigation a report with the results of the investigation and any punishment imposed, is made public. Is supposed to protect citizens interests.
National Ombudsman: Mr.Drs. M. Oosting
Substitute Ombudsman: Mr. N.A.M. Schipper
Secretary: Mrs. G. Zuidema

Ministry of Social Affairs & Work Opportunity.
Emancipation Policy Directorate.

address: Anna van Hannoverstraat 4 (Postbus 90801, 2509 LV) The Hague.
telephone: 070 3334444
fax: 070 3334033
Purpose: to promote the integration of (women's) emancipation policies. Creating possibilities for the support and stimulation of the emancipation process.

Ministry of Welfare, Culture & Public Health.
Refugees, Minorities & Asylum Seekers Directorate.

address: Sir Winston Churchillaan 362/366 (Bogaard Centre) (Postbus 5406, 2280 HK) Rijswijk.
telephone: 070 340 79
Purpose: to promote mutual acceptance between the indigenous population and ethnic groups, refugees and asylum seekers. Preventing discrimination and trying to obtain equal rights and opportunities for minorities.
Director: Drs. L. Elting

0064

발 신 전 보

WUS-3329   920716 1828 FN

번　　호 : _____　　　　종별 :

WCN -0758	WFR -1491
WGE -0994	WNR -0203
WSD -0422	WAU -0613
WJA -3133	WPH -0719
WMX -0498	WCZ -0385

수　　신 : 주　수신처 참조　　대사. 총영사

발　　신 : 장　관　　(연이)

제　　목 : 인권보장 관련기구

　　　　표제에 관한 기보고 사항에 추가하여 귀주재국 의회내 설치된 인권관련

기구의 성격, 주요활동 등에 대해 조사, 보고바람. 끝.

(국제기구국장　김재섭)

·　수신처　:　주미, 주캐나다, 주불, 주독, 주노르웨이, 주스웨덴, 주호주,

　　　　주일, 주필리핀, 주멕시코, 주칠레 대사

보안 통제	

앙고재	92년 2월 16일	42 과	기안자 성명 이		과장	심의관	국장 전		차관	장관		외신과통제

0065

	분류번호	보존기간

발 신 전 보

번 호 : WCZ-0384   920716 1827 FY   종별 : _____

수 신 : 주   체코   대사. 총영사 ♣♣♣♣

발 신 : 장 관   (연이)

제 목 : 인권보장 관련기구

연 : WCZ-0304

연호 보고시 귀주재국 의회내 설치된 인권관련 기구 관련사항도

포함바람. 끝.

(국제기구국장   김재섭)

	보 안	
	통 제	

앙고재	92년 7월 16일	4L2과	기안자 성명 이	과 장	심의관 전결	국 장	차 관	장 관	외신과통제

0066

발 신 전 보

번 호 : WAV-1111   920716 1828 FY   종별 :

수 신 : 주   오지리   대사. 총영사

발 신 : 장 관   (연이)

제 목 : 인권보장 관련기구

연 : WAV-0806

연호 보고시 귀주재국 의회내 설치된 인권관련 기구 관련사항도

포함바람. 끝.

(국제기구국장   김재섭)

보안통제

앙고재	92년 7월 16일	4∼2과	기안자 성명	과 장	심의관	국 장	차 관	장 관
			이					

외신과통제

관리 번호	92- 678

외 무 부

종 별 :

번 호 : GEW-1433

일 시 : 92 0720 1030

수 신 : 장관(연이)

발 신 : 주 독 대사

제 목 : 인권보장관련기구

대: WGE-0994

연: GEW-1088

대호 권세영 서기관이 7.16. 주재국 하원 외무위 SCHWUEPPE 전문위원을 접촉, 표제관련 문의한 바를 아래 보고함

가. 주재국 하원내에 인권관련 업무를 위해 설치된 별도의 기구는 없으며, 다만 인권관련 업무는 하원내 23 개 상임위원회중 군축 및 군비통제 업무, 대유엔 업무, 인권관련 업무, 대외문화정책등 4 가지 업무를 담당하고 있는 외무위원회의 소관사항임.

나. 외무위원회는 상기 4 가지 업무분야중 인권관련 업무 및 이와 관련된 대개도국 인도적 지원문제등을 예하 소위원회 (UNTERAUSSCHUSS)에 광범위하게 위임하고 있음.

다. 동 소위원회는 독일내 인권침해 사례는 최근 거의 문제시되고 있지 않으므로 주로 외국의 인권침해 사례등 현실적인 문제를 취급하고 있음. 예를들어 금년 하계휴가가 종료되면 동 소위원회는 페루의 인권상항에 관한 청문회를 개최하며, 동 청문회에는 유엔의 인권문제전문가, 독일및 페루의 인권문제 전문가등이 참가한다 함. 주재국 의회는 동 청문회 준비를 위해 인권상황 옵저버를 금년 6월 페류에 파견한바 있음.

동 청문회 결과는 외무위 이름으로 보고서로서 발표될 예정임.

라. 상기 소위원회는 외국의 인권침해 사례 취급외에도 유엔, 구주의회, EC및 주재국 내에서 인권관계 입법을 위해 활동을 하고 있음. 끝

(대사-국장)

예고:92.12.31. 까지

국기국	장관	차관	1차보	구주국	외정실	분석관	청와대	안기부

92.07.20   19:03

외신 2과   통제관 EC

0068

관리
번호 02
-6??

원 본

외 무 부

종 별 :

번 호 : USW-3611

수 신 : 장 관 (연이, 미일)

발 신 : 주 미 대사

제 목 : 인권보장 관련 기구

일 시 : 92 0720 1913

　　　대 : WUS-3329

　　주재국 의회내 설치된 인권전담기구로는 하원 외무위원회의 인권 및 국제기구 소위원회와 하원의 입법 보조기구인 인권 CAUCUS (CONTRESSIONAL HUMAN RIGHTS CAUCUS) 및 HELSINKI 조약에 따른 인권보장을 감독하는 유럽의 안보와 협력에 관한 위원회 (COMMISSION ON SECURITY AND COOPERATION IT EUROPE : 일명 HELSINKI 위원회)가 있는 바 관련사항은 아래와 같음.

　　1. 하원 외무위 인권 및 국제기구 소위

　　가. 구성 : 위원장 GUS YATRON 의원 (민-펜실베니아)의 9 명의 의원 (현재 1명 공석으로 총 9 명)

　　나. 관장업무 : 하기사항과 관련한 입법 및 감독

　　(1) UN 및 산하기구, 여타 국제기구

　　(2) 국제법, 세계인권선언의 이행 및 여타 인권관련 문제

　　(3) 작십자 국제위원회

　　(4) 국제 환경정책

　　(5) 국제 어업협약 감독

　　2. 인권 CAUCUS

　　가. 연혁 : 1983 년 기본인권 보장에 관심이 있는 하원의원들이 구성한 입법 보조기구

　　나. 구성 : 200 여명의 공화. 민주 하원의원으로 구성

　　- 공동의장 : TOM LANTOS (민-캘리포니아)

　　JOHN EDWARD PORTER (공-일리노이) 의원

　　- 집행위원회 : FOLEY 하원의장, FASCELL 외무위원장등 50 여명의 의원으로 구성

국기국	장관	차관	미주국	정와대	안기부	법무부

1 차번

PAGE 1

다. 담당업무

- 하원외무위 인권 및 국제기구 소위, 유럽의 안보및 협력에 관한 위원회 및 비정부 인권단체와의 유기적 접촉을 통하여 소속 의원에게 인권 활동에 대한 최신 정보 제공

- 인권박해의 피해자 및 이와 관련한 의회 활동에 대한 컴퓨터화된 최신정보와 의회내 인권 입법목록, 의원이 공동서명한 인권서한 목록 유지

- 인권관련 청문회, 브리피, 기자회견등 개최

3. 유럽의 안보와 협력에 관한 위원회

가. 연혁 : HELSINKI 조약상 인권규정 이행상태등을 검토하기 위하여 1976 년 입법에 따라 설립

나. 구성 : 18 명의 상. 하의원 및 3 명의 행정부 대표

- 위원장 : STENY H. HOYER 하원의원 (민-메릴랜드)

- 공동위원장 : DENNIS DECONCINI 상원의원 (민-아리조나)

다. 담당업무

- 1975 년 HELSINKI 조약상 인권규정등의 이행상태 감독 및 규정의 준수 독려

- 동서간 경제. 문화협력 증진을 위한 미국의 정부및 민간 프로그램 촉진 및 감독.끝.

(대사 현홍주-국장)

예고 : 92.12.31. 까지

PAGE 2

외 무 부

종 별 :

번 호 : SDW-0667

일 시 : 92 0722 1040

수 신 : 장관(연이)

발 신 : 주 스웨덴 대사

제 목 : 인권보장 관련기구

연:SDW-0528

대:WSD-0422

주재국 의회내 인권업무를 담당하는 별도의 기구는 없으나, 의회는 4 명의 OMBUDSMAN 을 임명, 인권침해 여부등을 포함, 국민의 권리보호 활동을 하고있음.끝

(대사 최동진-국장)

예고:92.12.31 까지

국기국   구주국

외 무 부

관리 번호	92 -682

종 별 :

번 호 : CZW-0684

일 시 : 92 0722 1800

수 신 : 장관(연이, 동구이)

발 신 : 주 체코대사

제 목 : 인권보장관련기구

대:WCZ-0385

1. 주재국의 경우 유엔헌장 및 CSCE 체제하 인권문제에 대처해 왔으나, 공산정권하에서는 한계가 있었음. 89.11. 공산정권 붕괴 및 특히 91.2. 구주이사회 가입계기, 회원국에게 부과되는 각종 국제적 인권조약에 가입하고 이를 시행해 오고 있음.

2. 의회내 기구는 다음과 같음.

가. 연방의회: 지금까지는 특별한 기구나 활동 없었으며, 지난 6 월 총선에 따라 구성된 의회는 "인권보호위원회(HUMAN RIGHTS PROTECTION COMMITTEE)" 신설 방침임. 다만, 현금 주재국의 연방분리 움직임에 비추어 실현성 여부는 미지수임.

나. 공화국 의회

1)체크공화국 의회: "청원.인권.소수민족 위원회(COMMITTEE FOR PETITION, HUMAN RIGHTS AND MINORITIES)"를 통한 입법 및 행정부 감시기능 수행

2)슬로바키아 공화국 의회: "청원. 법적보호 및 안전 위원회(COMMITTEE FORPETITION , LEGAL PROTECTION AND SECURITY)"를 통한 입법 및 행정부 감시기능수행

3. 주재국의 경우, 기본권에 관련된 사안에 대해서는 개인이 헌법재판소에 제소할 수 있는 바, 헌법재판소 판사[5H수 있는 바, 헌법재판소 판사는 의회가 추천하는 인사중에서 대통령이 임명토록 되어 있음. 끝.

(대사 선준영- 국장)

예고: 92.12.31 일반

국기국   차관   2차보   구주국   분석관

외 무 부

종 별 :

번 호 : CNW-0843　　　　　　　　　　일 시 : 92 0723 1700

수 신 : 장 관 (연일, 미일)

발 신 : 주 캐나다 대사

제 목 : 인권보장 관련기구

　　　대 : WCN-0758

　　　연 : CNW-0637

　　1. 주재국 의회에는 상임위원회로 인권 및 장애자 지위 위원회가 있으며, 여타 인권관련 기구는 없음.

　　2. 동 상임위원회의 주요임무는 인권 및 장애자 지위에 관한 법안을 심의하고, 인권위원회 (CANADIAN HUMAN RIGHTS COMMISSION, 연호로 기보고) 보고서를 검토하는 것임.

　　3. 관련 자료 파견 송부 예정임.

　　(대사 박건우- 국장)

　　예고 : 92.12.31. 까지

국기국　　　미주국

주체크슬로바크연방공화국대사관

U Mrazovky 17,
125 62 Praha 5 - Smichov
Czechoslovakia

/ 전화 (042-2) 54-2671

주체코(정) 92- 145

시행일자 : 1992. 7. 24.

선결			지시		
접수	일자시간		결재·공람		
	번호 43468				
	처리과				
	담당자				

수신 : 외무부장관

참조 : 국제기구국장

제목 : 인권보장 관련 기구

연 : CZW - 0684

주재국의 인권보장 관련 기구에 관한 자료를 별첨 보고합니다.

첨부 : 상기 관련 기사 1건. 끝.

주체크슬로바크연방공화국대사

0074

Human Rights Observance Activity in the CSFR

Human rights observance activity in the Czech and Slovak Federal Republic is concentrated especially in the program of the so-called Helsinki (peace) process, named after the meeting of the Conference for Security and Cooperation in Europe (CSCE) held in Helsinki in 1975. Its final act, also signed by the then Socialist Republic of Czechoslovakia, binds the signatories to observe human rights and fundamental freedom as a basic principle for security and cooperation among the signatory countries, i.e. as grave and as binding as respecting sovereignty, territorial integrity, non-interference and observance of international law. In practice however, the implementations for observing human rights came too short under Communist rule and the Czechoslovak civil movement of Charta 77 emerged as an umbrella civil organization to point out the shortcomings. Harsh persecutions imposed upon the Chartists, as the signatories of Charta 77 declaration in Czechoslovakia were called, by the police readily forced the movement out of bounds.

An essential progress in the Helsinki process was made in the eighties, when the threat of military confrontation between the East and the West was mitigated and measures for enforcing confidence and security, as well as disarmament in Europe were agreed (Madrid 1984-1986 followed by Stockholm at a later date).

With the beginning of Mikhail Gorbachev's Perestroika in the USSR, which also gave way to reform movements in Eastern and Central European socialist countries, human rights issue began to play a more important role in the CSCE meetings. Thus at the Vienna meeting in January 1989 the term "human dimension" gained a wider meaning, incorporating the question of human rights, humanitarian cooperation and direct contacts among the citizens of CSCE member countries. At the Paris meeting in June 1989, when Czechoslovakia was still under Communist rule, signatory countries bound themselves to inform each other on concrete human right issues and discuss "human dimension" question annually in the coming period (Paris Charter for a New Europe).

After the Communist regime was replaced by democratic forces in November 1989, Czechoslovakia actively participated in the Copenhagen meeting in June 1990, the meeting of CSCE experts on the question of minorities held in Geneva in 1991,and Moscow meeting in September 1991. The Copenhagen document defines in detail basic political rights, freedom of

0075

expression, association and peaceful demonstration, freedom of thought and religion, and emphasizes the right of the individual to leave any country including one's own and return to her. It also allows individuals and civic initiatives to watch and demand the observance of human rights internationally in the whole of CSCE. The right of sending observers and the obligation to receive human rights observers was also imposed on member countries. Other significant points in the Copenhagen document touch the rights of the child and the right of the individual to refuse military service with respect to his conviction, the rights of the minorities, etc.

The Moscow document of the CSCE emphasizes that the questions of human rights, basic freedoms, democracy and the lawful state are international issues, because the observance of these rights and freedoms represent one of the basic principles of international establishment. The document also defines in detail conditions for inviting, setting up and activities of foreign expert missions for human rights observance in a country. It also touches the jurisdiction in the protection of human rights of delinquents, freedom of expression of the individual and the mass media, the role of females in social and political activity, and cooperation in other spheres of the "human dimension".

The first document on human rights protection ratified by Czechoslovakia is the Convention on Slavery declared by the Association of Nations on September 1926. It was ratified by the first president of Czechoslovakia T.G. Masaryk in July 1930. The second similar document was the Charter of the United Nations Organization declared in June 1945, containing several human rights protection clauses. It was ratified by the next Czechoslovak president Edvard Benes in September 1945. During the Communist rule from February 1948 till November 1989, a number of international conventions and pacts on human rights were signed or ratified by Czechoslovakia, in some cases with some objections.

After democracy was restored in November 1989, human rights protection activity in Czechoslovakia intensified, both governmental and non-governmental organizations cooperated more widely with international counterparts. A section was created in the president's office, headed by the president's adviser Martin Bútora, which works out human rights policy and reports to the president. In the federal government, a section works on the subject and reports to deputy prime minister Jozef Miklosko, who is responsible for religious, cultural and human rights questions among other things. A constitutional law (Law no. 23/1991) was passed by the Federal Assembly of the CSFR in January 1991, assuring basic rights and freedom to all subjects and placing international conventions and treaties signed and ratified by CSFR before its own laws.

0076

Both the Czech Government and the Slovak Government recently confirmed that governmental departments for human rights questions will be founded soon, most probably after the June parliamentary elections.

Apart from the mentioned governmental bodies, at present there are several non-governmental organizations or civic initiatives working on protection of human rights in Czechoslovakia. For example, there is the Czechoslovak Helsinki Committee headed by the famous former dissident professor Jiří Hájek, the Helsinki Peace Assembly headed by Ivan Fiala, the Czechoslovak Section of the International Association for Human Rights, Slovak Union for Peace and Human Rights, Committee for Human Rights, Charta 77, Amnesty International, etc.

Besides the CSCE final documents and United Nations resolutions and declarations touching the sphere of human rights, the following is a list of main documents signed or ratified by Czechoslovakia : (i.e. excluding the already mentioned Convention on Slavery and the Charter of the United Nations)

Name and date of issue (month/year)	ratified or joined by Czechoslovakia
1. Convention on prevention and punishment of genocide crime (12/1948)	21.12.1950
2. Convention on political rights of women (12/1952)	6.4.1955
3. Convention on suppressing trade with people and exploitation of prostitution of other persons (12/1949)	14.3.1958
4. Supplementary convention on abolishment of slavery, trade with slaves and institutions and practice of similar slavery (9/1956)	13.6.1958
5. Convention on citizenship of married women (1/1957)	5.4.1962
6. Convention on fight against discrimination in education (12/60)	14.3.1963
7. Convention on agreement for marriage, on the lowest age for marriage and for registration of marriage (12/1962)	5.3.1965

0077

8. International convention on   29.12.1966
   removing all forms of racial
   discrimination (3/1966)

9. Convention on imprescriptibility   13.8.1970
   of war crimes and crimes against
   humanity (11/1968)

10. International pact on economic,   23.12.1975
    social and cultural rights
    (12/1966)

11. International pact on civil and   23.12.1975
    political rights (12/1966)

12. International convention on   25.3.1976
    suppression and punishment of
    apartheid crime (11/1973)

13. Convention on removing all forms   16.2.1982
    of discrimination of women (12/1979)

14. International convention against   29.7.1987
    apartheid in sports (12/1985)

15. Convention against torture and   7.7.1988
    other cruel, inhumane and humiliating
    treatment and punishment (12/1984)

16. Convention of the rights of the   7.1.1991
    child (11/1989)

17. European Convention on protection   18.3.1991
    of human rights and fundamental
    rights (11/1950)

18. Optional protocol to the   12.3.1991
    international pact on civil and
    political rights (12/1966)

19. Convention on the status of refugees   26.11.1991
    (7/1951)

20. Protocol on the status of refugees   26.11.1991
    (1/1967)

21. European Social Charter (10/1991)   signed 27.5.1992
    (on social rights of the individual)   ratification
                                             expected in
                                             Spring/1993

(Source: Department of Socio-Political relations and
Humanitarian questions, Government of the CSFR)

0078

Priliminary information

Human rights protection activity in CSFR

1.   Within the framework of the Federal Government, human
rights affairs fall under the office of the Deputy Prime
Minister Jozef Miklosko. Contact person: Dr. Hajsman,
Tel. 2102-398. He is sending by fax some documents on their
activity.

2.   In the Federal Ministry of Foreign Affairs, human rights
issues are handled by the CSCE committee. Contact person: Dr.
Kaloc Tel 2193-2718 or 2422. A list of main documents adopted
by CSFR can be picked up on 28/5 at the main gate of the FMFA.

3.   Helsinki Committee (contact person: Dr. Silhanová, Tel.
533361) recommends a brochure titled "Man and Human Rights.
State treaties and declarations. Publisher: Spektrum" sold at
the Faculty of Law, Charles University book shop. Information
on the activities of the Helsinki Committee will be sent by
fax.

4.   In the President's office, the section for human rights
headed by the President's adviser Martin Butora works only for
the President of the CSFR. No public documentation available.

5.   Charta 77 is now undergoing transformation. It may be
transformed into a non-governmental Association for Human
Rights in the near future.

0079

주 캐 나 다 대 사 관

캐나다(정) 720 - 582

92. 7. 24.

수 신 : 외무부장관

참 조 : 국제기구국장

제 목 : 인권보장 관련기구

대 : WCN - 0758

연 : CNW - 0843

연호 주재국 인권 관련 자료를 별첨 송부합니다.

첨부 : 1. 주재국 의회 인권 및 장애자 지위 위원회 관련 자료 1부.

2. Video Tape(인권위원회 토의과정등 수록) 1개

3. 기타 인권위원회 의사록등 10부. 끝.

주 캐 나 다 대 사

43204   0080

관리 번호	92 ~710		

외 무 부   원 본

종 별 :

번 호 : JAW-4203   일 시 : 92 0727 1749

수 신 : 장 관 (연이)

발 신 : 주 일 대사 (일정)

제 목 : 인권보장 관련 기구

　　　대 : WJA-3133

　　　연 : 주일(정)700-438

　　　대호 관련, 일본국회 (중의원 및 참의원)내에 별도로 설치된 인권관련 기구는
없음며, 인권관련 업무는 사안에 따라 외무, 법무, 예산등 각위원회에서
다루어지게됨. 끝

　　　(대사 오재희-국장)

　　　예고 : 92.12.31 일반

국기국

PAGE 1

外　務　部

종　별 :

번　호 : AUW-0626

일　시 : 92 0729 1500

수　신 : 장 관(연이)

발　신 : 주 호주 대사

제　목 : 인권보장관련 기구

　　　대:WAU-0613

　　　1. 주재국 의회내 설치된 인권관련기구의 관련사항을 아래 보고함.

　　　가. 기구명칭: 외교국방무역문제 상하원 합동위원회 산하 인권문제 소위원회(HUMAN RIGHTS SUBCOMMITTEE, JOINT COMMITTEE ON FOREIGN AFFAIRS, DEFENSE AND TRADE, PARLIAMENT)

　　　나. 설립배경:

　　　- 냉전체제 붕괴이후 인권문제가 중요한 국제관심사로 등장

　　　- 의회내 인권관련부서 설립에 대한 국제사면기구(AMNESTY INTERNATIONAL)로 부터의 요청(90.9)

　　　- 의회내에 인권문제에 관한 별도의 상하원 합동위원회를 설치하기 보다는 기존의 외교국방무역 합동위원회의 산하에 소위원회를 설립키로 결정(90.12)

　　　- 인권문제 소위원회로 공식 설립(91.3)

　　　다. 주요활동

　　　- 외무무역부로 하여금 매년 인권보고서를 의회에 제출케 하고, 동 보고서를 심사

　　　- 상기 외무무역부의 인권보고서는 인권보호를 위한 호주정부의 국제적 외교노력(선별적 사례)에 관한 것이며, 이점에서 세계 각국의 인권현황을 총망라하는 미 국무성의 대의회 인권보고서와는 성격이 상이.

　　　- 필요시, 주요 인권문제에 관한 청문회 개최 (예:91.11 EAST TIMOR 사태시)

　　　2. 주재국 인권정책의 기조및 상기 의회내 인권문제 소위원회의 설립 배경에 관한 관련 참고자료는 차파편 송부 예정임.끝.

　　　(대사-국장)

　　　예고:92.12.31.까지.

　　　国기국　　아주국

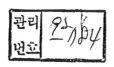

주 호 주 대 사 관

113 Empire Circuit, Yarralumla A.C.T. 2600 　　/(06)273 3044　　/(06)273 4839

문서번호　호주(정) 20228-33

시행일자　1992. 7. 29.(　　　　)

수신　장　관

참조　국제기구국장

선결			지	
접	일자시간		시	
			결	
수	번호		재	
처리과			공	
담당자			람	

제목　인권보장 관련기구

　　　대　:　WAU-0613

　　　연　:　AUW-

　　　연호관련, 인권문제에 대한 호주정부의 기본입장을 설명한 Evans 외무장관의
연설문 (92.7.17.) 및 의회내 인권관련기구의 설립배경에 관한 자료를 별첨
송부하오니 업무에 참고하시기 바랍니다.

　　　첨　부 :　1.　Evans 외무장관의 연설문 (인권문제에 대한 호주의 입장).
　　　　　　　　2.　의회 인권문제소위원장의 연설문 (인권문제소위원회 설립). 　끝.

접수 1992.8. 5

주 　호 　주 　대

0083

HUMAN RIGHTS IN AUSTRALIAN FOREIGN POLICY: WHERE TO FROM HERE?

Address by Senator the Hon Gareth Evans QC, Minister for Foreign Affairs and Trade, to the Centre for International and Public Law Conference on Human Rights, Canberra, 17 July 1992

From 1945 to 1991 the East-West divide, and what flowed from it, was the central organising principle of international affairs. The North-South divide - between the haves and have-nots - always mattered at least as much in human terms, but it is only now that it has assumed anything like the same prominence in international affairs.

In both East-West and North-South divides, the issue of attitudes to human rights has always constituted a particular fault line of its own. The latter years of the Cold War, particularly with the impetus given by the commencement of the Helsinki Process in 1975, saw the East-West human rights gap begin to be bridged. By the time of the anti-communist revolutions of the last three years, the process had become irresistible: the call for equal civil and political rights was, as much as any economic motivation, what produced the historical earthquake which has seen the disintegration of the USSR, the disappearance of communism as a ruling force in all but four countries, and the emergence of nearly twenty new states on the Eurasian landmass.

By contrast, in the North-South divide, differences of perception about what are human rights (or at least about which human rights matter most), and differences about what it is proper for the international community to do about human rights violations, still loom very large indeed.

For all the dramatic change in the international environment in recent times, we are still a long way from the advent of a

XVIII/92

0084

2

world, foreshadowed in the preamble to the Universal
Declaration of Human Rights, in which all human beings shall
enjoy freedom of speech and belief, with life and personal
liberty protected by the rule of law.

Today I want to suggest that, situated as we are in the Asia
Pacific region, and with our strong record of unswerving
commitment to human rights, Australia is uniquely placed to
help bridge the divide between North and South that will be a
central feature of the human rights debate in the nineties.

I want to suggest that while Australia's international human
rights efforts, both multilateral and bilateral, have worked
well enough to date, and while we should certainly continue to
pursue them, there are some new approaches to international
human rights protection which we are well placed to support
and endorse, and which should play a larger role in our
repertoire in the future. I want to refer to two such new
approaches in particular: first, the possibility of the
international community playing a more direct, hands-on role
in the resolution of certain "internal" problems; and
secondly, the role that countries like Australia can play in
human rights breach-prevention through so called institution-
building strategies.

Present Approach

Multilaterally, Australia's strategies to date have been
threefold: to encourage adherence to existing human rights
instruments, to ensure the effective operation of monitoring
machinery, and to expand the body of human rights treaties in
specific areas.

To establish a basis for encouraging others, Australia has
become party to all major international human rights
instruments. Amongst the more recent have been the Convention
on the Rights of the Child, which we played a major role in
developing and which we ratified on 17 December 1990. We also

0085

3

played a leading role in promoting wider adherence to the Second Optional Protocol of the International Covenant on Civil and Political Rights against the death penalty, and acceded to it on 2 October 1990.

To be credible internationally in promoting human rights we not only have to sign up to the relevant international legal instruments, but also have to acknowledge Australia's own deficiencies in the human rights area and commit ourselves to overcoming them. In that context, I am pleased that we have also now at last acceded, on 25 September 1991, to the First Optional Protocol. As a natural extension of that accession, the Government is currently supporting the candidature of Justice Elizabeth Evatt, who addressed the conference yesterday, for election to the Human Rights Committee established under the ICCPR. (As you would be aware, the convener of this conference, Professor Phillip Alston, is already a member of the Economic, Social and Cultural Rights Committee.)

We have complemented our activity in multilateral arenas by encouraging others to adhere to international human rights instruments, and by supporting UN mechanisms for monitoring human rights observance. We have pursued the latter particularly through the UN Commission on Human Rights, of which Australia is currently a member, and through the Third Committee of the UN General Assembly. We are also hoping that coordinated efforts to improve human rights will emerge from the Second World Conference on Human Rights to be held in Vienna next year, which will hopefully further define the relationship between democracy, development and human rights.

Encouraging wider adherence to existing instruments should continue to have a great prominence in our policy on human rights in coming years. There are, of course, many gaps remaining to be filled - for example, by the UN Declaration on Human Rights Defenders and on the Rights of Indigenous Peoples

0086

4

which are currently under consideration. Nevertheless, the broad legal foundations on which more universal respect for human rights can be built are now largely in place.

Our present human rights approach has a strong bilateral as well as multilateral dimension, extending both to states who clearly share our basic perspective and those who may not. Paying attention to the policies and practices of so called like-minded states on human rights issues can assist Australia's efforts towards achieving better human rights observance for a number of reasons. It should, for example, facilitate the adoption of common fronts on human rights issues, which can be immensely valuable. It is also important to have a sense of the extent to which we do in fact share the policy goals of 'like-minded' states. Actions and attitudes by such nations provide the context within which Australian actions will often be understood.

The record unfortunately shows, however, that some like-minded states pursue policy applications of human rights which we would not wish to support. Some states appear to be considerably less concerned about the gross violations of the rights of allegedly non-democratic opposition forces than with the rights of often self-proclaimed pro-democracy or "liberation" groups. A striking example of this is the practice of some countries in providing military advisers or even arms to nationalist or "democratic" governments or opposition groups as part of their efforts to encourage the growth of democracy and thus of human rights. Australian policy in such circumstances could be devalued by too close an association with aspects of others' policies.

In making human rights representations to countries who may not be so like-minded, we have sought to ensure that Australia's approach is characterised by a focus on the kind of rights which can readily be accepted as universal in character, by consistency, attention to detail, and –

0087

5

crucially - a willingness to respond frankly and fully to criticisms directed to us.

In the past five years, we have made over 2300 official representations to more than 120 countries - including to close allies such as the US; major trading partners such as Japan and China, the UK and other Western European countries; countries in the Middle East, Africa and Latin America; as well as to our regional neighbours including Indonesia, Papua New Guinea, Singapore and the Philippines.

Consistency means simply adopting so far as possible the same approach to all cases of alleged human rights abuse wherever they may occur, not picking and choosing between countries on other grounds.   This maintains a minimum but important protection against politicising an approach which aims to work impartially for a common good.   In some cases making diplomatic representations may be the only available measure, but they can also become an overly familiar and therefore less effective routine: consistency should not be viewed as adopting a standard process, but as a means of achieving policy goals.

There can be difficult conflicts arising from time to time between human rights objectives and other entirely legitimate national interests.   This need not be a reason to reduce engagement on human rights, but it is important to recognise that this engagement may not always be cost-free, at least in the short term.   Some countries do take non-economic factors into account in trade decisions, for example, particularly if the margin of economic advantage is slight.   And there can be other, more diffuse, side-effects of pursuing a policy which involves criticism of, and efforts to change, others' behaviour.

I remain convinced, however, that an effective human rights policy can be pursued with relatively little cost in terms of lost opportunities and serious friction in our external

0088

6

relations. It is a matter of handling human rights issues
sensitively - relying (other than in exceptional cases like
South Africa, China and Burma) on quiet persuasion rather than
punitive aid, trade or investment sanctions or over-strident
condemnations. To work in this way can in fact over the
longer term strengthen and broaden bilateral relations, not
least by providing a channel for the airing of conflicts and
interests and values which may otherwise go un-articulated.

Many human rights issues which arise in a North-South context
are not easily susceptible to definitive solution, because
they are embedded in decades - if not centuries - of political
and social battles, ideological debate and point scoring. If
these issues are to be resolved, I believe a very important
component of the process will be repeated practical exchanges
between countries on particular human rights problems, in
dialogue not just between governments but, to some extent,
between and within cultures. A good example of this has been
the constructive and ongoing dialogue initiated by the
Australian human rights delegation in its visit to China last
year, which is to be continued by a second visit later this
year.

New Approaches

All that said, there is nonetheless emerging in significant
portions of the international community a demonstrated
willingness to take strong collective interventionist, and
even punitive, measures in cases of widespread and gross human
rights abuse, in circumstances which might in the past have
been regarded as internal in character and thus beyond the
reach of any such international action.

The application of sanctions against South Africa by the
international community has always been seen as a special
case, but there are an increasing number of comparable cases
now emerging - e.g. the action taken under the auspices of the
United Nations to protect the Kurds in the aftermath of the

0089

7

Gulf War, and the increasing preoccupation with the traumas accompanying the break up of Yugoslavia.

The international community's commitment to Cambodia through the United Nations is perhaps the most interesting, and potentially far-reaching, example of all of a new international approach on human rights matters. The Comprehensive Settlement on Cambodia signed on 23 October last year - and now being implemented by nearly 16,000 troops, drawn from 29 countries, and a major civil administration component - provides various measures for the protection of human rights, including those to be enshrined in Cambodia's new constitution when it is drafted. The Settlement also provides in Article 5(4) of the Agreement on the Sovereignty, Independence, Territorial Integrity and Inviolability, Neutrality and National Unity of Cambodia, that "in the event of serious violations of human rights in Cambodia [the Parties to this Agreement] will call upon the competent organs of the United Nations to take such other steps as are appropriate for the prevention and suppression of such violations in accordance with the relevant international instruments".

In the discussions leading up to inclusion of this provision, there was some consideration given to inserting a direct reference to the possibility of international military intervention if necessary in such a case. While it was finally decided not to be quite so direct, it must nevertheless be said that this provision - and particularly the reference to "suppression" - is perhaps the strongest guarantee of internal human rights ever included in an international instrument. Its strength is even greater when you recall that the Agreement was signed by all permanent members of the UN Security Council, all of Cambodia's neighbours, and a number of other countries including, of course, Australia.

Some have argued that these various emerging precedents constitute a new international law principle, namely

0090

8

recognition of a "humanitarian right to intervene". Thus, for example, my friend and colleague Polish Foreign Minister (and distinguished international lawyer) Krzystof Skubiszewski, speaking at the UN General Assembly last year, drew attention to Secretary-General Perez Cuellar's statement in his annual report of that year that the principle of non-interference with the essential domestic jurisdiction of States cannot be regarded as a protective barrier behind which human rights could be massively or systematically violated with impunity", and went on to say:

> It should be made clear that the exception of domestic jurisdiction does not apply to any case where there is international regulation. And today practically all the multifarious human rights and fundamental freedoms are subject to treaty and other obligations. Hence their violation does not belong to the reserved domain of States, while individual or concerted action by Governments in defense of human rights does not constitute any interference or intervention in the internal affairs of the State.

One should certainly not overstate the extent to which any such intervention right is now recognised. One needs to retain a degree of healthy scepticism about the gap between rhetoric and action when it comes to countries applying similar responses in practice to what are in principle similar cases. A very careful case by case approach will in practice be adopted. But one can certainly say that the principle of non-intervention is no longer anything like as unquestionable as it was in the period of decolonisation.

Active interventionist measures are on any view ones of last resort. One has to acknowledge that the more frequent use of punitive sponsors linked to human rights issues could deepen the suspicion of many developing countries that those issues were being used by economically powerful states as an excuse to impose their own values or national interests on others. The international debate on this difficult issue could thus

0091

9

become frozen into unproductive confrontation between developing and developed states.

The focus of Australia's human rights policy on the universality of rights attempts to side-step precisely this sort of impasse. There is probably no surviving value system significant enough to underpin a culture which does not aspire - at least publicly - to increase human dignity and freedom from fear. Similarly, there are few governments which seriously argue that the Universal Declaration does not apply to them by virtue of some special and uniquely worthwhile features of their own culture.

But the existence of certain basic human aspirations and needs, and of international legal norms giving definition to human rights, does not remove the complexities either of pursuing human rights across cultural differences, or of a society reducing abuse within itself. It is true that it is often political pragmatism and expediency, rather than cultural difference, which motivates both violation of rights and the charge by some governments that criticism of even gross abuse is Western cultural imperialism. In these cases, common ground is more likely to be found with the victims of abuse than with governments.

Abuse can also be structurally embedded in ways that are difficult for governments to undo. Reducing abuse is not always simply a matter of a government refraining from action, but may require transforming, and sometimes simply improving, entire networks of social organisation and control. Abuse can also be deeply ingrained socially. This is exemplified by the systematic cruelty towards, and exploitation of, women in many parts of the world, sometimes despite the efforts of governments and not supported by the ethical ideals to which the particular culture aspires.

To the extent that the debate over cultural imperialism can be resolved, it will be achieved not in theory, but in the

0092

10

process of dialogue and collaboration on the concrete steps
needed to guard against abuse.   It would be particularly
productive, in my view, if we devoted more effort in future to
developing measures, incremental and well-targeted, to
strengthen the infrastructures or institutions contributing to
human rights observance.   Australia has, for example, been
active in providing advice to newly established human rights
institutions, including in Russia, India and Indonesia.   This
is one area where Australia's expertise can be used to
particularly good effect.   I am pleased that some foreign
governments have actively sought out advice and in some
institutional aspects apparently see us as a model.

At Australia's initiative, some members of the Commonwealth
are also considering coordinating, through the Commonwealth
Secretariat, assistance to developing country members in
strengthening the institutions which can protect human rights
observance.   This would in effect build on assistance
Australia has already given some Commonwealth members on
constitutional and electoral reform, and would extend the
growing Commonwealth role in providing election observers.

There is also considerable scope for encouraging more
enlightened attitudes through, for example, bilateral legal,
police and media exchanges, and these could be extended to
include the army and administration of indigenous peoples and
other minorities.   Such exchanges might show a way to make
progress on resolving in practical ways the dilemma of how to
give greater expression to universal aspirations without
repeating the histories of cultural domination.   Measures to
improve court systems, for example, or to reduce arbitrary,
destructive intervention in individuals' lives, can
demonstrate the interrelationships between political/civil and
social/economic rights in such a way that discussion between
officials can rarely do, and so help put to one side fruitless
arguments about which kinds of human rights have priority.   We
should also not assume that we would have nothing to learn
from this kind of collaborative exchange.

0093

11

Having the broader range of complementary tools that this sort
of approach implies - that is, encouragement and practical
assistance as well as criticism - should allow action on human
rights to be more closely tailored to particular conditions.
Institution-building measures can broaden the base of contact
a community has with ideas and ways of doing things that
promote respect for, and enjoyment of, human rights so that it
is not only ministers and officials who have regular contact
with human rights standards and their practical application.
Institution-building measures can also provide sectors within
a community with tools to push for change internally. The
issue of identifying common values without trampling on
cultural sensitivities can also be more directly tackled in
the context of working together on, for example, legal
processes in Vietnam or the humane delivery of birth control
in China.

To give substance to some of the ideas I have canvassed today,
I have directed my Department and our diplomatic missions
overseas to identify human rights priorities and the means
which would work against identified abuses, including
institution-building measures and joint action with like-
minded countries. Cataloguing what Australia already does in
the direction of institution-building, for example in aid and
exchange programs, will be an important element of this. We
will then be in a better position to judge how the priority
accorded to human rights objectives might be raised even
further within ongoing government activities. Some aid and
exchange programs, for example, already have a clear human
rights dimension: for instance, the provision of Tibetan
language textbooks in Tibetan minority areas.

If necessary, other government activities could be modified to
ensure that they serve - or at least do not work against -
human rights objectives. Military training programs, for
example, should ideally include a component on military law
and exclude training in techniques which could be used against

0094

12

civilian populations. By way of parentheses, let me point out that while we have demonstrated that we are prepared to cut off defence cooperation with governments which have perpetrated particularly gross abuses of human rights, such defence cooperation - especially training - is one of the few means we have to influence these armed forces' attitudes to human rights. Quite apart from formal training of military personnel in legal or other human rights matters, greater sensitivity to human rights issues can grow from exposure to societies and armed forces which do place importance on them. I am wary therefore of the knee-jerk reaction to any report of human rights abuse that we should immediately cut off defence cooperation. We need to consider the likely consequences of any particular measure.

As a further example of possible new directions for government action, my Department's Special Visitors Program could target visitors from sectors such as the media or the legal or penal systems. State and Federal government legal exchanges with other countries could extend beyond trade and commercial law, and similarly, State and Federal police could include, say, training in the presentation of evidence within their exchange programs.

Where feasible, the work of overviewing and building on activities already in train could be extended to the programs of non-government bodies such as LawAsia or the International Commission of Jurists. At the very least, these bodies could assist in the identification and targeting of programs relevant to their expertise. I am, for instance, aware of LawAsia's proposal for a Pacific Court of Human Rights. While this particular proposal may be somewhat ambitious, Australia has long supported the formation of a regional body for the protection of human rights, of the sort that exists in other parts of the world. It is pleasing that other countries in the region, including Indonesia and the Philippines, have now begun to promote this idea.

0095

13

The Government's human rights policy has in large part grown from Australian community values. It is therefore important that a wide cross-section of the public remains in touch with and broadly supportive of the policy. While links between my Department and human rights interest groups are good, some relevant sectors' of the community may have little understanding of the policy or of the need for it. I am certainly willing to meet, for example, with business people dealing with Asia or bilateral chambers of commerce to explain our human rights policy.

Such efforts will also be assisted, I believe, by such things as the production of a handbook of government human rights policy and the reasons for it, setting out the international legal context and establishing guidelines on the kinds of programs which could assist specific human rights objectives. My Department has started work on such a handbook and it will, of course, be publicly available when published.   The Department is also examining the possibility of offering training courses, both for our own officials who deal with human rights cases overseas and also for training officials from overseas countries, to give them a clear grasp of human rights policy objectives and instruments.

I should mention finally - not least because in the current budget discussions I am very conscious of where government resources are allocated - that our international human rights activities require significant Departmental resources, in Canberra and at posts. In some posts it is a major professional preoccupation. I want to maintain that effort, and at the high standard at which it is currently performed.

I realise that speaking to a group such as this falls very much into the category of preaching to the converted - and perhaps even to a few fundamentalist zealots! You are as well aware as I am of developments in the various international forums on specific aspects of human rights protection. I have thus sought to concentrate instead on perceptions of human

0096

14

rights in the post-Cold War world, and the capacity of the Australian Government to respond positively to changes in those perceptions.

It is a complex challenge which the Government - and I personally - look forward to meeting, not just with strong words and firm action, appropriate as these may be on occasion, but with whatever action is likely to be most effective in the particular circumstances. I look forward to a continuation of your support.

****

0097

PARLIAMENT OF AUSTRALIA

JOINT COMMITTEE ON FOREIGN AFFAIRS, DEFENCE AND TRADE
PARLIAMENT HOUSE, CANBERRA, ACT, 2600

HUMAN RIGHTS SUB-COMMITTEE

Senator Chris Schacht
Chairman

Hon. M J R MacKellar, MP
Deputy Chairman

Senator V W Bourne
Senator C M A Chamarette
Mr D M Connolly, MP
Mr L D T Ferguson, MP
Mr E J Fitzgibbon, MP
Mr C Hollis, MP
Mr M J Lee, MP

Secretary. Ms M Swieringa
(Tel: (06) 277 4306)

Administrative Assistant. Ms Denise Picker
(Tel: (06) 277 2395)

0098

PARLIAMENT OF AUSTRALIA

JOINT COMMITTEE ON FOREIGN AFFAIRS, DEFENCE AND TRADE
PARLIAMENT HOUSE, CANBERRA, ACT, 2000

SUB-COMMITTEE ON

HUMAN RIGHTS

TERMS OF REFERENCE

To consider and report on an annual Report by the Department of Foreign Affairs and Trade on the Government's international efforts to promote and protect human rights.

0099

DIPLOMACY TRAINING PROGRAM
UNIVERSITY OF NEW SOUTH WALES
6 JANUARY 1992

I speak to you today as the Chairman of the Joint Committee on Foreign Affairs Defence and Trade but, more particularly, as the Chairman of the new Human Rights Sub-Committee. This is a new committee of the parliament established after considerable discussion and some angst. Human rights is a relatively new concern of foreign relations, at least in the formal sense and it is an area of great sensitivity in diplomatic relations, coloured as it is by moral values. It is certainly an area of expanding interest since the end of the Cold War. I would like to begin by briefly outlining the origins and establishment of the committee.

Parliamentary committees have a role in monitoring the implementation of government policy and of keeping parliament informed of the work and policy directions of the government. One aspect of foreign policy which has grown in importance and which seemed in the past to get scant, or at best haphazard, attention has been human rights. This was not because human rights was seen to be unimportant. This Australian Government has always accorded human rights a high priority and Australia's international reputation as a promoter of human rights through international fora is a good one. Moreover, the support for a strong human rights stand is bipartisan and broadly based in the community.

0100

The Joint Committee on Foreign Affairs, Defence and Trade has long been the focus for appeals and representations from many groups within the Australian community which, because of their ethnic background, have an interest in the human rights situations in other parts of the world. Many people have come to Australia to escape repression at home.

In particular, Amnesty International has worked closely with the Committee as a source of information on human rights abuses throughout the world. It was Amnesty which perceived the need for a more focussed and formalised reporting mechanism on human rights issues. They wrote to the Committee in September 1990 proposing that some mechanism be established whereby the Minister for Foreign Affairs should provide an annual report to Parliament on its work in this field and that this report should be referred to the Joint Committee on Foreign Affairs, Defence and Trade for examination. The intention was to 'expand parliamentary responsibility and community support for the continued development of human rights protection.' The emphasis was to be on the record of the Australian Government in its activities to promote and protect, not an examination either of individual cases or of the human rights records of other countries.

The Committee considered the proposal very closely. Members were surveyed as to the best mechanism for such a review. Would it be through the Parliamentary Amnesty group, a group that was well established and widely supported on both sides of the Parliament? However, despite the energy and dedication of this group, it did not have the status or the legal authority invested in a parliamentary

2

0101

committee. It was thought best to maintain the process within the Committee system.

A separate, new joint committee was also considered, but given that the portfolio responsibility for human rights fell to the Minister for Foreign Affairs and that the issue is often linked with other foreign policy issues, it was decided to create a new sub-committee within the Joint Committee on Foreign Affairs, Defence and Trade.

The proposal gained approval and support from the Minister, Senator Gareth Evans, in December 1990 with the proviso that details of individual cases raised with other governments should not be placed on the public record and that the Committee recognise the often delicate nature of human rights negotiations.

Resources have proved to be another restraint. When the Committee looked at the work of the United States Congressional Committee on Human Rights which considers the Annual report of the State Department, running to 1700 pages, it was necessary to set our sights somewhat lower than that most comprehensive review of the human rights records of the world. Neither our Department of Foreign Affairs and Trade nor the Joint Committee of the Parliament could produce or review such a report.

The Human Rights Sub-Committee was established in March 1991 and received its first referral from the Minister on 7 May 1991. Its terms of reference are to consider and report on an annual report by the Department of Foreign Affairs and Trade on the Government's

3

0102

international efforts to promote and protect human rights.

The Department's first annual report came to the Committee in November 1991. The inquiry was then advertised nationally with a view to receiving submissions by the end of January. The Committee is interested to receive submissions from organisations and individuals who are concerned with human rights issues and who seek to comment on the Report. Early next year the Committee intends to hold a series of public hearings based on the submissions.

The first public hearing of the Human Rights Sub-Committee was held on 2 December, made necessary by the tragic situation of the massacre in Dili on 12 November. On that occasion the Committee took oral evidence from Mr Bob Muntz, the Community Aid Abroad worker who was injured during the shooting in Dili, written evidence from Russell Anderson, Amy Goodman and Allan Nairn, three other Western eyewitnesses to the killings, as well as statements from Amnesty International and the Department of Foreign Affairs and Trade. The intention was to place the eyewitness accounts on the record.

This hearing was an unusual one created by unusual circumstances. The intention was not to conduct a definitive inquiry into what happened in Timor but to place factual information about the events of 12 November 1991 on the public record. The Committee does not expect to conduct hearings of this kind into the many and dreadful human rights abuses that occur in the world. However, it may from time to time have such hearings on matters of public interest to Australia. Timor fell into this category because of its proximity, its historical links

4

0103

with Australia, its sizeable refugee community living here and because of the interest that exists over our policy towards both Timor and Indonesia.

It was important for the committee to hear first hand accounts of what happened as soon as possible after the event and be prepared to make an informed judgement on whether the Government's response seemed adequate and whether the government's policy on Timor was in line with the priorities it accorded human rights in other areas.

Furthermore, the Committee was able to send the evidence collected that day to the Djaelani Commission investigating the incident in Indonesia.

The Committee is very aware of the delicacy and sensitivity of the issue of human rights. One other function that I see as important for the Human Rights Sub-Committee is, through debate, to clarify and enunciate the nature and role of human rights in international relations.

Since the Second World War, international relations theorists have been embroiled in a debate on the limits to national sovereignty. It is a lively and significant debate. The idea of national sovereignty accompanied the rise of the nation state as the building block of international order. Non-intervention of one state in the affairs of another was a logical concomitant to liberal democracy. If people were organised into groups of their own free will, then the type of government they wished to give themselves was entirely their own affair. States did not interfere with

5

0104

the internal affairs of one another.

Therefore, intervention (or aggression) brought the right to international sanction and retaliation as against Hitler or Saddam Hussein. Although it should be noted that consistency was never absolute and size and strategic importance mattered. Hungary and Czechoslovakia were invaded by the Soviet Union with impunity and Poland and East Germany were suppressed for many years; Chile, the Dominican Republic, Vietnam, Afghanistan and East Timor have experienced considerable interference in their affairs with little international sanction. The constraints here were often the great power politics of the Cold War. With the decline and disintegration of the Soviet Union, the particular competition of East and West has been taken out of the equation.

Moreover, the world is internationalising as a result of communications technology and the deliberate policy of nations which sought to establish institutions such as the League of Nations, and later the United Nations, to protect the world against the madness of world war. However, the Charter of the United Nations is much broader than simply establishing a mechanism against aggression. Support for underdeveloped nations, the protection of children and notably the declaration on human rights, formalised in 1948, are all included.

These 'other' concerns of the United Nations reflect increasing interest in a minimum standard of justice for all. The inequalities in the world need to be addressed. Within the UN the wealth of the West and North is set against the poverty of the East and South. The tension arises out

6

0105

of decolonisation. Decolonisation has, however, led to two contradictory tendencies. Opposition to and sensitivity about all forms of imperialism has led to the assertion of local cultures and systems against Western ones but at the same time Western economy, Western principles of nationalism and self-determination are espoused as useful weapons against their authors. This is as it should be.

The doctrine of human rights comes within this argument about what are applicable universal doctrines. It is often asserted that the concept of human rights is a Western construct, part of the cultural imperialism of the West to try and shape developing societies in their own image and likeness. It is seen to relate to the Western political development of liberal democracy where the rights of the individual are enshrined within constitutions and legal systems which seek to protect freedom of speech and association, freedom from arbitrary arrest and the right to a fair trial, free elections and rights to privacy and property.

Against this developing nations assert the primacy of economic and social rights - the right to a standard of living adequate to health and well being, the right to social security and civil order. So the argument is not whether human rights exist but what they consist of. It seems they have different priorities in different societies.

The Chinese Government's criticism of the United States for the poverty and violence within US society is a justification of the priority they choose to give to economic rights as the most basic human right, as is their oft stated claim that strong government in China is a prerequisite for social order and efficient economic distribution. The claim has some

7

0106

validity, but I suspect it is also a justification of the maintenance in power of the governing elite. Like St Augustine whose cry was 'Lord make me pure, but not yet' their cry is liberty, yes, but some time in the future.

It is possible that economic/social rights and political rights are not so separate. The Communist regimes which countered the Capitalist nations' emphasis on individual liberty with their superior ability to provide equality of material welfare have failed largely because the trade off proved false. Without freedom of speech and association and the free exchange of ideas, economies seem to stagnate.

In the end a distinction needs to be drawn between governments and peoples; between the claims that are made by regimes, Eastern or Western, Northern or Southern, which seek to use doctrines of cultural relativism to preserve their own power and to entrench themselves in office, and the aspirations of ordinary people who would choose a different path if given a free choice. The society of all humankind often stands opposed to the club of states.

We do not want to trespass on the legitimate internal arrangements of nations which choose to organise themselves differently from us. Nevertheless there are situations where all people can find agreement. Wherever you go in the world you find that individuals in every society share the same aspirations. The freedom fighter in Eritrea, the peasant farmer in China, the monk in Burma, the black activist in South Africa: they all want the security of food and shelter, and the safety of knowing that they have freedom of expression and association without the fear

8

0107

of being punished, tortured and killed for their views.

Irrespective of cultural and political heritage, can anyone find a person who likes the idea of being woken up in the middle of the night to be dragged off by a bunch of Government thugs and held indefinitely without trial. What people do want is to be able to live with comfortable amenity knowing that their families will be safe, and that their children will have an opportunity in the first place to live, and in the longer term, progress to a higher standard of living.

The common people of the Third World do not need to know the details of the United Nations Covenant on Political and Civil Rights to know what they want as basic human rights. They know they do not want a corrupt government which will arrest them arbitrarily, or confiscate their property or demand bribes for its services; they know they do not want their teenage children conscripted to fight in wars against their own people; and they know they do not want ruthless, brutal and anti-democratic regimes foisted upon them.

What they also know is that they'd like to live in peace free from fear; they'd like to have a say in who governs them.

I believe that Australia as a democratic, pluralistic and relatively wealthy nation, has an international responsibility to accept its share of the burden in assisting those nations which do not enjoy anywhere near the standard of living to which we have access. Secondly, there is a moral duty to raise our voice on behalf of those peoples throughout the world who have none of the political freedoms or rights to dissent,

9

0108

which we simply take for granted.

The question must be asked: What form should our assistance, our support for international human rights take? I would also draw a distinction between words and action. Debate and argument are the basis of our system. Criticism, therefore, for us is always a right. It is intrinsic to our culture of free speech, but, of course, it should be accurately based. We believe that human judgement is best informed by debate. So we should not hesitate to voice our views or our values where we believe there is abuse of human rights, economic, social or political, either within our own country or in others.

No culture is spotless or pure or inviolate. All theory and practice, including our own, should be subject to scrutiny, both internally and internationally. For this reason, I believe we are fair game to be scrutinised and criticised for our historical relationship with our aboriginal people. One of the fiats of all governments is to protect its citizens and all governments can be judged by their success or failure in that. At core, I believe there is a common humanity that is reflected in the philosophical theories underpinning all societies. These theories value and respect human life and decry cruelty and tyranny. This is so for Islam and Christianity, Confucianism and Buddhism, as well as Humanism.

It is this belief in a core of rights that attach themselves to human beings that gives confidence to the Australian position on human rights. Therefore, in its submission to the Human Rights Sub-Committee, the Department of Foreign Affairs and Trade says that it chooses to take

10

0109

a leading role in the promotion of international rights because it 'is conscious of its moral obligation to reflect in its foreign policy the democratic and individual values of Australian society.' Furthermore the Department noted:

> that the observance of the rights and principles of the Universal Declaration—of Human Rights would result in a more just international order;

> that the application of these standards transcends national borders; and

> therefore they are a legitimate subject for international scrutiny and concern.

Action is more difficult. The imposition of a moral truth is often unwise and usually ineffective. Intervention to redress human rights abuses, either through economic sanctions or military force, should be reserved for conduct that has 'outraged the conscience of the world'. The difficulty is that intervention itself may prove more costly in human lives than the original abuse and it may entrench and prolong the rule of an oppressive regime rather than lessen its hold. Moreover, distinguishing motives for intervention can be difficult. Humanitarian concerns can, and often are, linked to strategic or economic gain.

There are, however, examples where intervention on purely humanitarian grounds has seemed justified:

  · India's invasion of East Pakistan in November 1971 because

11

0110

10 million refugees had fled to India after Pakistani troops had killed as many as 3 million Bengalis. They left in 1972.

. In 1978 when Vietnam invaded Kampuchea after a quarter of the population had been murdered by Pol Pot. They finally left in 1989.

. In 1979 when Tanzanian troops invaded Uganda to prevent the continuing slaughter of the population by Idi Amin. They withdrew in June 1981.

. The creation of a Kurdish enclave in Northern Iraq this year.

Actions such as these are taken in extreme cases. For the most part, Australia makes representations through the various human rights organisations in the world. The new Human Rights Sub-Committee of the Australian Parliament is another avenue.

Human rights are on the political agenda and that is important. I believe, as I think do most Australians, in liberty and the democratic ideal, in a society that promotes justice and equality for all, in a society that strives to meet the aspirations of all its citizens. In this, I hope, that government can be a civilising power. The protection and promotion of human rights internationally is a step in the direction of extending, beyond the borders of the individual state, the simple expectation that human beings will treat each other well.

Senator Chris Schacht
Chairman
Human Rights Sub-Committee

12

0111

외 무 부

종 별 :

번 호 : PHW-0876

일 시 : 92 0730 1520

수 신 : 장 관(연이,아동)

발 신 : 주 필리핀 대사

제 목 : 인권보장 관련 기구

대:WPH-719

연:PHW-598

1. 주재국 의회내 인권관련 기구로서 상, 하 양원 각각 상임위원회의 하나인 인권위원회를 두고 있음.

가. 하원 인권 위원회는 전체 43 개 상임위워노히중 하나로서 의장, 부의장을 포함 24 명의 상임위원과 3 명의 직원을 가진 사무국을 두고 있으며, 주요 활동은 인권관련 법률제정 심의에 국한되고 있음.

나. 상원 인권관련 기구는 법사 및 인권위원회로서 이는 전체 33 개 상임위원 회중 하나인바, 9 명의 상임위원과 사무국으로 구성되고 있으며, 기능은 인권관련 법률심의임.

2. 주재국은 또한 대통령 소속하에 대통령 인권위원회를 두고 있으며, 그 기능은 주재국내 인권 상황 점검, 행방불명 또는 불법감금된 가족의 소재 파악을 포함한 인권관련 대통령 자문 기관임. 동 위원회 위원은 법무부 장관이 의장이며, 연호 언급 인권위원회의장, 대통령 법률고문, 국방부, 상원, 하원에서 각각 1 명의 대표자, 민간 인권단체 대표 2 명등으로 구성되어 있음.끝.

(대사 노정기-국장)

예고:92.12.31. 까지

국기국   아주국

* 원본수령부서 승인없이 복사 금지

외신 2과 통제관 BS

0112

대 한 민 국
주 오스트리아 대사관

오스트리아 20730-<del>754</del>

수 신 : 장관

참 조 : 국제기구국장

제 목 : 주재국 인권보장 관련 기구 현황

199 2 . 7 . 30 .

(보존기간 :   )

대 : WAV-0806, IIII

표제 관련 사항을 다음과 같이 조사하여 보고합니다.

I. 주재국내 인권보장 기구

　가. 성격

　　(I) 주재국 내에는 다양한 인권보장 기구가 설치되어 있으나 대부분이 AMNESTY INTERNATIONAL, INTERNATIONAL HELSINKI FEDERATION FOR HUMAN RIGHTS, INTERNATIONAL SOCIETY FOR HUMAN RIGHTS 등과 같은 국제적 인권기구의 오스트리아 지소의 성격을 띠고 있음.

　　(2) 오스트리아내 독자적인 인권보장기구로는 다음의 세 기구가 있으며 이들은 정부와는 관련없이 독자적인 인권활동을 전개하고 있음.

　- ÖSTERREICHISCHES INSTITUT FÜR MENSCHENRECHTE

　- LUDWIG BOLTZMANN-INSTITUT FÜR MENSCHENRECHTE

　- ÖSTERREICHISCHE LIGA FUR MENSCHENRECHTE

　나. 기능 및 활동

　(I) ÖSTERREICHISCHES INSTITUT FÜR MENSCHENRECHTE

　- 구주 평의회(COUNCIL OF EUROPE) 의 권고에 의해 1979년 창립

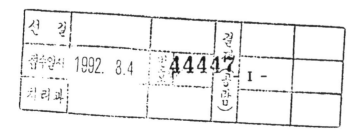

0113

- 회원의 분담금, 각종 재단의 보조금 및 기부금에 의해
운영되는 사적 기관
- 인권 문제에 관해 오스트리아 법원의 판결을 검토하고
오스트리아의 인권보장에 관한 유럽 조약 준수 여부를 감시하며 정기 보고서를
구주평의회에 제출
- 인권 관련 법원 판결의 DATA BANK 역할, 인권보장에 관한
연구 진흥, 일반인에게 인권 문제를 홍보하는 기능 등을 수행함.
- 정부는 기본권에 관련된 입법 과정에서 동 협회의 자문을
구하는 경우가 많음.

(2) LUDWIG BOLTZMANN-INSTITUT FÜR MENSCHENRECHTE
- 최근인 92년 2월 창설되었으며 아직 조직 정비 단계에 있음.
- OSLO, COPENHAGEN, UTRECHT 등에 소재하는 여타 유럽
인권보장기구들과의 유기적 연관하에 국제적 DOCUMENTATION NETWORK 형성
- 인권 문제에 관한 연구 조사 기능
- 정부의 인권 관련 입법 과정에 참여하기 위해 정부 부처들과
접촉 중
- 동 기구는 LUDWIG BOLTZMANN-FOUNDATION, PRIVATE SPONSOR
및 공공기구로부터 재정 지원을 얻어 운영됨.
(3) ÖSTERREICHISCHE LIGA FÜR MENSCHENRECHTE
사적 기구로서 상기 기구들과 역사한 기능 수행
2. 외무성의 인권보장 관련 업무

가. 외무성 SEKTION I (CENTRAL AFFAIRS) ABTEILUNG I.7 에서 담당
나. 내용
- 전반적 인권 문제 관련 사항
- 인도적 문제, 소수 민족의 권리 등에 관한 국제법 해석

- 2 -

0114

- 국제인권법정에서 오스트리아를 대표
- 비정부 간 인권보장기구와의 접촉 유지
- 인권문제에 관한 각종 정보 수집 및 사기구와의 정보 교환

3. 기타 정부 부처의 인권보장 관련 업무

가. 수상실
- 인권보장 관련 헌법적 문제에 관한 사항
- 인도적 문제에 관한 헌법 및 국제법 관련 사항
- UN HUMAN RIGHTS COMMITTEE 에서 오스트리아를 대표

나. 내무성
- 난민의 수용에 관한 제반 사항 : 망명 접수 여부, 망명이
  거부된 자의 처리, 오스트리아내 난민 수용소의 운영 등
- 오스트리아내 외국인의 등록에 관한 사항
- 국제 난민기구와의 접촉 및 정보 교환

4. 국회의 인권보장 관련 업무

오스트리아 국회내에는 인권보장 관련 별도 기구가 설치되어 있지 않고
외교정책위원회, 국내정책위원회, 법사위원회 및 노동.사회위원회 등 관련
위원회에서 사안에 따라 인권업무를 처리함.

첨부 : 주재국의 인권보장 관련 참고 자료   끝.

주 오 스 트 리 아   대 사

0115

주 필 리 핀 대 사 관

주비정 700 - **0670**   1992. 7. 31.

수 신 : 장관

참 조 : 국제기구국장

제 목 : 주재국 인권보장관련 기구

        연 : PHW - 0876

        연호 2항 주재국 대통령 인권위원회 관련 자료를 별첨 송부

합니다.

별 첨 : 상기 자료 3건.   끝.

(예고: 92.12.31까지(일반))

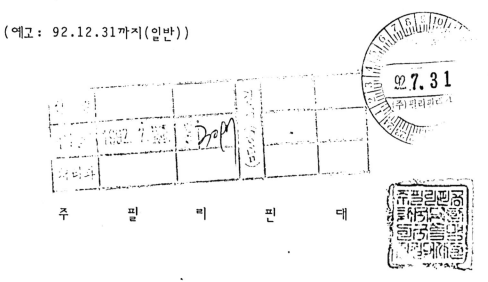

주 필 리 핀 대

0116

PLANS, PROGRAMS AND ACTIVITIES
OF THE PRESIDENTIAL HUMAN RIGHTS
COMMITTEE (CREATED BY ADMINISTRA-
TIVE ORDER NO. 101, DATED
DECEMBER 13, 1988) FOR 1990

1. To request the Commission on Human Rights, thru its Chairman, to furnish the Committee/Secretariat monthly reports of cases it has filed with Provincial/City Prosecution Offices, NAPOLCOM, JAGO, and the Courts, indicating the docket number, parties involved, date filed, and status of case, to enable the Human Rights Committee (HRC) to monitor and follow-up said cases and ensure their early prosecution and resolution.

2. To prepare and monitor a hit list of 10 priority cases for 1990.

3. To issue a Department Circular directing Provincial and City Prosecutors to submit the names of the Prosecutor and his alternate whom they have designated to assist and to attend to human rights complaints and requests for assistance as provided under DOJ Department Circular No. 37, dated December 12, 1988.

4. The Committee may decide, on a case to case basis, to assist or participate in fact-finding missions so as to monitor accurately the situation whenever there are reported human rights violations.

To support, through the facilities of mass media (news-papers, radio, television, and dissemination of posters and brochures/leaflets), a more effective country-wide information campaign on human rights and the rights of individuals, particularly on the rights of persons against unwarranted arrests, unreasonable search and seizure, and the rights of detainees, and the duties and obligation of law enforcement and military officers under the Constitution towards detainees and suspects under custodial investigation.

6. To work for the repeal of P.D. 1850.

7. To endorse and support the enactment into law of pending bills in Congress providing for a Witness Protection Program.

8. To direct the Department of National Defense, thru its representative in the Committee, to submit to the Committee the list and location of PC/INP and military detention centers throughout the country, and the names of the detainees confined thereat.

0117

9. To assist the Department of Foreign Affairs and the Commission on Human Rights in the preparation of national position papers for presentation before international human rights bodies.

> – Approved and Adopted Unanimously
> by the Members of the Human Rights
> Committee Present during its Meeting
> of January 30 , 1990.

N.B. – As of June 25, 1990, Nos. 2, 3 and 8 have already been implemented while Nos. 1 and 4 are being effected from time to time.

0118

MALACAÑANG
MANILA

ADMINISTRATIVE ORDER NO. 101

CREATING A HUMAN RIGHTS COMMITTEE WITH REPRESENTATIVES FROM THE EXECU-
TIVE, CONGRESS, THE COMMISSION ON HUMAN RIGHTS AND PRIVATE SECTOR
HUMAN RIGHTS GROUPS.

WHEREAS, the Constitution provides in the Declaration of Principles and State Policies that, "The State values the dignity of every
human person and guarantees full respect for human rights";

WHEREAS, this Government is firmly committed to protect human
rights and promote its observance by all;

WHEREAS, there is a need for a standing body with representatives
from the Executive, Congress, the Commission on Human Rights, and
private sector human rights groups to assess and monitor, on a continuing basis, the Philippine human rights situation and to advise the
President on the proper measures that ought to be taken without delay.

NOW, THEREFORE, I, CORAZON C. AQUINO, President of the Philippines,
by virtue of the powers vested in me by law, do hereby order:

SECTION 1. There is hereby created a Human Rights Committee, to
be composed of:

The Secretary of Justice as Chairman
The Chairman of the Commission on Human Rights, the Presi-
dential Legal Counsel, a representative of the Department of
National Defense, a Senator and a Congressman as the Senate
President and the Speaker of the House of Representatives may
wish to designate and two representatives of private human
rights groups to be nominated by said groups and appointed by the
President, as Members.

SECTION 2. The Committee shall exercise the following functions
and duties:

a. To assess and monitor the Philippine human rights situation
and advise the President so that proper measures can forthwith be
taken effectively;

b. To assist relatives to locate persons who have disappeared
and are believed to be detained illegally; and

c. To perform such other functions and duties as may be necessary to meet the objectives of the Committee.

SECTION 3. The Committee shall have a Secretariat which shall be
located in the Department of Justice. The Secretariat shall provide staff
support to the Committee.

SECTION 4. The amount of One Hundred Thousand (₱100,000.00) Pesos, or so much thereof as may be necessary, is hereby authorized to be released from the Compensation and Organizational Adjustment Fund in the 1988 General Appropriations Act or from such other lump-sum appropriations as may be determined by the Department of Budget and Management for the operational requirements of the Committee.

SECTION 5. This Administrative Order shall take effect immediately.

DONE in the City of Manila, this 13th day of December, in the year of Our Lord, nineteen hundred and eighty-eight.

Corazon C. Aquino

By the President:

CATALINO MACARAIG, JR.
Executive Secretary

MALACAÑANG
MANILA

ADMINISTRATIVE ORDER NO. 243

FURTHER RECONSTITUTING THE MEMBERSHIP OF THE HUMAN RIGHTS COMMITTEE
CREATED UNDER ADMINISTRATIVE ORDER NO. 101, SERIES OF 1988

I, CORAZON C. AQUINO, President of the Philippines, by virtue
of the powers vested in me by law, do hereby order:

SECTION 1. The Human Rights Committee created under Administrative Order No. 101, series of 1988, is hereby further reconstituted,
as follows:

Chairman   - Secretary of Justice

Members   - A representative each from the -

                Office of the President
                Department of Foreign Affairs
                Department of National Defense
                Department of the Interior and Local Government
                Department of Health
                Department of Social Welfare and Development
                Department of Labor and Employment
                Two representatives from non-government
                    organizations on human rights to be
                    designated by the President

Upon the designation by the Honorable, the President of the
Senate, the Honorable, the Speaker, House of Representatives, and the
Honorable, the Chairman, Commission on Human Rights, of their respective representatives in the Committee, such representatives so
designated shall become regular members of the Committee representing
their respective agencies.

SEC. 2. The provisions of Administrative Order No. 219 dated
6 May 1991 and of other issuances inconsistent herewith are hereby
repealed or modified accordingly.

SEC. 3. This Administrative Order shall take effect immediately.

Done in the City of Manila, this 21st day of October, in the
year of Our Lord, nineteen hundred and ninety-one.

[signature: Corazon C. Aquino]

By the President:

[signature]
FRANKLIN M. DRILON
Executive Secretary

CERTIFIED COPY:
[signature]
AURORA T. AQUINO
DIRECTOR IV

0121

FUNCTIONS AND DUTIES OF THE SECRETARIAT,
HUMAN RIGHTS COMMITTEE (HRC)

1. The Secretariat, headed by an Undersecretary of Justice or any DOJ official who may be designated by the Secretary of Justice, shall have two sections or units: (a) the clerical and utility staff and (b) the investigative/prosecution support staff.

2. The Clerical and Utility Staff shall be charged with record keeping and maintenance and cleanliness of the office of the Committee. It shall record all proceedings of the Committee, transcribe stenographic notes thereof, type and or computerize all communications of the Committee and/or the Chairman, and prepare the reproduction of documents or reports of human rights violations and/or requests for assistance relative thereto, and other materials that may be needed during the monthly regular meetings (usually the last Tuesday of the month) or special meetings of the Committee.

This unit shall also be charged with the service of communications, as well as subpoenas that the members of the investigative and prosecution staff may issue concerning specific cases of human rights violations assigned by the Committee for investigation and/or prosecution.

3. The Investigative and Prosecution Staff shall be manned by four (4) state prosecutors who shall attend to the investigation and prosecution of special cases of violations of human rights which the Committee may assign from time to time. The members of the staff may also be sent to the field to investigate, in behalf of the Committee, reports of human rights violations, or attend exhumations of bodies of alleged victims of human rights violations. This staff or unit shall also be charged with assisting the head of the Secretariat in the preparation of the agenda for the regular and/or special meetings of the Committee, and in the preparation of drafts of communications and/or recommended actions on matters involving human rights violations coming from the public, government and non-government organizations, and people and NGOs from other countries of the world.

It shall also conduct an inventory of all cases involving human rights violations that are pending before all Provincial/City Prosecution Offices and the Courts. It shall monitor all said cases, with particular emphasis on: (a) compliance with the timetable imposed by the Secretary of Justice within which the prosecution should complete the presentation of its evidence, and (b) the conduct of court trials of special human rights cases, certified as such by the Secretary of Justice, in accordance with the respective Trial Briefs which prosecutors will be required to submit.

0122

4. It shall undertake the computerization of reports and records of cases of violation of human rights and the up-dated status thereof.

5. The Secretariat shall perform such other functions and duties that may be assigned to it by the Committee.

외 무 부

종 별 :

번 호 : FRW-1657

일 시 : 92 0818 1700

수 신 : 장관(연이,구일)

발 신 : 주 불 대사

제 목 : 인권보장 관련기구

대:WFR-1491

1. 주재국 의회내에 인권문제를 전담하는 별도의 위원회는 없음

2. 다만 하원내에 인권문제를 위한 정당간 실무구룹(INTERGROUPE SUR LES DROITS DE L'HOMME) 이 88.12 에 결성되었으나, 현재까지 특기할 만한 활동이 없었으며, 상원내에도 인권문제 연구구룹(GOUPE D'ETUDES DES DROITS DE L'HOMME) 이 있으나, 활동은 전무한 실정이라함. 끝

(대사 노영찬- 국장)

예고: 92.12.31 까지

국기국   구주국

92.08.19   04:40

외신 2과 통제관 FM

0124

각국 인권보장 관련기구 현황

1. 독립 기구

국 명	기 구 및 성 격	주 요 활 동
캐나다	○ 캐나다 인권위원회, 공식언어 위원회, 프라이버시 위원회등 5개 위원회 - 캐나다 정부로부터 보조금을 지급받는 준정부기관	
일 본	○ 인권옹호위원 - 일본의 독특한 인권보장 제도 - 임기 3년의 12,548명의 위원으로 구성 - 위원은 지방자치단체장의 추천에 의거 법무대신이 위촉	1) 자유인권사상에 관한 계몽 선전 2) 민간의 인권옹호운동 조장 3) 인권침해 사건에 대해 조사 하여 법무대신 및 관계기관에 보고 및 권고 4) 빈곤자에 대해 소송원조 등 인권옹호를 위한 구제수단 강구 5) 기타 인권옹호 일반에 관한 활동
필리핀	○ 인권위원회(헌법기관) - 헌법상 독립기구(의장 및 4명의 위원)	1) 인권침해상황 조사(인권침해 호소시 또는 기구 자발적 으로) 2) 내부규칙 제정 3) 국내외 필리핀 국적 보유자 인권보호를 위한 법적구제 조치, 인권피보호 대상자에 대한 인권침해 예방 조치 4) 구치소, 형무소 등에 대한 방문

1

0125

국 명	기 구 및 성 격	주 요 활 동
필리핀		5) 인권신장을 위한 연구, 교육, 홍보 6) 의회에 대하여 인권침해자에 대한 적절한 보상조치 마련 촉구 7) 정부의 인권관련 국제규약 준수 여부 감시 8) 인권침해 사실 조사에 협조한 증인 보호 9) 정부 각 기관에 대해 인권 보호활동에 필요한 협조 요구 10) 자체인사조직 11) 기타 법률로 규정된 사항
멕시코	O 국가인권위 - 내무성 산하 외청 　(독립기관) - 위원장과 임기 3년의 　10명 위원	1) 인권수호정책 입안, 제의 2) 국내외 관련기관과의 협력 3) 국제문제에 있어 외무성과의 협력 4) 관련 조약, 협정체결 수행을 위한 계획수립 및 조치 제의

2. 정부 담당기관

국 명	외 무 부	기타 정부내 담당기관
미 국	○ 국무부 인권 및 인도적 업무 담당국 (Bureau of Human Rights and Humanitarian Affairs) - 양자 업무과 - 다자 업무과	○ 법무부 인권국 (Civil rights Division)
캐 나 다	○ 인권사회과	○ 법무부 인권과 ○ 보사부 인권과
스 웨 덴	○ 외무부 국제협력처, 정부7국 (국제기구담당) ○ 외무부 법률4국	
호 주	○ 외무부 국제기구국 인권과	○ 법무성 인권과
일 본	○ 외무부 국제연합국 인권 난민과	○ 법무성 인권옹호국
영 국	○ 외무부 유엔과내 인권정책 부서 (Human Rights Policy Unit)	○ 내무성 형사사건 및 헌정과 (The Criminal Justice and Constitutional Department)
노르웨이	○ 정무국(Department of Political Affairs)내 인권 관계 특별고문이 국제인권 문제 담당 ○ 법무국(Department of Legal Affairs) 제1법무과	○ 법무부 입법과(Division of Legislation Affairs)

3

0127

국 명	외 무 부	기타 정부내 담당기관
프랑스	○ 유엔국 인권부국 ○ 법무국 인권부국	○ 법무성 인권실 ○ 수상비서실 인권문제 담당 보좌관 ○ 내무성 인권국
독 일	○ 인권문제 조정관(유엔국장) - 정부부처내 인권문제 관련 협의 및 조정업무 담당 ○ 인도적 지원, 외국 긴급 재난 및 난민지원 담당과	○ 내무부 ○ 법무부 공법담당 국장
필리핀	○ 외무부 유엔6과	없 음
칠 레	○ 외무부 차관실 직속 인권 문제 담당관실 (Asesoria de Derechos Humanos)	없 음
헝가리	○ 국제기구국 인권과(Human Right Desk, 직원 3명)	없 음
러시아	○ 외무성 인권문화국	○ 내무성 ○ 법무성 ○ 공민권 위원회(대통령실 산하)

4

0128

3. 기타 인권기구

국 명	기 구 및 성 격	주 요 활 동
독 일	○ 인권문제 국제기구 (Internationale Gesell-schaft fur Menschenrechte) - 민간단체(1972년 설립, 프랑크프르트 소재)	1) 연례보고서 발간 2) 주요문제 발생시 사법당국에 제소 3) 인권관련 홍보 및 교육 4) 42개국에서 인권향상을 위한 개발 프로젝트 참여
미 국	○ 민권위원회 (Commission on Civil Rights)	1) 인종, 피부색, 종교, 성, 연령에 따른 차별에 관한 정보 수집 2) 동 사실 및 개선 건의안을 대통령.의회에 보고
캐나다	○ 100여개 민간단체	
헝가리	○ 헝가리 인권센타	1) 국제 인권관련 의무와 국내법과의 조화문제 연구 2) 인권관련 잡지 발간 3) 국제회의 개최 및 참가
러시아	○ 난민권 보고 위원회	
노르웨이	○ 노르웨이 인권연구소	1) 국제적 인권제도 및 각국 인권 연구 2) 유럽의 인권, 특히 동구, 구소련의 인권문제 3) 개발도상국의 인권 및 남북 관계에 있어서 인권문제 4) 국제적 인권과 각 문화 및 규범에 따른 갈등

5

0129

각국의 인권보장기구 현황 조사, 1992 335

국 명	기 구 및 성 격	주 요 활 동
프랑스	o 인권협의 위원회(70명으로 구성)	
칠 례	o 대중인권보호 위원회 o 칠례 인권위원회 - 비정부 독립 민간기구 (78.12.설립)	1) 유엔 인권위 및 미주 인권위 등 국제 인권관련 기구에 대한 칠례 인권 상황 자료제공 2) 인권위반 감시 3) 인권구조 4) 인권보호 5) 타국 인권기구와 연대활동 6) 인권관련 홍보 및 교육 7) 상.하원 인권위 및 정부에 대한 자문 및 인권관련 법안에 의견 제출

6

0130

4. 의회내 기구

국 명	기 구 및 성 격	주 요 활 동
헝가리	O 인권, 소수민족 및 종교 위원회 - 국회내 상임위원회 (27명의 국회의원)	1) 인권문제 발생시 국회에서 결의 채택 2) 인권관련 입법활동 적극 추진
러시아	O 인권위원회 - 최고회의내(입법부) 설치	O 인권관련 입법조치 및 정책 심의
영 국	O Parliamentary Human Rights Group - 의회내 초당적 인권보장 기구	

7

0131

정 리 보 존 문 서 목 록					
기록물종류	일반공문서철	등록번호	2021010058	등록일자	2021-01-12
분류번호	734.29	국가코드		보존기간	30년
명 칭	인권업무 현황 및 추진계획, 1992				
생 산 과	국제연합2과	생산년도	1992~1992	담당그룹	
내용목차					

0001

공   란

공　　　란

공   란

공   란

공　　　란

인 권 업 무 현 황

1992. 1.

국 제 기 구 국
국 제 연 합 2 과

0007

- 차 례 -

0008

0009

인권업무 현황

1. 경사리산하 인권관계 주요기구

가. 유엔 인권위원회(Commission on Human Rights)

1) 설립근거

   ○ 경사리 결의(5(Ⅰ), 9(Ⅱ))에 의거, 1946년 설립

2) 구 성

   ○ 경사리에서 선출되는 임기 3년의 53개 위원국으로 구성

3) 회의일정

   ○ 매년 1-3월중 6주간 일정으로 제네바에서 개최

   * 제48차 회의 : 92.1.27-3.6

4) 주요임무 및 조직

   ○ 아래 인권문제 전반에 대하여 토의, 동 결과를 경사리에 보고
   - 세계 인권상황 검토
   - 고문등 재소자 인권문제 검토
   - 각종 인권협약 평가
   - 아동, 소수민족, 이주노동자등 인권취약계층의 인권보호문제
   - 발전의 권리, 법조인 독립문제등 특정분야에 대한 성문화 작업
     및 성문화 내용 이행여부 검토

1

o 상기 임무수행을 위하여 아래 특별보고관(Special Rapporteur),
  특별대표 또는 실무위원회(Working Group)를 한시적으로 임명,
  특정업무를 조사, 보고케 함.
  - 국가별 인권문제 관련
    . 남아공관련 전문가 실무위(5명)
    . 피점령하의 쿠웨이트 인권상황 특별보고관
    . 쿠바문제 특별대표
    . 루마니아문제 특별보고관
    . 이라크문제 특별보고관
    . 엘살바돌문제 특별대표
    . 아프가니스탄문제 특별보고관
    . 이란문제 특별대표
    . 하이티문제 특별보고관
    . 적도기니문제 특별대표
  - 주제별 인권문제 관련
    . 용병문제 특별보고관
    . 비상사태문제 특별보고관
    . 불법구금문제 실무위(5명)
    . 고문문제 특별보고관
    . 강제실종 실무위(5명)
    . 불법처형문제 특별보고관
    . 경제.사회.문화적 권리 관련 특별보고관

5) 아국과의 관계
  o 아국은 매년 회의에 주제네바대사를 수석대표로 외무부, 법무부
    담당관으로 구성된 옵서버대표단을 파견

2

0011

o 아국 인권관련사항으로는 주로 3-4개 민간인권단체(NGO)가 시국관련
  사건을 거론

  - 아측은 답변권 행사등을 통해 대응

    * 북한 인권관련, 최근 미국 및 일부 NGO는 북한의 체제 및
      기본적 인권침해상황을 거론

o 아국은 92.4월 경사리 조직회의에서 선출예정인 인권위원국 선거에
  입후보하고 있음.

나. 유엔 인권소위원회(Sub-Commission on Prevention of Discrimination and
    Protection of Minorities)

 1) 설립근거

    o 1947년 인권위원회 결정에 따라 설립

 2) 구 성

    o 인권위원회에서 선출되는 임기 4년의 26명의 위원으로 구성

      - 동 위원은 정부의 지명에 의해 인권위에서 선출되나, 개인자격으로
        활동

 3) 회의일정

    o 매년 8월중 4주간 일정으로 제네바에서 개최

      * 제44회의 : 92.8.3-8.28

 4) 주요임무

    o 인권전반에 관한 연구활동(각종선언 및 협약초안 마련)

    o 인권관련 차별방지 및 소수자 보호에 관하여 인권위에 권고

    o 기타 경사리 및 인권위에서 위임하는 인권문제 토의

    * 최근 인권소위는 인권위와의 업무중첩 및 과도한 업무확대 현상,
      위원의 독립성 문제와 관련, 비판을 받고 있으며, 이에따라 업무개선
      방안을 논의중임.

3

0012

5) 아국과의 관계

　　o 아국은 매년회의에 주제네바대사를 수석대표로 외무부, 법무부

　　　담당관으로 구성된 옵서버대표단을 파견

　　o 남북한 인권상황을 일부 NGO가 거론하는 사례가 있음.

　　　- 아측은 답변권 행사등을 통해 대응

2. 인권협약산하 주요조직

가. 인권이사회(Human Rights Committee)

　1) 설립근거

　　o 1976년 발효한 시민적, 정치적 권리에 관한 국제규약(International
Covenant on Civil and Political Rights) 제28-32조에 의거, 설립

　2) 구 성

　　o 규약당사국회의에서 선출된 임기 4년의 18명의 당사국 출신 위원으로
구성

　　　- 현재 규약당사국 : 99개국

　3) 회의일정

　　o 매년 3차례 회의개최

　　　- 1회는 뉴욕, 2회는 제네바에서 개최

　　　* 제44차 회의 : 92.3.23-4.10, 뉴욕

　　　　제45차 회의 : 92.7.13-7.31, 제네바

　4) 주요임무

　　o 당사국이 제출한 정기보고서 심의

　　　- 최초보고서는 규약발효후 1년이내 제출

　　　- 이후에는 매 5년마다 제출

4

0013

○ 규약 선택의정서(Optional Protocol to the International Covenant on the Civil and Political Rights)에 따라 제출된 진정서를 심의, 결정

　　* 선택의정서 당사국 : 58개국

○ 위원회 활동을 매년 유엔총회에 보고

5) 아국과의 관계

○ 동 규약은 아국에 대하여 90.7.10.발효

　　* 동 규약 선택의정서는 아국에 대하여 90.7.10.발효

○ 아국은 90.7월 최초보고서를 제출

　　- 동심의는 92.3월 회의시 있은 계획이었으나, 법무부 요청을 고려, 92.7월 회의로 심의를 연기하여 줄것을 인권사무국에 요청중

　　* 북한은 81년 규약가입 이후 1차례 보고서를 제출, 심의를 마쳤으나, 87.12월까지 제출키로 되어있는 2차 보고서를 아직 제출치 않고 있음.

나. 경제적, 사회적, 문화적 권리위원회(Committee on Economic, Social and Cultural Rights)

1) 설립근거

○ 1976년 발효한 경제적, 사회적, 문화적 권리에 관한 국제규약 (Interntional Covenant on Economic, Social and Cultural Rights)과 관련, 경사리 결의에 따라 실무위원회가 구성된바 있으며, 85년 경사리 결의에 따라 현재와 같은 형태로 구성됨.

5

0014

2) 구 성

　　○ 규약 당사국회의 추천에 따라 경사리에서 선출된 임기 4년의 18명의

　　　당사국 출신 위원으로 구성

　　　- 현재 규약당사국　:　103개국

3) 회의일정

　　○ 매년 1회 3주간의 일정으로 제네바에서 개최

4) 주요임무

　　○ 당사국이 제출한 정기보고서 심의

　　　- 최초보고서는 규약발효 다음해 6.30까지 제출

　　　- 이후에는 매 5년마다 제출

　　○ 위원회 활동을 매년 경사리에 보고

5) 아국과의 관계

　　○ 동 규약은 아국에 대하여 90.7.10. 발효

　　○ 아국은 92.6.30까지 최초보고서를 제출예정임.

　　* 북한은 81년 규약 가입이후 최초보고서(제3부)를 제출, 동 심의가

　　　91.12월 개최된바 있음.

다.　기타 협약산하위원회

위 원 회 명	근 거 협 약	구 성	회의일정	아국과의 관계
인종차별철폐위 (Committee on the Elimination of Racial Discrimination : CERD)	International Convention on the Elimination of All forms of Racial Discrimination - 69.1.4.발효 - 당사국 : 129개국	임기 4년의 18명 위원	매년 2회 제네바에서 개최	- 79.1.4.발효 - 80년이래 6차의 정기 보고서 제출 - 현재 제7차 보고서 준비중

6

0015

위 원 회 명	근 거 협 약	구 성	회의일정	아국과의 관계
여성차별철폐위 (Committee on the Elimination of Discrimina- tion against Women : CEDAW)	Convention on the Elimination of Discrimina- tion against Women - 81.9.3.발효 - 당사국 : 108개국	임기 4년의 23명 위원	매년 1회 비엔나와 뉴욕에서 교대로 개최	- 85.1.26.발효 - 제2차 보고서 는 93년도 위원회에서 심의예정
아동권리위원회 (Committee on the Rights of the Child)	Convention on the Rights of the Child - 90.9.2.발효 - 당사국 : 108개국	임기 4년의 10명 위원	매년 1회 개최	- 91.12.20발효 - 발효후 2년 이내 보고서 제출 의무
고문방지위원회 (Committee against Torture)	Convention against Torture and other Cruel, Inhuman or Degrading Treat- ment or Punish- ment - 87.6.26.발효 - 당사국 : 61개국	임기 4년의 10명 위원	매년 2회 제네바에서 개최	- 협약 미가입

7

0016

3. 유엔체제내 인권보장관련 주요절차

가. 총회에서의 토의

1) 토의방식

o 총회(제3위원회)에서의 인권문제 토의는 당해년도 인권위원회와
경사리에서의 토의 및 결의중 중요내용이 토의·결의되는 경향임.

2) 제46차 총회(91) 주요토의결과

o 인권문제 접근방식에 대한 선후진국간 이견 노정

o 특정국가 및 지역의 인권상황 거론
- 남아공, 이스라엘, 이란, 이락, 미얀마, 베트남, 스리랑카,
아프가니스탄, 하이티, 과테말라, 엘살바돌, 쿠바, 소말리아,
수단, 자이레, 케냐

o 국별인권상황 및 주제별 인권문제 결의안 채택
- 국별결의안 : 이라크, 피점령하의 쿠웨이트, 미얀마, 엘살바돌,
아프가니스탄
- 표결을 통해 채택된 주제별 결의안
. 정기적 선거실시 원칙 강화(미국제안)
. 국가주권 및 국내선거에서의 불간섭 원칙 존중(쿠바제안)
. 발전의 권리등 인권의 효율적 향유방안(쿠바제안)

나. 1503 절차(상세내용 : 별첨 2)

o 1970년 경사리 결의 1503호에 의거, 시행되고 있는 인권 및 기본적
자유의 침해에 관한 진정서 비밀처리절차임.
- 72-88년간 35만여건의 진정서 처리
- 73-88년간 인권위에서 44개국의 국별인권상황이 토의됨.

8

0017

o 동 절차는 개별적인 사건을 다루는 것이 아니라 지속적 형태의
   인권위반상황, 즉 장기간에 걸쳐 다수의 사람들에게 영향을 미치는
   인권상황을 다루는 절차임.

다. 선택의정서상의 절차(상세내용 : 별첨 3)

o 시민적, 정치적 권리에 관한 국제규약(B규약) 선택의정서 당사국이
   B규약상 권리를 침해한 경우 피해당사자는 인권이사회에 진정서를
   제출할수 있음.

o 진정서가 일정요건을 구비한 경우, 이사회는 당사국 정부가 제출한
   답변자료를 검토, 진정서를 심의하고, 이사회의 견해(views)를 채택,
   당사국 정부 및 진정인에게 송부함.

o 상기 의견은 법적집행력은 없으나, 강력한 법적의견으로서 당사국에
   대해서는 도덕적, 정치적 권위를 가짐.

라. 특별보고관 활동

o 최근 유엔의 인권활동중 두드러진 현상의 하나는 인권위원회 산하에
   특정국가별 또는 특정주제별 특별보고관등을 임명, 조사.보고토록
   하는 것임.
   - 현재 14명의 특별보고관 및 특별대표, 3개 실무위 활동중.

o 이들중 아국의 인권상황과 관련 활동에 관심을 가져야할 특별보고관
   및 실무위는 아래와 같음.
   - 고문문제 특별보고관
     . 85년 활동시작
     . 88년 방한한바 있으며, 최근 매년 아국관계 2-3개 사건 질의
       및 정부답변내용을 보고서에 수록

9

0018

- 불법구금문제 실무위

  . 91년 활동시작

  . 아직 아국관련 사례는 없음.

마. 유엔전문기구내 진정서 절차

1) UNESCO

o 교육, 과학, 문화 및 정보의 분야에서 유네스코의 관할하에 있는
  인권의 침해에 관하여 개인, NGO등이 제출한 진정서(Communication)를
  심사하는 절차임.

o 유네스코 집행위원회 산하의 협약 및 권고위원회(Committee on
  Conventions and Recommendations)는 진정서에 대한 심사여부 및
  동 진정서에 대한 결정을 당사국 정부의 답변자료등을 검토, 결정,
  동 위원회 결정은 집행위원회에 보고됨.

  - 상기 결정은 법적 구속력은 없으나, 심의과정에서 당사국 정부와의
    대화를 통하여 문제해결을 모색하는등 정치적 효과가 있음.

o 현재 협약 및 권고위원회에는 아국관계로 장의균, 임수경 및 문규현
  사건이 심사여부 결정단계에 있음.

2) 국제노동기구(상세내용 : 별첨 4)

o 국제노동기구는 단결권, 단체교섭권등 기본적 노동권문제뿐만 아니라
  아동노동, 빈곤층 문제, 직업훈련, 사회보장등 광범위한 문제에
  관하여 다양한 구제절차를 운영하고 있음.

  - "협약 및 권고의 적용에 관한 전문가위원회", "협약 및 권고의
    적용에 관한 총회위원회"에서 담당

10

4. 국제민간단체 현황

가. 현 황

1) 유엔 인권회의 참가 NGO 자격

○ 유엔 경제사회이사회와 협의관계(Consultative Relations)에 있는
NGO로서 3개 등급(Category I , II , Roster)이 있으나, 실제로
회의에 참여하고, 발언하는데 있어서는 등급에 따른 차이가 별로
없음.

- 경사리 산하의 NGO 위원회에서 매 2년에 1회씩 자격부여 심사

2) 주요활동

가) 인권회의등 참가

○ 유엔 인권위, 인권소위등 관련회의에 옵서버로 참가하여
발언하거나, 서면 발언문을 제출하여 유엔 사무총장이
배포토록 함.

- 유엔 인권소위에서는 특히 NGO의 인권관련 정보제공 역할을
고려, 회의시 발언순서를 위원, NGO 대표, 옵서버 국가
대표순으로 부여하고 있음.

○ 1503 절차에 의거, 인권관련 진정서를 유엔 인권사무국에
제출함.

나) 인권관련 협약 초안 및 선언문 작성 실무회의 참가

○ 인권위 및 인권소위 참가활동의 일환으로 인권관련 협약 초안
및 각종 선언문 작성 실무위 활동에 참가함.

- 최근의 예로 아동권리협약, 이주 노동자 및 가족의 권리
보호협약 초안 작성 작업등이 있음.

11

0020

다) 인권관련 세미나 및 회의참석

　　　o 인종차별주의 철폐등 인권관련 주제에 관한 NGO 회의 및
　　　　세미나에 참석함.

3) 최근 인권회의시 NGO활동 평가

　　o 통상 유엔 인권위에는 130여개 NGO, 인권소위에는 90여개 NGO가
　　　참여함.

　　o 상기 NGO중 대부분이 각기 특정지역 및 특정국가의 인권상황만을
　　　집중적으로 언급하는 실정이며, 전반적인 세계인권상황에 대한
　　　언급과 인권문제에 대한 이론적 분석 및 접근을 시도하고 있는
　　　NGO는 20-30여개에 불과함.

나. 아국과의 관계

　　o 아래 NGO들이 방한활동, 아국관계 보고서 발간, 유엔 인권위등
　　　회의에서의 아국 인권문제 거론등의 활동을 통해 아국 인권상황에
　　　관심을 표명
　　　- AI(국제사면위원회), Asia Watch, ICJ(국제법률가 위원회),
　　　　International Human Rights Law Group, International League
　　　　for Human Rights, WCC(세계교회협의회) 산하 국제문제위원회등

　　o 아래 친북 NGO는 임수경사건등 시국사건에 관해 유엔 인권위에서의
　　　발언, 1503 절차에 따른 진정서 제출 활동을 전개
　　　- International League for the Rights and Liberation of Peoples,
　　　　International Union of Students, International Confederation
　　　　of Free Trade Unions, World Federation of Democratic Youth
　　　　International Association of Democratic Lawyers

12

0021

5. 인권관련 주요현안

가. 유엔가입이후 유엔체제내 인권토의 참여확대

o 유엔내 주요 인권활동 조직인 인권위(인권소위), 경사리 및 총회
  토의에 적극적, 유기적 참여를 통하여 유엔내 인권토의내용 파악,
  각종협약 및 선언등 인권관련 규범의 국내도입 및 활용을 적극
  추진하는 것이 바람직

o 상기관련, 인권위 위원국 진출(기입후보), 경사리 이사국 피선을
  추진

o 본부, 주유엔대표부 및 주제네바대표부 담당관의 효율적 회의참여
  방안 강구 필요

나. 각종협약에 대한 아국보고서 작성체제 확립

o 그간 아국이 인권관련협약 가입을 적극 추진한 결과, 동 협약들에
  의거한 정기보고서 작성업무의 비중이 증대됨.

o 향후 제출하여야 할 보고서
  - 인권규약(A) : 92.6.30. 최초보고서 제출, 이후 매 5년마다 제출
  - 인권규약(B) : 91.7.30. 최초보고서 기제출, 이후 매 5년마다 제출
  - 인종차별철폐협약 : 92.2월말 제7차 보고서 제출, 이후 매 2년마다
                      제출
  - 여성차별철폐협약 : 90.1월 제2차 보고서 기제출, 이후 매 4년마다
                      제출
  - 아동권리협약 : 93년말까지 최초보고서 제출, 이후 매 5년마다 제출

13

0022

ㅇ 인권규약(B) 보고서는 법무부에서 관계부처와 협의, 보고서 초안
(국문본)을 작성하고, 외무부에서 영문 최종본을 작성 제출한바
있으며, 인종차별 및 여성차별철폐협약은 외무부에서 전담 작성하고
있음.

ㅇ 보고서 작성을 위한 정부내 협의회 구성등을 법무부등 관계부처에
제의 계획

다. 세계인권회의 대책

ㅇ 유엔총회 결의애 의거, 93.6월 베를린에서 개최예정이며, 동 준비를
위한 회의가 아래와 같이 개최예정
- 제2차 준비회의 : 92.3.30-4.10, 제네바
- 아주지역 준비회의 : 92.8.17-8.21, 방콕
- 제3차 준비회의 : 92.9.14-9.25, 제네바
- 제4차 준비회의 : 93년 전반기 개최

ㅇ 동 회의는 68년도 테헤란 회의 이후 최초로 유엔주관하에 세계인권
상황을 평가하고, 향후 유엔을 중심으로한 인권활동 방향을 토의
예정인바, 유엔내에서의 점증하는 인권업무의 중요성에 비추어 적극
참여가 바람직

라. 남북합의서 채택이후 북한 인권문제 대응
ㅇ 관련 검토자료 별첨(1) 참조

첨부 : 1. 남북합의서와 북한 인권문제
2. 1503 절차
3. 선택의정서상의 절차
4. 국제노동기구에서의 제소절차
5. 제46차 유엔총회 인권관계 결의안 표결현황   - 끝 -

14

0023

공   란

공   란

공 란

공　　란

공   란

1503 절차 내용

1. 1503 절차 연혁

o 1959년도 경사리 결의 728F에 의거, 인권침해 진정서(Communication) 비밀 List를 인권위 및 인권소위에 배포토록 함.

o 1967년도 경사리 결의 1235에 의거, 인권위 및 인권소위가 모든 국가에서의 심각한 인권침해 관련정보를 조사하고, 인권위가 지속적인 형태의 인권 위반상황에 대한 철저한 조사를 행하여 이를 경사리에 보고하며, 권고를 행할수 있도록 함.

o 1970년 경사리 결의 1503에 의거, 인권 및 기본적 자유의 침해에 관한 진정서 처리절차(1503 절차)가 채택됨.
   - 72-88년간 35만 여건의 진정서 처리
   - 73-88년간 인권위에서 44개국의 국별인권상황이 토의됨.

2. 1503 절차의 특징

o 1503 절차는 개별적인 사건(individual case)를 다루는 것이 아니라, 지속적 형태의 인권위반상황(situations which reveal a consistent pattern of violations of human rights) 즉, 장기간에 걸쳐 다수의 사람들에게 영향을 미치는 상황을 다루는 절차임.
   - 개별적 사건을 다루는 인권규약 선택의정서에 의한 진정서 절차와 구별됨.

o 1503 절차에 의한 모든조치는 경사리에 보고되기 전까지 비밀로 함.
   관련회의는 비공개로 진행되며, 회의기록 및 문서의 비밀은 유지됨.
   - 다만 1978년 이래로 인권위 의장은 인권위 회의에서 인권상황에 대한
     심의를 받는 국가 및 더이상 심의를 받지않는 국가명을 발표하고 있음.
   - 또한 경사리는 특정국 인권상황에 대한 조사가 완료된후 비밀을
     공개할 것을 결정하기도 함.(85년 알젠틴, 우루과이, 86년 필리핀)

3. 진정서의 요건

o 진정서가 검토되기 위해서는 아래 요건을 구비해야 함.
   - 유엔헌장, 세계인권선언 및 기타 인권협약의 원칙에 합치되어야 하며,
     정치적 동기가 없어야 함.
   - 지속적 형태의 심각하고 입증된 인권침해가 있다고 믿을만한 합리적인
     근거가 있어야 함.
   - 진정서는 피해당사자 또는 침해내용을 직접적으로, 근거를 갖고
     알고있는 개인 및 그룹, 또는 침해내용에 대해 직접적이고 근거있는
     증거를 갖고 있으면서 선의로 활동하는 민간단체(NGO)에 의해
     제출되어야 함.
   - 오직 언론보도에 근거한 익명의 진정서는 접수되지 않음.
   - 표현이 남용적이거나, 관련국가에 관한 모욕적 언급을 포함하여서는
     아니됨.
   - 국내적 구제절차가 완료되어야 하며, 여타 기존의 절차와 중복되거나,
     유엔의 의해 이미 다뤄진 내용을 반복 제출하여서는 아니됨.

21

4. 1503 절차의 내용

o 유엔 인권사무국은 매달 접수된 진정서 내용을 진정서 사건 관련국 정부에 통보하면서 답변을 요청함.

o 인권소위 위원 및 인권위원국은 매달 진정서 List(진정내용 요약 및 정부답변 포함)를 통보받음.

o 매년 임명되는 5명의 인권소위 위원으로 구성된 진정서 심의 실무위원회가 매년 인권소위 개최 2주전에 개최되어 모든 진정서 및 정부답변을 검토, 지속적 형태의 심각한 인권침해를 입증할 것으로 추정되는 사건을 선정, 인권소위에 보고함.
   - 동 실무위에서 기각된 진정서에 대해서는 추가 조치가 없음.

o 인권소위는 선정된 진정서를 심의, 지속적 형태의 인권침해로 추정되는 상황을 인권위에 제출할지 여부를 결정함.

o 인권위 산하 진정서 실무위(Working Group on Situations)은 인권소위 자료를 검토, 개별사건과 관련 향후 취한 조치를 인권위에 권고함.

o 인권위는 특정상황(particular situation)에 대한 철저한 조사(study)가 필요한지 여부를 결정하여 경사리에 보고 및 권고를 제출함.
   - 진정서 관련 당사국은 인권위에서의 자국문제 토의 및 결정시 회의에 참석할 권리가 있음.

22

0031

선택의정서상의 절차

1. 진정절차의 개요

o   B규약 선택의정서 당사국이 B규약상 권리를 침해한 경우 피해당사자 및
    대리인은 인권이사회에 진정서를 제출할수 있으며, 이사회는 당사국이
    제출한 서면정보를 고려, 이를 심의하고 이사회의 견해(views)를 채택함.

o   상기 견해는 당사국 및 진정인에게 통보되며, 유엔총회에 보고됨.

o   동 진정서는 당사국 관할권 아래 있는 피해당사자 및 대리인만이 제기
    할수 있어 1503 절차에 의한 진정서에 비해 절차상 보다 엄격함.
    -   진정서에 대한 심의는 진정서 제출자와 당사국 정부가 제출한
        문서로된 정보에 근거하여 이뤄짐. 따라서 심의시 출석발언, 증인
        심문등이 허용되지 않음.

o   진정서는 모든 국내적 구제절차가 완료된후 제출되어야 하며, 익명이거나
    진정서 제출의 권리를 남용한 것으로 판단되는 진정서는 접수되지 않음.
    또한 동 문제가 여타 국제적 조사 및 해결절차에 따라 검토되고 있어서는
    아니됨.
    -   당사국에 대하여 B규약과 선택의정서가 발효한 날 이후에 발생한
        사건(아국의 경우 90.7.10)을 대상으로 함. 다만 인권침해가 그이전에
        발생하더라도 침해상태가 계속되거나 또는 그 자체가 규약위반을
        구성하는 효과를 가지는 경우에는 예외로 함.

0032

2. 현   황

o 77년-91.7월간 인권이사회에 접수된 B규약 선택의정서에 의한 진정서는
   총 468(36개국)건이며, 인권이사회는 이중 119건에 대한 의견(view)을
   채택하였음.
   - 심의가 허용되지 않은 것   : 124건
   - 종결 또는 취소된 것   : 70건
   - 심의가 진행중인 것   : 46건
   - 심의여부가 결정되지 않은 것 : 103건

3. 진정서 처리절차

o 인권사무국은 접수된 진정서 목록 및 진정내용 요약을 정기적으로
   인권이사회 위원에게 통보함.

o 인권이사회는 진정서 토의(Consideration) 여부를 결정함.
   - 동 심의와 관련, 당사국 정부 및 진정서 제출자에게 진정서 관련정보
     및 의견을 서면으로 제출할 것을 요청할수 있음.
   - 당사국 정부가 진정서 내용을 통보받고 의견서를 제출할 기회를 부여
     받은 후에야 진정서 토의 여부에 대한 결정이 내려질수 있음.

o 진정서 토의 여부가 결정되면 당사국 정부 및 당사자에게 즉시 통보됨.

o 진정서가 인권이사회에서 토의되는 것으로 결정된 경우, 당사국은
   6개월내에 진정내용에 대한 정부답변서를 제출하여야 하며, 동 사건관련
   구제조치가 있었을 경우 동 내용도 인권이사회에 통보하여야 함.
   동 정부 답변서는 당사자에게 전달되며, 당사자는 이에 대해 추가의견서를
   제출할수 있음.
   - 이사회는 정부의 상기 답변내용을 검토, 동건 토의결정을 재심의
     할수 있음.

24

0033

o 인권이사회는 정부의 답변서 및 당사자의 의견서를 검토, 진정서에 관한
  이사회 의견(view)을 채택하며, 동 의견을 당사자 및 당사국 정부에
  통보함.

o 상기 진정서 처리내용은 경제사회이사회를 거쳐 총회에 제출하는
  인권이사회 연차 보고서에 포함됨.

o 진정서 관련 인권이사회 활동은 비공개로 진행되나, 이사회는 일반 및
  언론을 위해 Communique를 배포할수 있음.

25

0034

국제노동기구에서의 제소절차

1. 제소 발생사유

가. 비준협약 위반

o 회원국이 비준협약을 위반한 경우, 그 협약을 비준하고 있는 다른
  회원국을 포함하여 어느나라의 노.사단체나 협약위반 회원국을
  ILO에 제소할수 있음.(헌장 제24조 및 제26조)

나. 근로기본권 침해

o 결사의 자유.단결권.단체교섭권등 노동기본권에 관한 침해가 발생할
  경우, 회원국이나 노.사단체는 노동기본권을 침해한 회원국을 ILO에
  제소할수 있음.(ILO의 확립된 관행)

다. 협약 미비준과 제소

o 신규회원국의 경우 가입이전의 기존협약에 대하여 법적 비준의무는
  없음.

o 그러나 제87호 협약(결사의 자유 및 단결권 보호)과 제98호 협약
  (단결권 및 단체교섭권)의 경우에는 미비준시에도 협약준수의무가
  발생하는 것으로 봄.(ILO 입장)

2. 대아국 제소 대상분야

가. 비준협약 위반

o 아국이 비준한 협약이 있을 경우 동협약 위반으로 제기될 가능성은
  희박

26

0035

- ILO 설립이후 비준협약 위반을 이유로 노.사 단체가 제출한 진정 (representation)은 총 31건이며, 헌장 제26조에 따라 회원국 또는 이사회가 제기한 이의(complaint)는 총 14건임.

나. 근로기본권 침해

ㅇ 아래 근로기본권에 침해문제와 관련, 제소가 가능할것임.
- 복수노조금지
- 공무원 노조.교원노조 금지
- 노조설립 신고제
- 근로자 구속
- 노조의 합리적 정치활동금지

3. 근로기본권 침해사건 제소처리 절차

가. 절차 개관

접 수 → 관련위원회 회부 → 심사 및 권고안 작성 →

이사회에 권고안 제출 → 권고안 채택 → 관련국에 시정조치 요구

나. 단계별 주요내용

1) 접 수

ㅇ 노.사단체와 회원국 정부는 각각 진정(representation)과 이의 (complaint)를 ILO에 신청할 수 있음.

2) 위원회 회부

 o 노동기본권 침해를 다루는 위원회는 "결사의 자유위원회"
   (Committee on Freedom of Association), "사실조사.조정위원회"
   (Fact-Finding and Conciliation Commission), "심사위원회"
   (Commission of Inquiry)등 3개임.

 o "결사의 자유위원회"가 사실상 거의 대부분의 사건을 취급함.
   - 동 위원회는 51년 설립이래 연평균 약 40건의 제소사건을 처리

 o 사실조사.조정위원회는 50년 설립이래 5건만 처리함.

 o 심사위원회의 경우 45년이후 7차례 설치되었으며, 83년 폴란드
   자유노조문제를 다루기 위해 "결사의 자유위원회"의 권고에 따라
   설치된 심사위원회가 가장 최근의 예임.

3) 심사 및 권고안 작성

 o 결사의 자유위원회
   - 주로 문서에 기초하여 조사활동을 실시(해당 정부의 사전동의 불요)

 o 사실조사.조정위원회
   - 관련정부의 동의를 전제로 조사단 또는 전문가를 구성.파견하여
     사실조사등 실시

 o 심사위원회
   - 사실조사.조정위원회의 경우와 같이 조사활동등 수행

 o 위의 조사활동등에 기초하여 이사회에 제출할 권고안 작성

4) 이사회의 권고안 채택

 o 이사회는 위원회가 제출한 권고안을 채택 또는 거부할수 있으나,
   수정은 허용되지 아니함.

28

0037

5) 시정조치 요구

  o 이사회는 권고안에 따라 해당국 정부에 시정조치를 요구

  o 시정조치 불수행시 해당국가에 동조치의 이행을 반복 요구함으로써
    정치적 압력 가중

  * 폴란드의 경우 ILO의 계속적 압력에 대항하여 84년 ILO에 탈퇴의사
    통보후 87년 복귀

29

0038

제46차 총회 인권관련 결의안 표결 현황

결 의 안 제 목	표 결 결 과	비 고
인권의 효율적 향유방안 (L.34/Rev.1) * 제안국 : 쿠바	표결 채택 (찬성 123- 반대 2 - 기권 34)	아국 : 찬성 북한 : "
국가주권 및 국내선거에서의 불간섭원칙 존중(L.60) * 제안국 : 쿠바, 북한등	표결 채택 (찬성 102- 반대 40 - 기권 13)	아국 : 반대 북한 : 찬성
이락의 인권상황(L.53) * 제안국 : 미국	표결 채택 (찬성 129- 반대 1 - 기권 17)	아국 : 찬성 북한 : 불참
이락 점령하의 쿠웨이트 인권상황(L.57) * 제안국 : 미국	표결 채택 (찬성 155- 반대 1 - 기권 0)	아국 : 찬성 북한 : "
정기선거실시 원칙 강화 (L.61/Rev.1) * 제안국 : 미국등	표결 채택 (찬성 134- 반대 4 - 기권 13)	아국 : 찬성 북한 : 반대
고문희생자 자발적 기금(L.40)	Consensus 채택	
인권관련 국제협약상의 보고 의무등 국제협약의 효율적 이행(L.41)	〃	
아동권리협약 이행(L.42)	〃	
국제인권협약(L.49)	〃	
이민노동자 권리보호협약 (L.52)	〃	
소수인 차별금지 및 보호 (L.31/Rev.1)	〃	
세계인권회의(L.26)	〃	
인권센타 강화(L.36)	〃	
정신장애자 보호(L.37)	〃	
사법행정에 있어서의 인권 (L.38)	〃	

결 의 안 제 목	표 결 결 과	비 고
인권과 빈곤(L.39/Rev.1)	Consensus 채택	
현대적 형태의 노예제도 철폐기금(L.44)	"	
개발권(L.46)	"	
인권보호 및 증진을 위한 국내기구(L.48)	"	
강제실종 문제(L.50)	"	
인권 및 과학기술 발전(L.54)	"	
인권과 대량이동(L.55)	"	
세계토착 원주민의 해(L.56)	"	
인권분야에서의 비선별성, 중립성 및 객관성 원칙을 통한 유엔활동 강화(L.59)	"	
모든형태의 종교탄압 철폐 (L.63)	"	
미얀마 인권상황(L.43)	"	
엘살바돌 인권상황(L.51)	"	
아프가니스탄 인권상황(L.58)	"	
고문방지협약 지위(L.45)	"	
인종차별철폐협약 6조 개정 (L.47)	"	

0040

인권업무 추진방안

1992. 3.

국 제 기 구 국

- 차   례 -

0042

인권업무 추진방안

1. 인권문제에 대한 인식 전환 필요성

가. 국제질서 개편과정에서의 인권의 중요성 대두

　ㅇ 최근 전체주의 체제의 몰락과 민주선거제도의 확산으로 인권의
　　중요성에 대한 인식이 다자 및 양자 차원에서 전세계적으로 부각

나. 유엔가입 이후 국제인권정책 수립 필요

　ㅇ 우리의 유엔가입 이후 유엔의 주요활동의 하나인 인권보장 활동에
　　동참하고, 국내 민주화 추세에 맞춰 세계 인권문제 토의에 참여하기
　　위하여 주요 인권문제에 대한 우리입장 정립이 필요

다. 북한 인권문제 제기 문제

　ㅇ 남북관계의 실질적 진전을 위하여는 북한 주민에 대한 기본적 인권
　　보장등 북한 체제 변화가 필요

　ㅇ 북한당국이 인권의 중요성을 인식하고, 인권부재 상황을 개선하도록
　　하기 위하여는 국내적, 국계적 여론을 환기하며, 국제적으로 가능한
　　압력 방안을 강구

1

0043

2. 주요 인권회의 현황

가. 인권위원회 (Commission on Human Rights)

1) 특 성

O 53개 위원국으로 구성된 유엔내 인권문제 담당 위원회

- 매년초 6주간 회의 개최

2) 최근 토의경향

O 세계 주요 인권 위반사례 비판

- 이라크, 이란, 쿠바, 중국(티베트 포함), 미얀마, 인니(동티몰), 중남미 일부 국가, 남아공, 피점령 팔레스타인 지역

O 고문등 피구금자 인권문제, 소수민족, 토착민, 이주 노동자 인권 문제

O 경제.사회 개발과 인권의 문제

* 아국은 93-95년 임기의 위원국으로 피선 예정

나. 인권 소위원회 (Sub-Commission on Prevention of Discrimination and Protection of Minorities)

1) 특 성

O 개인자격의 26명의 전문가로 구성된 인권위 산하 조직

- 매년 8월 4주간 회의 개최

2) 최근 토의경향

O 인권위 토의내용과 유사하며, NGO 참가활동이 활발함.

O 인권위와 역할이 중첩된다는 비판에 따라 활동 개선방안 논의중

O 90년 이래 비밀투표제 도입등 의사규칙 개정을 통하여 특정국가 (중국, 쿠바등)에 대한 인권 결의안을 채택, 인권위 활동을 선도

2

다. 총 회 (General Assembly)

1) 특 성

　o 당해년도 인권위 및 경제사회이사회에서의 토의 및 결의중 중요
　　내용이 토의, 결의되며, 향후 인권위등에 대한 지침을 결정

2) 최근 토의경향

　o 91년도 제46차 총회시 이라크 및 미얀마 인권 관련 결의안이
　　최초로 채택되어 유엔의 인권분야 기능 강화 가능성을 시현

　o 미국등이 주도, 유엔이 개별국가의 선거 지원활동을 수행할수
　　있는 법적장치가 마련됨.

라. 인권협약 산하 위원회

1) 현 황

　o 인권이사회

　o 경제적, 사회적, 문화적 권리 위원회

　o 인종차별 철폐 위원회

　o 여성차별 철폐 위원회

　o 아동권리 위원회

　o 고문방지 위원회

2) 특 성

　o 10-23명으로 구성된 위원회로서 매년 1-3차례씩 회의를 개최,
　　각국이 제출한 보고서 심의 및 진정서 처리등의 협약상 임무 이행

　o 인권관련 협약의 상호 연관성에 따라 협약 산하 위원회간 협력
　　강화 문제, 보고서 제출 및 심의의 실효성 증대 문제가 대두

3

0045

마. 세계 인권회의 (World Conference on Human Rights)

1) 회의 개요

O 93년 개최 예정 (장소 미정)

O 동회의 준비를 위하여 향후 3차례 준비회의 개최

2) 개최 의의

O 68년 테헤란 회의에 이어 개최되는 유엔주관 회의로서 세계
인권상황을 평가하고, 향후 인권보장을 위한 국제적, 국내적
활동방향 및 인권조직 강화 문제를 논의

3. 유엔회의에서의 남.북한 인권문제 제기 현황

가. 한 국

O 최근 인권상황 개선으로 인권위등 유엔회의에서 아국 인권문제를
거론한 정부대표는 없었음. 다만 북한이 89.8월, 92.2월 임수경
사건을 언급한 바 있으며, 92.2월 주한미군 주둔문제를 간략히 거론
하였음.

O 인권위 및 인권소위시 친북한 국제민간단체 및 WCC등 3-4개 단체가
주로 아국의 시국사범 문제와 재소자 인권문제를 거론한 바 있음.

O 진정서 심의절차 (1503 절차)에 의거, 인권사무국에 접수된 아국 인권
관계 진정서는 85-91년간 9건 이었으나, 인권소위 진정서 실무위에서
모두 기각됨.

4

0046

나. 북 한

O 90년도 이전 인권위에서 북한 인권문제는 거의 제기되지 않았으나,
  90.2월 이래 미국이 북한의 전체주의 체제등 기본적 인권 부재상황을
  간략하나 강도있게 비판함. 92.2월 러시아는 자국내 북한 유학생
  및 노동자 인권문제를 제기함.

O 91년도 46차 총회시 오지리가 북한 독재체제를 언급함.

O 인권위 및 인권소위에서는 89.8월 이래 2-3개 국제 민간단체가
  전체주의 체제의 인권문제를 비판하면서 북한을 언급함.

O 북한 인권문제에 대한 진정서는 전무한 상태
  - 91.11월 국제 인권옹호 한국연맹이 유엔 인권사무국에 제출한
    북한 숙청인사 관련 진정서가 확인된 유일 사례

4. 인권업무 추진대책

가. 기본 대책

1) 인권관계 회의 적극 참가

  O 그간 아국 인권문제 비판에 대한 대응을 위주로 한 소극적 참가
    에서 탈피, 금년도 인권위원국 피선을 계기로 인권위 등에서
    주요 인권문제에 대한 입장을 밝히고, 인권관련 성문화 작업에
    참여하는 등 적극적 참가대책 수립
  O 93년 세계 인권회의 적극 참여를 통하여 인권에 대한 우리정부
    및 국민의 인식을 확대

5

2) 주요 인권의제에 대한 입장 정립

 O 유엔가입 이후 총회, 경사리 및 인권위등에서 주요 인권문제
    (국가별, 주제별)에 대한 토의 및 결의안 표결 참여에 대비,
    우리입장 정립
    - 중국, 미얀마, 이란 관계 결의안 표결시 입장 수립

3) 국제 인권문제에 대한 인식 확산 추진

 O 국내 학계인사중 적격자를 선정, 인권회의 대표단에 포함하여,
    인권문제에 대한 학계의 인식을 높이고, 장기적으로는 인권기구에
    진출할 전문가로 양성

4) 인권관련 양자 현안 대응시 국제 Forum 활용

 O 인권의 범세계성 및 정치적 민감성을 감안, 인권적 요소가 포함된
    양자 현안 대응시 유엔 인권회의 등을 활용
    - 정신대 문제 등

5) 인권관련 협약상 의무 성실 이행

 O 인권협약 관련 보고서 제출 등 협약상 의무를 성실히 이행, 우리의
    인권보장 의지를 과시
    - 인권규약(A) 보고서 제출 (92.6.30까지), 인권규약(B) 보고서
      심의 (92.7월)

 O 보고서 작성과정을 통해 관계부처가 협약규정의 국내적 이행 의무를
    재인식 하도록 추진

6

0048

나. 우리 인권문제 제기시 대응책

1) 유엔 관련기관의 제기

ㅇ 아국관련 진정서, 인권위 산하 특별보고관 및 실무위원회의
정부입장 문의 및 자료요청에는 적극 대응

2) 인권관련 회의시 정부 또는 민간단체의 제기

ㅇ 우방국 정부대표의 아국문제 제기는 그 사례가 드물 것으로
예상되나, 필요한 경우에는 동 대표 발언 전후에 비공식적으로
우리 입장을 전달

ㅇ 민간단체가 수개국의 인권문제와 함께 아국 문제를 거론할
경우에는 대응치 아니함. 다만 친북한 단체등이 우리 인권
상황을 집중적으로 거론할 경우에는, 인권관련 회의의 관행에
비추어 답변권을 행사, 대응토록 함.

다. 북한 인권문제 제기

1) 필요성

ㅇ CSCE 활동에서의 인권의 역할이 동구 자유화에 크게 기여한 것으로
평가되고 있어 최근 인권의 중요성이 더욱 부각

ㅇ 북한 인권상황에 대한 유엔등 국제사회의 관심을 제고함으로써
북한 당국이 인권의 중요성에 대한 인식을 갖도록 하는데 기여

ㅇ 유엔 인권회의에서 일 국가의 인권문제가 심각히 거론되고,
관련 결의안등이 채택될 경우 해당국가는 국제여론 완화를 위한
일련의 대응조치를 취하는 것이 일반적 추세

7

0049

2) 고려사항

O 타방 인권문제를 거론하는 것을 내정간섭 또는 비난으로 간주
   하는 국내외적 시각이 상존하는 현실에서 우리 정부가 다자 및
   양자차원에서 직접 북한 인권문제를 제기할지 여부는 국내여론
   및 북측 예상 대응을 고려, 결정하여야 할것임.

O 유엔회의에서 타국가, 특히 분쟁 상대국가 인권문제를 거론할
   경우, 인권침해 내용에 대한 논의 보다는 상호 비난의 정치
   선전장화 되는 경향이 있음. 따라서 북한문제 제기를 위하여는
   회의 의제, 토의방법 및 회의 분위기등에 적합한 방법을 선택
   하여야 함.

3) 대 책

   가) 기본방향

   O 북한 인권상황 개선의 시급성에 대한 국내외적 인식의
      확산을 추진

   O 유엔등 국제사회에서 북한 인권문제에 대한 비판여론을
      조성, 이를 북한사회의 개방과 연계되도록 함.

   나) 유엔 인권관련 회의 대책

   O 주요 우방국이 총회 및 인권위 등에서 북한 인권문제를
      지속적으로 거론하도록 사전 협의 시행
      - 양국간 정책 협의회등 활용

   O 국제민간단체(NGO)와의 지속적인 협력 및 객관적 자료
      제공등을 통하여 북한 인권문제에 대한 관심 및 대응활동을
      촉구

8

0050

* 현 단계에서 NGO의 유엔 등록을 우리 정부가 추진하는 것은
  절차적 측면에서 어려움.

O 국내 인권단체가 북한 관련 개별적 인권침해 사례에 관하여
  유엔에 진정서를 제출토록 유도함.

  - 1503 절차 및 강제실종 실무위원회 활동등 활용

9

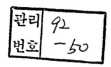
외 무 부

110-760 서울 종로구 세종로 77번지 / (02) 723-8934 / (02) 723-3505

문서번호 연이 20314-53

시행일자 1992.3.23.

(경유)

수신 수신처 참조

참조

취급		장 관	
보존			
국 장	전결		
심의관			
과 장			
기안	김종훈		협조

제목 인권업무 추진계획

　　　　인권업무에 관한 당부 추진계획을 별첨과 같이 수립하였으니 귀실.국의
관련업무 추진에 참고하여 주시기 바랍니다.

첨부 : 인권업무 추진계획 1부. 끝.

예고 : 93.12.31.일반

검토필 (1992. 6 .30.)	전
검 토 필(1992. 12. 31.)	서
검 토 필(19 93. 6 .30.)	계

수신처 : 외교안보연구원장, 외교정책기획실장, 아주국장, 미주국장, 구주국장,
　　　　　중동아프리카국장, 문화협력국장

0052

인권업무 추진계획

1992. 3.

국 제 기 구 국

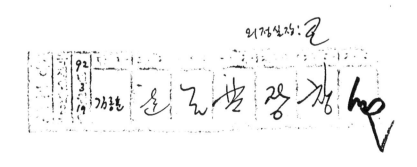

0053

- 차 례 -

1. 인권문제에 대한 인식

2. 최근 인권문제 토의 추세

3. 남.북한 인권문제 제기 현황

4. 인권업무 추진방안

   가. 국제 인권문제

   나. 아국 인권문제 제기 대응

   다. 북한 인권문제 거론

   라. 기타 인권업무

첨부 : 1. 92년도 인권관계 회의 참가계획

       2. 인권관련 NGO 현황

예고 : 93.12.31. 일반

0054

1. 인권문제에 대한 인식

가. 국제질서 개편과정에서의 인권의 중요성 부각

- O 냉전종식 이후의 신국제질서 형성과정에서 인권의 중요성과 범세계성(universality)에 대한 인식이 고조되고 있음.
  - 전체주의 체제의 퇴조 및 민주선거제도 확산 추세와 병행
- O 92.1. 안보리 정상회담에서도 인권의 중요성이 부각된 바 있으며, 국제 인권관련 회의등 다자차원에서 뿐 아니라 양자관계에서도 인권외교가 고도화되고 있음.

나. 유엔 회원국으로서 국제인권정책 수립 필요

- O 우리의 유엔가입 이후 회원국으로서 유엔의 주요활동의 하나인 인권보장 활동에 동참하기 위해 세계 인권문제 토의에 적극 참여 필요
- O 국내 민주화 추세를 바탕으로 우리의 대외관계 확대 등을 감안, 주요 인권문제에 대한 우리입장의 정립이 요구됨.

다. 남.북한 관계에 있어서 인권 존중원칙 견지

- O 남북관계의 실질적 진전을 위하여는 궁극적으로 북한 주민에 대한 기본적 인권보장등 북한 체제의 변화 필요
- O 북한당국이 인권의 중요성을 인식하고, 인권부재 상황을 개선하도록 하기 위하여는 국제적 여론환기 및 가능한 압력 방안 강구 필요
  - 92.1. 부쉬 미국대통령은 방한시 기자회견을 통하여 북한 인권 상황 개선이 미.북한간 관계개선의 선결사항임을 천명
  - 최근 서구국가등에서도 북한 인권상황 개선 필요성 대두

1

0055

2. 최근 인권문제 토의 추세

가. 제46차 유엔총회 (91.9-12.)

O 동서냉전 종식에 따라 비동맹권이 상대적으로 위축된 상황에서
  미국을 중심으로 하는 서방그룹이 토의를 주도하여 최초로 이라크
  및 미얀마 관련 결의안이 채택되도록 함으로써 유엔총회의 인권분야
  활동 강화를 시사함.
  - 동구권 국가들도 서방국가들의 주도에 동참

O 또한 미국의 주도로 민주화 추세를 실질적으로 장려하기 위한 목적의
  결의안을 채택함으로써 유엔이 개별국가의 선거지원 활동을 수행할수
  있는 법적, 제도적 근거를 마련함.

O 아국은 제3위 토의시 인권문제에 대한 일반발언외에도 회원국으로서
  최초로 인권문제 표결에 참여함.
  - 이라크 관련 결의안 및 유엔의 선거지원 활동 관련 결의안에
    찬성표명

나. 제48차 인권위 (92.1.27-3.6)

O 미국이 쿠바, 이란, 이라크, 중국, 북한, 미얀마 등 전체주의 국가의
  인권탄압 상황을 집중 거론함으로써 향후 국제적 압력 지속 시사

O 개별사안으로서는 동티몰, 티베트, 중남미 등의 인권문제가 각국 및
  NGO들에 의해 강력 제기된 한편, 팔레스타인 및 아파타이트 문제등은
  상대적으로 퇴색

O 주제별로는 고문등 피구금자 인권문제, 소수민족, 토착민, 이주
  노동자 인권문제 등이 중점 거론

O 아국도 옵서버로서 정식 발언을 통하여 국제 인권문제에 대한 관심과
  기본입장을 표명
  - 전체주의 국가의 인권상황 개선을 중점적 과제로 지적

2

0056

3. 남.북한 인권문제 제기 현황

가. 한 국

O 최근 인권상황 개선으로 인권위등 유엔회의에서 아국 인권문제를
거론한 국가는 없었음.

- 다만 북한이 89.8월, 90.2월 임수경 사건 및 92.2월 주한미군
주둔문제 언급

O 인권위 및 인권소위에서 친북한 국제민간단체 및 세계 교회 협의회
(WCC)등 3-4개 단체가 주로 아국의 시국사범 문제와 재소자 인권문제를
거론한 바 있음.

O 진정서 심의절차 (1503 절차)에 의거, 인권사무국에 접수된 아국 인권
관계 진정서는 85-91년간 9건 이었으나, 인권소위 진정서 실무위에서
모두 기각됨.

나. 북 한

O 90.2월 제46차 인권위 이래 매년 인권위에서 미국이 북한의 전체주의
체제와 기본적 인권 부재상황을 강도있게 비판해오고 있음.

O 91년도 46차 총회시 오지리가 북한 독재체제를 언급하였으며, 92.2월
러시아는 북한당국에 의한 자국내 북한 유학생 및 노동자의 인권침해
문제를 제기함.

O 인권위 및 인권소위에서는 89.8월 이래 2-3개 국제 민간단체가
전체주의 체제의 인권문제를 비판하면서 북한을 언급함.

O 북한 인권문제에 대한 진정서는 전무한 상태

- 91.11월 국제 인권옹호 한국연맹이 유엔 인권사무국에 제출한
북한 숙청인사 관련 진정서가 확인된 유일 사례임.
(동건은 92.7월 인권소위 강제실종 실무위에서 심의 예상)

3

0057

4. 인권업무 추진방안

가. 국제 인권문제

1) 인권관계 회의 적극 참가

○ 93-95 임기의 인권위원국 진출을 계기로 총회, 인권위 등에서
   인권문제의 실질적 토의 및 인권관련 성문화 작업에 적극 참여

○ 93년 세계 인권회의 및 동회의 준비과정에의 적극 참여를 통하여
   인권문제에 대한 우리의 관심 표명 및 국내 인식 확대
   - 각료급 규모 대표단 파견 검토 (관계부처 및 전문가 포함)

* 92년 인권관계 국제회의 참가계획 별첨

2) 주요 인권의제에 대한 입장 정립

○ 유엔가입 이후 총회, 경사리 및 인권위등에서 주요 인권문제
   (국가별, 주제별)에 대한 토의 및 결의안 표결에 대비, 우리 입장
   정립 필요
   - 46차 총회시 표명한 입장을 기초로 발언 및 표결에 대처
   - 특히, 미얀마, 이란, 남아공, 이스라엘 관계 결의안 대비
   - 오지리의 인권침해 조사 긴급절차 제의 및 코스타리카의
     고문방지 선택의정서 제안등 검토

3) 인권문제에 대한 국내 인식 확산

○ 국내 학계인사중 적격자를 선정, 인권회의 대표단에 포함하여,
   장기적으로는 인권기구에 진출할 전문가로 양성

○ 동인들의 연구발표, 신문기고 등을 통해 인권문제에 대한 국내
   인식 확산

4

0058

나. <u>아국 인권문제 제기 대응</u>

   1) 유엔 관련기관의 제기

      O 아국관련 진정서, 인권위 산하 특별보고관 및 실무위원회의
        정부입장 문의 및 자료요청에 적극 대응
        - 현재 불법구금 실무위에서 보안법 위반자 관련 조사 요청
          접수, 관계부처와 정부입장 협의중

   2) 정부 또는 민간단체의 제기

      O 인권관련 회의시 민간단체가 수개국의 인권문제와 함께 아국
        문제를 거론할 경우에는 일일이 대응치 아니하나, 친북한
        단체등이 우리 인권상황을 집중적으로 거론할 경우에는, 회의관행
        및 상황에 따라 답변권 행사

다. <u>북한 인권문제 거론</u>

   1) <u>필요성</u>

      O CSCE 체제내에서의 인권논의가 동구의 개방 및 민주화에 기여한
        사실 및 최근 전반적 민주화 개혁 추세를 바탕으로 전체주의
        국가들의 인권탄압에 대한 국제사회의 압력이 가중되고 있는
        상황에서 북한 인권문제를 부각시키는 것은 시의에 적합함.
      O 대내적으로 남북한 합의서를 토대로 남북대화의 진전과 함께
        대외적으로 북한의 개방 개혁을 촉진하기 위한 국제사회의
        압력이 병행되도록 추진하는 것이 효과적임.
        - 남북대화가 진행되고 있다는 사실 때문에 우방국들이 북한
          인권 탄압상황을 간과할 우려도 있음.

5

공 란

라. 기타 인권업무

1) 인권관계 협약에 따른 보고서 제출 및 심의

- O "B"규약 보고서 심의 (92.7, 제네바) 대비 사전준비 철저
  - 법무부와 협조, 답변자료 등 준비중
- O "A"규약 보고서 작성 (92.6. 기한)
  - 청와대, 외무부, 법무부 주관으로 보고서 작성중
    (법무부 관계부처 자료 종합; 외무부 최종정리)
- O 기타 각 협약에 따른 보고서 제출 및 심의
  - 인종차별 철폐협약 보고서 92.3. 제출 예정
  - 아동권리협약 보고서 93.12.한 제출
  - 여성차별 철폐협약 제2차 보고서 : 93년 상반기 심의 예정
- O 보고서 작성 및 심의과정을 통해 국내 각 부처의 협약규정 이행
  및 인권존중 의식 확산

7

0061

* 일본은 동국내 정신장애자 문제에 관하여 인권위 토의시
  제기등 국제여론 확산에 따라 국내법을 개정한 사례가 있음.

첨부 : 1. 인권관련 주요 NGO 현황
       2. 인권관련 위원회 구성 현황

8

인권관련 주요 NGO 현황

가. 전세계적 또는 아시아지역 인권상황 관심 단체

O 국제사면 위원회 (Amnesty International) :
   1 Easton Street, London Wcix 8DJ, United Kingdom

O 국제법률가 위원회 (International Commission of Jurists) :
   109 route de chene, B.P. 120, 1224 Chene-Bougeries, Switzerland

O Human Rights Watch(Asia Watch) :
   485 Fifth Avenue, New York, NY 10017-6104, U.S.A.

O Commission of the Churches on International Affairs (WCC) :
   150 route de Ferny, 1211 Geneve 20, Switzerland

O International Federation of Human Rights :
   27 rue Jean-Dolent, 75014 Paris, France

O International Human Rights Law Group :

O International League for Human Rights :
   432 Park Avenue South, Room 1103, New York, NY 10016, U.S.A.

O Pax Christi-International Catholic Peace Movement :
   Plantin en Moretuslei 174, 2018 Antwerp, Belgium

O Pax Romana :
   37/39 rue de Vermont, 1202 Geneve, Switzerland

O International Educational Development :
   1324 North Capitol, NW, Washington, DC 20002, U.S.A.

O International Confederation of Free Trade Unions :
   37-41 rue Montagne-aux-herbes-potageres, 1000 Bruxelles, Belgium

O Four Directions Council :
   4733 175h Avenue, NE No. 37, Seattle, WA 98105, U.S.A.

O Human Rights Advocates :
   2918 Florence Street, Berkeley, CA 94705, U.S.A.

나. 친북한 단체

O International Association of Democratic Lawyers :
   263 Avenue Albert, 1180 Bruxelles, Belgium

O International League for the Rights and Liberation of Peoples :
   C.P.315, 1211 Geneva 4, Switzerland

0063

인권관련 위원회 구성 현황

1. 인권위원회(Commission on Human Rights, CHR) : 53국

가. 아프리카

　　O 앙골라, 브룬디, 가봉, 감비아, 가나, 케냐, 레소토, 리비아,
　　　마다가스칼, 모리타니아, 나이지리아, 세네갈, 소말리아,
　　　튀니지, 잠비아

나. 아 시 아

　　O 방글라데시, 중국, 사이프러스, 인도, 인도네시아, 이란, 이라크,
　　　일본, 파키스탄, 필리핀, 스리랑카, 시리아

다. 중 남 미

　　O 알젠틴, 바베이도스, 브라질, 칠레, 콜롬비아, 코스타리카, 쿠바,
　　　맥시코, 페루, 우루과이, 베네주엘라

라. 서방그룹

　　O 호주, 오스트리아, 카나다, 프랑스, 독일, 이태리, 네덜란드,
　　　폴투갈, 영국, 미국

마. 동 　 구

　　O 불가리아, 체코, 항가리, 러시아, 유고

2. 인권 소위원회(Sub-Commission on Prevention of discrimination and Protection Minorities) : 26인

가. 아프리카

O Judith Sefi Attah(나이지리아), El Hadji Guisse(세네갈),
Ahmed Khalifa(이집트), Fatma Zohra Ksentini(알제리),
Halima Embarek Warzazi(모로코), Said Naceur Ramadhane(튀니지)
Fisseha Yimer(이디오피아)

나. 아 시 아

O Awn Shawkat Al-Khasawneh(요르단), Rajindar Sachar(인도),
Ribot Hatano(일본), Jin Tian(중국), Kuksum-Ui-Hakim(방글라데시)

다. 중 남 미

O Leandro Despouy(알젠틴), Miguel Alfonso Martinez(쿠바),
Claude Heller(멕시코), Gilberto Verger Saboia(브라질),
Clemencia Forero Ucros(콜롬비아)

라. 서방그룹

O Mrs. Erica-Irene A. Daes(그리스), Asbjorn Eide(노르웨이),
Louis Joinet(프랑스), Ms. Claire Palley(영국), Linda Chavez(미국),
Marc Bossuyt(벨지움)

마. 동 구

O Stanislav Valentinovich Chernichenko(러시아), Ioan Maxim(루마니아),
Volodymyr Boutkevitch(우크라이나)

3. 인권이사회(Human Rights Committee) : 18인

F.J. Aguillor Urbina(코스타리카), Janos Fodor(헝가리), Rosalyn
Higgins(영국), Rajsoomer Lallah(모리셔스), Andreas Mavrommatis
(사이프러스), Rein A. Myullerson(러시아), Fausto Pocar(이태리),
A. Serrano Caldera(니카라과), Amos Wako(케냐), Nisuke Ando(일본),
Christine Chanet(프랑스), Vojin Dimitrijevic(유고), Omran El Shafei
(이집트), Kurt Herndle(오스트리아), Birame N'Diaye(세네갈),
Waleed Sadi(요르단), Julio Prado Vallejo(에쿠아돌),
Bertil Wennergren(스웨덴)

4. 경제적, 사회적, 문화적 권리 위원회(Committee on Economic, Social and Cultural Rights) : 18인

Vassil Mrachkov(불가리아), Mikis D. Sparsis(사이프러스),
Philippe Texier(프랑스), Mohamed L. Fofana(기네), Kenneth O. Rattray
(자마이카), Juan Alvarez Vita(페루), Wladyslav Neneman(폴란드),
Samba Cor Konate(세네갈), M. de los Angeles J. Butragueno(스페인),
Philip Alstone(호주), Abdel Halim Badawi(이집트), Virginia Bonoan-
Dandam(필리핀), Luvsandanzangiin Ider(몽고), Valeri Kouznetsov(러시아),
Alexandre Muterahejuru(루안다), Jaime Marchan Romero(에쿠아돌),
Bruno Simma(독일), Javier Wimer Zambrano(멕시코)

0066

＊ 일본은 동국내 정신장애자 문제에 관하여 인권위 토의시
　　제기등 국제여론 확산에 따라 국내법을 개정한 사례가 있음.

첨부 : 1. 92년 인권관련 국제회의 참가계획

　　　 2. 인권관련 주요 NGO 현황

8

92년도 인권관계 주요회의 참가계획

회 의 명	기간 및 장소	토 의 내 용	아국 참석범위(안)
제48차 유엔 인권 위원회	1.27-3.6, 제네바	○ 세계인권상황 토의	○ 수석대표 : 주제네바대사 ○ 대표 : 본부, 주제네바대표부, 법무부 관계관
세계인권회의 제2차 준비위원회	3.30-4.10, 제네바	○ 세계인권회의 의제 선정 * 세계인권회의는 유엔주관 회의로서 68년도 테헤란회의 이후 최초로 개최 되는 평가회의	○ 수석대표 : 주제네바 대사 ○ 대표 : 본부, 주제네바대표부 담당관
제45차 인권이사회	7.13-7.31, 제네바	○ 아국 최초보고서 심의	○ 수석대표 : 추후 검토요 ○ 대표 : 본부 및 법무부 담당관
제44차 유엔 인권 소위원회	8.3-8.28, 제네바	○ 세계인권상황 토의	○ 수석대표 : 주제네바대사 ○ 대표 : 본부, 주제네바, 주유엔 대표부, 법무부 관계관
세계인권회의 아주 지역 준비회의	8.17-8.21, 방콕	○ 세계인권회의 토의 의제관련 아주지역 국가간 협의	○ 본부 담당관 또는 주제네바대표부 관계관
세계인권회의 제3차 준비위원회	9.14-9.25, 제네바	○ 세계인권회의 토의 내용 구체적 토의	○ 수석대표 : 주제네바 대사 ○ 본부 국장급 및 담당관, 주제네바 대표부 및 법무부 관계관 * 93년 본회의 대비 대표단의 지속성 유지 필요

인권관련 주요 NGO 현황

1. 유엔 인권회의 참가 NGO 자격

O 유엔 경제사회이사회와 협의관계에 있는 NGO로서 3개 등급(Catergory
   I, II, Roster)이 있으나, 실제로 회의에 참여하고, 발언하는데
   있어서는 등급에 따른 차이가 거의 없음.

2. 주요 역할

가. 인권회의등 참가

O 유엔 인권위, 인권소위 및 인권관련 세미나 등 관련회의에 옵서버로
   참가하여 발언하거나, 서면 발언문을 제출하여 유엔 사무총장이
   배포토록 함.

O 1503 절차에 의거, 인권관련 진정서를 유엔 인권사무국에 제출

나. 인권관련 협약 초안 및 선언문 작성 실무회의 참가

O 인권위 및 인권소위 참가활동의 일환으로 인권관련 협약 초안 및
   각종 선언문 작성 실무위 활동에 참가함.

3. 최근 인권회의시 NGO 활동 평가

O 통상 유엔 인권위에는 130여개 NGO, 인권소위에는 90여개 NGO가 참여함.

O 상기 NGO중 대부분이 각기 특정지역 및 국가의 인권상황만을 집중적으로
   언급하는 실정이며, 세계 인권상황에 대한 전반적 언급, 인권문제에 대한
   이론적 분석 및 접근 등 활발한 활동을 하고 있는 NGO는 20-30여개에
   불과

0069

4. 주요 NGO

가. 전세계적 또는 아시아지역 인권상황 관심 단체

o 국제사면 위원회 (Amnesty International)

o 국제법률가 위원회 (International Commission on Jurists)

o Asia Watch

o Commission of the Churches on International Affairs (WCC)

o International Federation of Human Rights

o International Human Rights Law Group

o International League for Human Rights

o Pax Christi International

o Pax Romana

o International Educational Development

o International Confederation of Free Trade Unions

o Four Directions Council

o Human Rights Advocates

나. 친북한 단체

o International Association of Democratic Lawyers

o International League for the Rights and Liberation of Peoples

0070

외 무 부

110-760 서울 종로구 세종로 77번지   /   (02) 723-8934   /   (02) 723-3505

문서번호 연이 20314- 74

시행일자 1992.3.27.

(경유)

수신 주제네바 대사, 주유엔대사

참조

취급		장 관	
보존			
국 장	전결		
심의관			
과 장			
기안	김종훈		협조

제목 인권업무 현황자료

　　　본부에서 작성한 인권업무 현황자료를 별첨 송부하오니 귀 업무에 참고하여

주시기 바랍니다.

첨부 : 상기자료 1부. 끝.

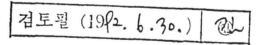
검토필 (1992. 6. 30.)

1992. 12. 31. 대 대공문에
의거 일반문서로 재분류됨

1. 국제민간단체(NGO)의 북한 인권관련 조사내용

가. A.I.

○ A.I. 대표단 방한시 귀순한 북한 유학생 면담 (90.10월)

- 소련 및 동독 유학생

○ 평양 IPU 총회시 A.I. 대표단 방북 (91.5월)

- 북한 사법체제 조사활동

- 방북 보고서는 아직 발표되지 않음.

나. Asia Watch

○ 88.12월 Minnesota Lawyers Int'l과 공동으로 북한 인권상황에 대한 종합 보고서 ("Human Rights in the Democratic People's Republic of Korea") 발표

2. 국내 NGO 현황

○ 세계 인권옹호 한국연맹

- 회 장 : 김연준 (68년도 테헤란 회의에 고문으로 참가)

- 91.11월 재소 고려인 연합회를 대신하여 유엔 인권사무국에 북한 숙청인사 생사 관련 진정서 제출

0072

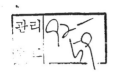

외   무   부

110-760 서울 종로구 세종로 77번지 / (02) 723-8934 / (02) 723-3505

문서번호 연이 20314-305

시행일자 1992.4.1.

(경유)

수신 수신처 참조

참조

취급		장 관	
보존			
국 장	전결		
심의관			
과 장			
기안			협조

제목 인권업무 추진계획

　　　1. 본부가 수립한 인권업무 추진계획을 별첨 송부하니 동 추진계획의
시행과 관련한 귀관 의견있을시 회보하여 주시기 바랍니다.

　　　2. 본부는 금년 4월말 경제사회이사회 조직회의에서 실시될 인권위원회
(Commission on Human Rights) 위원국 선거에 아국의 입후보 의사를 표명하여
이미 아시아그룹의 추천을 획득한 바 있음을 참고하시기 바랍니다. (지역그룹
추천시 특별한 사정이 없는한 4월 선거에서 투표없이 그대로 선출됨.)

첨부 : 인권업무 추진계획 1부. 끝.

예고 : 1993.12.31.일반.

수신처 : 주유엔대사, 주제네바대사, 주EC대사, 주일대사, 주호주대사, 주미대사,
　　　　　주영대사, 주불대사, 주독대사, 주러시아대사, 주오스트리아대사
　　　　　주북경대표부 대표.

주카나다 대사

0073

검토필 (1992. 6. 30.)

법토필 (1992. 12. 31.)

검토필 (1993. 6. 30.)

	분류번호	보존기간

발 신 전 보

번 호 : WUN-0900   외 별지참조   종별 :

수 신 : 주   수신처 참조   대사. ♣♣♣♣

발 신 : 장 관   (연이)

제 목 : 인권업무 추진계획

연 : 연이 20314-305 (92.4.1.)

1. 연호, 인권업무 추진계획에 따른 세부시행과 관련, ~~귀관 자체~~
~~추진사항등~~ 귀견 보고바람.

2. 북한인권 관련 각종 정보 및 참고자료 입수시 수시 보고바람. 끝.

(국제기구국장   김재섭)

예고 : 93.12.31.일반

수신처 : 주유엔, 주제네바, 주EC, 주일, 주호주, 주미, 주카나다, 주영,
주불, 주독, 주러시아, 주오스트리아 대사, 주북경대표부 대사

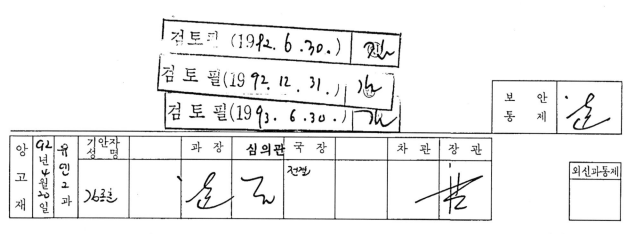

0074

관리 번호	9↓ -78

외 무 부

종 별 :

번 호 : AUW-0328

일 시 : 92 0421 1700

수 신 : 장관(연이)

발 신 : 주 호주 대사

제 목 : 인권업무 추진계획

대:WAU-0336

1. 대호 추진계획과 관련, 별다른 의견이 없음.

2. 북한 인권관련 정보는 입수시 수시 보고위계임.끝. (대사 이창범-국장)

예고:93.12.31. 일반.

검토필 (1992. 6. 30.)	김

검토필(1992.12.31.)	김

검토필(1993. 6.30.)	김

국기국   아주국

PAGE 1

외 무 부

종 별 :

번 호 : CPW-1657

일 시 : 92 0422 1200

수 신 : 장 관(연이)

발 신 : 주 북경 대표

제 목 : 인권업무 추진계획

　　대: WCP-0940

　　연: CPW-1096

1. 대호 본부 계획에 특별한 의견 없음.

2. 인권문제에 관한 중국의 입장을 연호 참고바람. 끝.

(대사 노재원-국장)

예고:92.12.31 일반

검토필 (1992. 6. 30.)

1992. 12. 31. 의거 일반문서로 재분류함

국기국　　아주국

공　　　란

공　　　란

공   란

공　　　란

공   란

공 란

공   란

공　　　란

공 란

K

```
┌─────────┐
│ 관리 92 │
│ 번호 -85 │
└─────────┘
```

외 무 부

종 별 :

번 호 : CNW-0508

수 신 : 장관(연이)

발 신 : 주 캐나다대사

제 목 : 인권업무 추진계획

일 시 : 92 0424 1800

대:WCN-0406

1. 대호 계획 관련, 당관 이견없음.

2. 단 주재국 외무부 관계관은 냉전체제하에서는 쏘련 및 동구의 인권문제가 전략적 문제도 부상되었으나, 이제는 인권문제가 주로 전략적 중요성이 별로 없는 제 3 세계 국가들의 문제라는 점에서 G-7 등 서방 선진국간 협의시 인권문제에 대한 관심이 다소 퇴조되고 있다는 관측이 다소 퇴조되고 있다는 관측을 하고 있는바, 참고 바람. 끝

예고:92.12.31. 일반

```
┌──────────────────────────┐
│ 검토필 (1992. 6. 30.)  印 │
└──────────────────────────┘
```

1992 12 31 대 예고문에 의거 일반문서로 재분류됨

국기국

PAGE 1

92.04.25   09:09

외신 2과 통제관 CE

0086

공   란

공   란

공   란

원 본

외 무 부

종 별 :

번 호 : UKW-0775

일 시 : 92 0505 1700

수 신 : 장관(연이)

발 신 : 주 영 대사

제 목 : 인권업무 추진계획

대: 연이 20314-305, WUK-0709

1. 대호 인권업무 추진계획에 대해 당관은 특별한 이견없으며, 동 계획중 당관 해당사항에 대해 아래와 같이 업무추진 계획임.

-당지소재 국제사면위원회(AI)와 긴밀한 협의유지, 인권관련 진전사항에 대한 수시 정보제공등으로 아국의 개선된 인권상황에 대한 올바른 인식유도

-북한의 인권탄압 실상에 대한 주재국 및 인권단체의 주의환기 노력

. 제 3 국 및 민간인권단체 자료활용

-주재국의 92 년도 한반기 EC 의장국 취임관련, EC 국가들에 의한 지속적인북한 인권문제 거론을 위한 주재국의 협조요청

-주재국에서 개최되는 인권관련 회의에 아국대표의 참석노력 강화

2. 북한 인권관련 정보 및 자료 입수시 수시 송부 예정임.끝

(대사 이홍구-국장)

예고: 92.12.31 일반

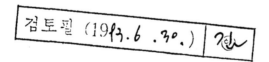

검토필 (19r3.6.30.)

국기국   구주국

인권업무 세부 추진사항

1992. 5.

국 제 기 구 국

0091

- 차 례 -

예고 : 93.12.31.일반

0092

공   란

공   란

공 란

공　　　　　란

2. 국제 및 국내 인권문제 대응

가. 인권에 대한 정부 기본정책 천명

O 아래 주요 인권관련 현안에 대한 정부입장을 제47차 유엔총회 제3위
  연설을 통해 종합적으로 밝힘으로써 인권에 대한 정부 기본정책
  정립을 추진
  - 타국 인권문제 제기와 내정간섭
  - 인권보장을 위한 보편성과 지역적.국가적 특수성의 조화
  - 발전의 권리 등 경제적.사회적 권리와 시민적.정치적 권리의 관계
  - 소수민족 보호 등 새로운 인권문제에 대한 대응
  - 인권보장을 위한 유엔의 역할

O 상기 정부 기본정책에 근거하여 국가별.주제별 주요 인권문제에 대한
  입장 결정

나. 주요 인권관련 의제에 대한 입장 정립

O 총회에서 쟁점이 될 주요 인권문제(국가별, 주제별)에 대한 세부입장
  및 결의안 표결입장 결정
  - 미얀마, 이란, 남아공, 이스라엘 관련 결의안 대비
  - 오지리의 인권침해 조사 긴급절차 제의 검토
  - 티벳, 동티몰 문제에 대한 내부 입장 마련

7 - 5

0097

다. 유엔 인권위 회의 및 세계인권회의 적극 참가

　　O 93-95년 임기의 인권 위원국 자격으로 제49차 유엔 인권위(93.2월)
　　　에서 주요 인권문제에 대한 입장을 발언 또는 투표를 통해 개진
　　　- 고문, 재소자 인권, 세계 인권상황 등 주요의제에 대해 관계부처와
　　　　협의, 세부입장 수립
　　　- 회의 대표단에 학계인사 포함 문제 적극 검토
　　　- 회의에서 채택된 결의가 국내적으로 이행 또는 활용되도록 관계
　　　　부처에 대한 홍보활동 전개

　　O 세계인권회의(92.6월, 비엔나), 동 준비회의(92.4월, 93.4월, 제네바)
　　　및 지역회의(92.12월, 방콕)에서 주요 인권현안에 대하여 일관된 아국
　　　입장 표명
　　　- 세계회의 대표단은 68년 회의에 예를 감안, 각료급 수석대표,
　　　　관계부처 담당관, 학계 및 민간단체 대표로 구성하며 국회인사
　　　　포함도 검토
　　　- 준비회의 및 지역회의 진행사항 상세 파악, 적극 대처

라. 인권보고서 작성 및 심의 대비 체제 확립

　　O 각종 인권관련 협약의 가입에 따라 인권보고서 작성 및 심의 업무의
　　　중요성 부각
　　　- 보고서 작성 협약　:　인권규약(A), 인권규약(B), 인종차별철폐
　　　　　　　　　　　　　　　협약, 여성차별철폐 협약, 아동권리 협약

7 - 6

0098

O 보고서 작성을 단순히 협약 이행 현황을 취합하는 작업으로 간주하기 보다는 관계부처에서 협약 이행상의 문제점을 파악, 개선하는 기회로 활용

  - 보고서 작성을 관계부처 의견취합 후 일개 부처에서 작성하는 기존의 방식에서 관계부처간 협의 체제에 의한 작성으로 발전 필요

O 보고서 심의의 중요성에 대하여 관계부처의 인식 제고

O 보고서 작성 및 심의를 위한 국내 체제를 92년말까지 확립

  - 93년도에는 인권규약(A), 여성차별철폐 협약 보고서 심의, 아동권리 협약 보고서 작성 예정

마. 국내 민간 인권단체 육성

O 인권문제에 대한 인식 제고를 위해 세계 인권옹호 한국연맹 등 기존의 국내 민간 인권단체와 협조관계 유지

  - 동 국내단체가 주요 국제 민간단체에 북한 인권관련 자료를 제공 하도록 추진

  - 북한 관련 개별적 인권침해 사례에 관하여 유엔에 진정서 제출을 유도

O 새로운 인권단체의 발굴, 육성

  - 인권문제의 국제적 논의 현황에 대한 이해 제고를 위해 각종 자료 제공

7 - 7

0099

공   란

공   란

공   란

공   란

주 러 대 사 관

주러정 20276- 56   92.7.7

수신 : 외무부장관

참조 : 국제기구국장

제목 : 인권업무 추진계획

대 : 연이 20314-305, WRF-1548
연 : RFW-2547

　　　　표제건 관련, 연호 참고바라며 아울러 당지에서의 북한인 인권문제에

대한 객관적인 비판 및 거론을 위해서는 주재국의 민간 인권관계기관을 활용

하는 방안도 검토하시기 바랍니다.

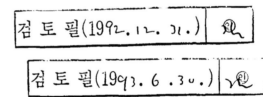

첨부 : 동 단체목록
예고 : 93.12.71. 일반

주　　　러　　　대　　　사

0104

LIST OF GENERAL NON-GOVERNMENTAL
ORTHODOX ORGANIZATIONS OF RUSSIAN
FEDERATION

I. Lawprotecting group of "MEMORIAL" society. Chairman - Dmitry Leonov; address: Moscow, 127550, Dmitrovskoye chausse 45, building 3, apart.63, tel. 976-03-43.

2. Moscow Helsinki group. Coordinator - Alexei Smirnov, executive secretary - Mikhail Alexeyev; address: Moscow, Novo-slobodskaya ulitsa 14/19, tel.116-76-82.

3. Moscow department of antifascist centre. Chairman - Eugene Victorovich Prosheikin, tel. 496-35-80.

4. Non-governmental organization "Civil assistance"(Moscow). Chairwoman - Grafova Lidiya Ivanovna, Deputy - Strelnikov Sergei Ivanovich, tel. 208-88-02(O), 231 -30-65(H) - Grafova; tel.208-91-46 (O), 474-45-08 (H) - Strelnikov; fax: 202-02-48; telex: 411-294.

5. Moscow Russian-American Bureau on human rights. Co-Directors - Proslavsky Vladimir Eugenyevich, Berman Irina Victorovna; adress: 103030, Moscow, Novoslobodskaya ulitsa 14/19, building I, public council of Moscow Bureau, tel. 258-94-67, fax: 973-39-28.

6. Russian Committee of Advocates for human rights protection. Chairman - Yuri Shmidt, address: 119194, Moscow, Saint-Petersburg, Chaikovskogo 28, tel.553-86-58.

7. Committee of Russian refugees. Chairman - Radayev Ivan Ivanovich; address: Moscow, proyezd Sapunova 13, tel.928-26-92.

8. Moscow Committee for refugee's rights protection. Chairwoman - Mirzabekyan - Svetlana Artashovna; address: Moscow, Tverskaya street 13, tel. 200-54-62.

0105

외교문서 비밀해제: 한국 인권문제 18
한국 인권문제 민주화 관련 기타 자료 3

초판인쇄 2024년 03월 15일
초판발행 2024년 03월 15일

지은이 한국학술정보(주)
펴낸이 채종준
펴낸곳 한국학술정보(주)
주 소 경기도 파주시 회동길 230(문발동)
전 화 031-908-3181(대표)
팩 스 031-908-3189
홈페이지 http://ebook.kstudy.com
E-mail 출판사업부 publish@kstudy.com
등 록 제일산-115호(2000. 6. 19)

ISBN 979-11-7217-072-1 94340
979-11-7217-054-7 94340 (set)